T0346698

Police Deception and Dishonesty

Police Deception and Dishonesty

The Logic of Lying

LUKE WILLIAM HUNT

OXFORD
UNIVERSITY PRESS

OXFORD
UNIVERSITY PRESS

Oxford University Press is a department of the University of Oxford. It furthers the University's objective of excellence in research, scholarship, and education by publishing worldwide. Oxford is a registered trade mark of Oxford University Press in the UK and certain other countries.

Published in the United States of America by Oxford University Press
198 Madison Avenue, New York, NY 10016, United States of America.

© Oxford University Press 2024

Library of Congress Cataloging-in-Publication Data
Names: Hunt, Luke William, author.
Title: Police deception and dishonesty : the logic of lying / Luke William Hunt.
Description: New York, NY : Oxford University Press, [2024] |
Includes bibliographical references and index.
Identifiers: LCCN 2023033840 (print) | LCCN 2023033841 (ebook) |
ISBN 9780197672167 (hardback) | ISBN 9780197672181 (epub)
Subjects: LCSH: Police—Professional ethics. | Law enforcement—Moral and
ethical aspects. | Deception. | Police-community relations.
Classification: LCC HV7935.H86 2024 (print) | LCC HV7935 (ebook) |
DDC 363.2—dc23/eng/20231005
LC record available at https://lccn.loc.gov/2023033840
LC ebook record available at https://lccn.loc.gov/2023033841

DOI: 10.1093/oso/9780197672167.001.0001

Printed by Sheridan Books, Inc., United States of America

For my parents

Contents

Preface

When a person learns that I quit my job as an FBI special agent to become a philosophy professor, they have questions. Or if they don't have specific questions, they simply want me to help them with their bewilderment. I like to respond that I thought FBI-agent-to-philosopher was the natural career progression. After getting that bad joke out of the way, I eventually receive this question: But *why* did you leave the FBI?

Making significant career and life changes are difficult and complex for most people. In my case, I certainly value the unique experiences I had in the FBI and I am grateful for them all—both the good ones and the bad ones. Although I have no major regrets about my unusual career path, I think it is fair to say that my personality was not suited to all aspects of the job.

When I was preparing to go through the FBI's lengthy application process—leading to a spot at Quantico for New Agent Training—I was also studying for the Graduate Record Examinations (GRE). The GRE is the standardized test that has historically been required for admission into doctoral programs. Considering my bookish interests and introversion, I was drawn to academia from the beginning. It was a close second to Quantico. The FBI just had what seemed like a more multidimensional (intellectual, physical, public service) appeal.

I was thrilled when I finally received a spot at Quantico, and the training itself is something I will always appreciate. It was exhilarating to experience and learn about so many different things: firearms (pistol, shotgun, and M4), defensive tactics, physical fitness obstacle courses, interviewing, interrogation, operational skills (conducting surveillance, executing search warrants, arrest warrants, and so on), investigative techniques and tactics (including those relying on dishonesty and deception), as well as a number of academic topics (such as the various legal and administrative rules governing FBI agents).

After posing for a picture shaking Director Mueller's hand and receiving my FBI credentials, I was sent into the field as an FBI agent. Many of my early experiences on the job were rewarding, with respect to both the work and the friendships with colleagues and mentors. It felt as if life and work were converging seamlessly and with increasing momentum. But in fact, looking back now, I recall journal entries from the earliest days of my career in which I tried to calm my doubts about being an FBI agent. Basically, I was trying to convince myself that the FBI was as good as it gets and that it would be irrational to think there were better options (such as academia), all things considered.

My doubts became more pronounced as the years went by. Some of them stemmed from new domestic circumstances. Naturally, my life was changed when my wife gave birth to our first son. Priorities began to shift and my time (which was in short supply) became more precious.

On the other hand, some of my misgivings about the job were more idiosyncratic, including those related to my introverted need for space and autonomy. Such needs are not exactly a good fit for FBI agents considering that agents must always be available and must account for almost everything they do—from documenting phone calls to vacation itineraries. Never alone and always under the Bureau's watchful eye, I felt like I was losing my sense of self. It didn't help that FBI agents are routinely polygraphed (both during the application process and while on the job) to determine whether they might be a threat to national security. I recall irrationally fearing that I would lose my job for, say, confessing to the (deceptive) polygrapher that I sometimes took a bathroom break without locking my computer (which is a potential security threat).

To be sure, it is reasonable to think that such oversight is good, at least to a certain point. If the FBI puts too much trust in its agents—or doesn't know where and what agents are doing on their vacations—then perhaps they cannot be held accountable (a concept that is important in this book). So I am quite open to the idea that some facets of my personality were simply not a good fit for the FBI.

I was nevertheless having a successful career—both operationally in the field through securing federal indictments in my investigations, as well as professionally through promotion to Supervisory Special Agent. This brings me to a final, philosophical reason that contributed to my leaving the FBI— the reason that is relevant to this book.

As everyone knows, FBI agents—like most law enforcement officers— routinely rely on tactics involving deception and dishonesty. Consider the use of confidential informants (or "sources"), whom agents (and other law enforcement officers) use to secretly gather information and evidence in support of investigations (or simply to gather intelligence to better understand a department's operating environment). I do not think that all use of informants is unjustified, though the practice is inherently dishonest and deceptive. For example, agents direct informants to conceal from others their relationship with the FBI, direct informants to participate in constructed (fake) criminal schemes, and direct informants to secretly record encounters with those ensnared in the schemes.

Of course, I cannot reveal anything about the informants with whom I dealt. Generally, though, it is worth noting how this sort of deception and dishonesty gave me another reason to question my career path. Suppose, hypothetically, I had an informant who was in a position to gather information or evidence about criminal or national security matters in another country. Suppose further that engaging in such operational activity would be dangerous (for example, if targets in the other country learned that the informant was an informant). Finally, suppose the informant desperately did not want to engage in such operational activity, including because the informant had regular, domestic concerns regarding safety and family commitments (not unlike myself).

Why would such a person agree to operate for law enforcement and intelligence agencies? There are many possible reasons, but one reason is that such agencies often have leverage over informants—such as evidence that the informant committed a crime. In exchange for gathering evidence, the officer or agent might agree to ask the prosecutor to consider reducing the informant's criminal exposure. In other words, a bargain is reached between the informant and the law enforcement officer, even if the bargain is steeped in deception and dishonesty. Did the informant have a "real choice" given the nature of the government's leverage? Was the government justified in subjecting the informant to the risk of harm in order to acquire evidence?[1]

The broader point is that one reason these situations troubled me was that I could identify with the informants I handled. That may sound odd. But even if our lives appeared to have taken dramatically different paths (which wasn't always the case), I could typically see how I (or anyone) could end up in the informant's position had things been slightly different. I was especially uncomfortable with the institutional power—the power to compel one to engage in dangerous operations relying on deception and dishonesty—law

---

[1] I examined these questions in *The Retrieval of Liberalism in Policing* (New York: Oxford University Press), ch. 4.

enforcement officers had over people who weren't much different from you and me (aside from a few chance twists and turns in life).

So that is a long, multipart way of answering the question about why I left the FBI. I suppose that sort of answer isn't a surprise given that I now work in a field known for verbosity. If this brief biographical sketch isn't interesting, I hope it at least illustrates a central point about why I wrote this book: Police deception and dishonesty—and the way it plays a role in communities and the lives of countless individuals—is something we should all care about.

It is for this reason that I tried to write the book for everyone—regardless of whether you are a professional academic or simply someone who cares about institutions and ethics. If you fall into the latter group, then perhaps you will be most interested in the real-world cases studies examined in the second part of the book. If you find the theoretical material in the first part of the book a bit monotonous, I encourage you to move to the Interlude and then jump right into the second part of the book. You can always pick your way around the theoretical material when the mood strikes. If you are a professional academic, then perhaps your reading interests will be the opposite. The book is not intended to be precious, and I hope readers will focus on the parts they find most interesting.

A related point is that I hope the book's discussions of theory and practice are ecumenical—that is, I hope they are more or less general in their extent and application, regardless of your moral and political views. I'll give you two examples, one scholarly and one political.

First, there are three prominent philosophical approaches to ethical reasoning: (1) *consequentialist ethics*, which generally suggests that decisions about what we ought to do should be based on the consequences of our decisions; (2) *deontological ethics*, which generally suggests that decisions about what we ought to do should be based on rules and duties that reach beyond the consequences of our decisions; and (3) *virtue theory*, which is generally about examining and understanding the nature of virtue (moral character) instead of consequences and deontological duties.

As we will see, the arguments in this book are sympathetic to each of these three approaches to ethical reasoning. It seems clear that one reason unconstrained police deception and dishonesty is problematic is that it can have bad consequences—from the erosion of community trust to wrongful convictions (as when a deceptive and dishonest police interrogation compels people to confess to crimes they did not commit). Empirical data confirms these consequences.[2] On the other hand, one of the book's central themes is that it can be wrong for the police to deceive and lie *even if* the deception and dishonesty results in *good* consequences (though I am not a radical Kantian, as I will explain in the Introduction). This view is based on assumptions regarding political morality, including authority, legitimacy, and constraints on the *means* the police may use to bring about good consequences such as enhanced security. Finally, the book considers how honesty may be construed as a *virtue* that is relevant to both individuals and institutions. Some will see this sort of ecumenical approach as problematic, but staking out entrenched positions and failing to look for common ground is often a mistake.

Now for the political example. There is no doubt that policing is a controversial, hot-button topic. There are loud calls not only to "defund the police," but also to *abolish* the police. On the other end of the spectrum, some pundits argue that we need *more* policing—or simply that policing needs only minor reform. I have written about this debate elsewhere—and will return to it briefly in the book's Epilogue—but I hope there are at least some points in the book on which we can all agree.[3] In one sense, some of my conclusions will sound radical (police need to be less proactive and more reactive), but I suppose the conclusion is decidedly less radical when considering arguments in favor of getting rid of the police altogether.

* * *

That is the story of how and why I came to write this book. All writers are in some sense influenced by their life stories, and I want to be candid about the possible ways my story might have influenced this book, wittingly or not. In any case, this Preface will mercifully conclude the memoir aspects of the book, though I will occasionally incorporate professional anecdotes in the coming chapters where appropriate. I hope to do this with humility and the understanding that mine is but one perspective on policing.

L.W.H., Tuscaloosa, Alabama, Summer 2023

[2] For example, Innocence Project, a nonprofit legal organization focused on exonerating people who have been wrongly convicted, has documented that false confessions (which may be based on police deception and dishonesty during interrogation) account for almost 30 percent of wrongful convictions. See "Explore the Numbers: Innocence Project's Impact," Innocence Project, https://innocenceproject.org/exonerations-data/ See also Saul Kassin's extensive scientific study of the connection between false confessions and police interrogation practices, including *Duped: Why Innocent People Confess—and Why We Believe Their Confessions* (Lanham: Prometheus Books, 2022).

[3] I examined "defunding the police" and "police abolition" in "The Limits of Reallocative and Algorithmic Policing," *Criminal Justice Ethics* 41, no. 1 (2022).

The Logic of Lying

Five Presumed Justifications for Police Dishonesty

1. Cover

The police seek to enter a man's home to investigate an alleged crime. The man refuses to let the police in his home without a warrant; the police enter anyway, tackling the man and pinning him to the floor. The man is handcuffed and taken to sit in jail for two days. The police file a criminal complaint charging the man with resisting arrest to cover for their use of force. Prosecutors eventually drop the charges.

Thompson v. Clark (2022)

2. Control

The police tell a woman she is facing a forty-year prison sentence for a drug charge unless she serves as a police informant. The police want the woman to have oral sex for money with the target of an investigation so the police can charge the target with soliciting a prostitute. The police wire the woman to record the encounter and give her a napkin, instructing her to spit the target's semen into it to provide physical evidence of the sex act. The woman completes the act. In fact, she was only facing a six-to-ten-year sentence for the drug charge.

Alexander v. DeAngelo (2003)

3. Catch

FBI agents construct an undercover sting operation to arrest a man in a terrorism plot. The investigation relies heavily on an FBI informant, who poses as a terrorist to provoke the man by inspiring, planning, financing, and equipping the proposed terrorist attack. The man is convicted and sentenced to serve a twenty-five-year prison sentence as a result of his involvement with the FBI informant.

United States v. Cromitie (2013)

4. Confess

A teenager is interrogated by the police about his involvement in the rape of a woman in a park. The teen says he didn't do it. The police say they know the teen is lying because they have fingerprints from the victim's pants— though no fingerprints exist. The teen confesses and is incarcerated for several years. It is later discovered that the teen was not the rapist.

"Central Park Five" case (1989)

5. Convict

Three suspects carjack a cabdriver, forcing him out of his vehicle and stealing his vehicle. The police show the victim photographs of men who fit the description of the carjackers, but the victim initially recognizes only one carjacker. A detective testifies that he then prepared two photo lineups that included the additional two suspects and that the victim identified the two suspects from the lineup. The two additional suspects were charged with the carjacking. In fact, the photo lineups were fabrications; some of the photos in the lineups did not even exist at the time the detective testified that he administered the lineup.

Eastern District of New York, Docket No. 18-CR-97 (PKC) (2018)

Introduction

On Beating a Broken Bone with a Boot

Would you tell a lie to a criminal if it meant he would stop beating your broken arm with a boot? Martin Scorsese's film, *The Departed*, is based on Boston's real-life Winter Hill Gang—a group of mostly Irish American mobsters led by Whitey Bulger from the late-1970s to the mid-1990s. In the film, Billy Costigan (played by Leonardo DiCaprio) is a newly minted police officer who goes undercover to infiltrate the criminal organization run by Irish mob boss Frank Costello (a character based on Bulger, played by Jack Nicholson).[1] His cover is a criminal conviction for assault and battery, followed by probation and court-ordered counseling. The cover helps provide Costigan with the requisite street credibility to join Costello's crew.

But there's a problem: Given Costigan's background as an officer, how can Costello trust that Costigan has truly left the police and embraced a life of crime? On their initial meeting, Costello takes Costigan into a backroom in a bar. Costigan's right arm is encased in a plaster cast to protect a bone he broke in a recent fight. After Costigan's cast is forcibly removed, Costello repeatedly slams a boot onto Costigan's broken arm while screaming the question: "Are you still a cop?" Costigan—in excruciating pain—yells a lie to Costello repeatedly: "I am not a fucking cop!" Satisfied, Costello stops the beating and welcomes Costigan into the fold.

The film sticks out to me because it was released the same year (2006) that I graduated from the FBI's New Agent Training at Marine Corp Base, Quantico, in Virginia. In fact, Costello (like Whitey Bulger in real life) was an FBI informant.[2] So both the film and real life include multiple layers of deception and dishonesty—coinciding with the wide variety of deceptive tactics that I learned during New Agent Training at Quantico. After several

---

[1] Jeremy Kagan, *Director's Closeup 2* (Lanham: Scarecrow Press, 2013), 50.
[2] Adam Nagourney and Ian Lovett, "Whitey Bulger Is Arrested in California," *New York Times*, June 23, 2011.

Police Deception and Dishonesty. Luke William Hunt, Oxford University Press. © Oxford University Press 2024.
DOI: 10.1093/oso/9780197672167.003.0001

years as an FBI Special Agent, I made the natural career transition to academic philosophy (there's my joke). Oddly enough, I soon realized that Enlightenment-era philosopher Immanuel Kant had something to say about Officer Costigan's lie to Costello.

In his infamous essay, *On a Supposed Right to Lie from Philanthropy*, Kant indicates that it would be wrong to, say, lie to a knife-wielding stranger who shows up at your door looking for your friend. Suppose you think the stranger is a would-be murderer hunting your friend (who happens to be hiding in your bedroom). And yet Kant seems to suggest that it would be wrong to lie to the stranger about your friend's location.[3] This is a decidedly unusual conclusion to reach about the limits (or lack thereof) of honesty. Indeed, it sounds like the sort of implausible conclusion many people have come to expect from philosophers. Surely it can't be wrong to lie to a murderer at your door in order to protect your friend. Likewise, surely it can't be wrong for an undercover police officer to lie to a crime boss who's mercilessly beating the officer's broken arm with a boot.

Let me assure you that I'm sympathetic to the worry that Kant's commitment to honesty is a bit extreme. But perhaps it's not quite as extreme as it seems. Kant's position is not that you owe something to the murderer personally (beyond the basic duty to treat the murderer as a person, not an object).[4] The murderer at your door is clearly acting unjustly, and so you don't owe him the truth specifically.[5] The reason that Kant might think truth-telling is justified in such cases is based on the value of truth-telling to the *moral community* generally.[6]

---

[3] Immanuel Kant, "On a Supposed Right to Lie from Philanthropy," in *Practical Philosophy*, trans. Mary Gregor (Cambridge: Cambridge University Press, 1996), 605–16.

[4] I am not a consequentialist, but someone sympathetic to consequentialism might argue that a liar does not necessarily treat another person as a "mere means" if the liar lies for the good of someone other than the person to whom the lie is directed; perhaps the liar could fully recognize the intrinsic value of the person on the receiving end of the lie, but think that the harm caused to that person is outweighed by the good that the lie brings about. We will consider a variety of ways to think about these and related issues.

[5] For example, Allan Wood interprets Kant to mean that not telling the truth to a murderer at the door is a wrongful lie only if the speaker's declaration was not coerced or extorted by the murderer (and the speaker's declaration was necessary). Allan Wood, *Kantian Ethics* (Cambridge: Cambridge University Press, 2008), 248. It is worth noting that Kant is not terribly concerned about the morality of deception that does not include lying. For insightful analysis and critique, see Thomas Carson, *Lying and Deception: Theory and Practice* (Oxford: Oxford University Press, 2010), ch. 3. For an approach to police lying that is sympathetic to Kantiansm (while recognizing problems with Kantian absolutism), see Sam Duncan, "Why Police Shouldn't Be Allowed to Lie to Suspects," *Journal of the American Philosophical Association* 9, no. 2 (June 2023): 268–283.

[6] See Karen Stohr, *Choosing Freedom: A Kantian Guide to Life* (New York: Oxford University Press, 2022), 176–184, for an incisive, accessible discussion of these points.

The Book's Thesis

Although I won't dwell on Kant's work (mercifully), this book pursues a related thesis: human society—including especially institutions such as the police—requires cooperative relations steeped in honesty in order to be viable. That is a big, sweeping claim that will require a lot of unpacking, but I think the evidence will bear it out. The idea is that the police institution cannot function in society effectively without honesty as a normative foundation. Think about the police role in society for a moment. They investigate crimes, they use force to make arrests, they patrol cities and highways, they search for missing persons, they respond to emergencies, they respond to non-criminal social problems, they address crowd-control at large public events—the list goes on and on. In short, the police are often the primary point-of-contact between citizens and the state—the agents that we see in public on a day-to-day basis.

As a direct point-of-contact between citizen and state, the police institution presents the community with an accessible opportunity to evaluate the state's trustworthiness. We can do our best to acquire knowledge on our own through experience—by doing our homework and learning about the world directly. But to survive in a political community, we all must rely on others at some point.[7] Relying on others—at both an individual and institutional level—requires a degree of trust and mutual forbearance that cannot exist under widespread conditions of deception, dishonesty, and fraud. Now think about the significance of this idea with respect to political institutions such as the police—an institution that has profound power and authority over the community. It's plausible to think that honesty and trust are crucial if we want any semblance of a viable, functioning society—including a viable, functioning police institution.

Empirical research bears out these points.[8] For example, researchers have recently used survey data to explore the relationship between *social trust* (general trust among members of a society) and *legal trust* (trust in legal institutions such as the police) in African states, concluding that trust in the legal system (such as the police institution) is a function of social trust. One

---

[7] Kant says that there can be no society if people do not express their thoughts genuinely. Immanuel Kant, *Lectures on Ethics*, trans. Louis Infield (Indianapolis: Hackett Publishing, 1963), 224.

[8] See, e.g., *Social Trust*, ed. Kevin Vallier and Michael Weber (New York: Routledge, 2021): part I (empirical work on social trust); as well as Ben Bradford, Jonathan Jackson, and Mike Hough, "Trust in Justice," in *The Oxford Handbook of Social and Political Trust*, ed. Eric M. Uslaner (New York: Oxford University Press, 2017), 633–654.

important takeaway from this research is that social and legal trust are only connected when legal officials (such as the police) are viewed as representative of most members of society.[9] We should thus ask: To what extent have deception and dishonesty been normalized for the police compared to other members of society? Relatedly, empirical research in the United States and the United Kingdom suggests a deep relationship between trust, legitimacy, and justice: legal trust is important to public cooperation with authorities such as the police, meaning that both the public *and* the police have a lot at stake.[10]

Even if you're on board with the value of trust, I suspect you're still skeptical of Kant's conclusion about the concrete case of the murderer at your door. Likewise, I suspect you're skeptical that it's always wrong for a police officer to lie to a suspected criminal. I'm skeptical of these sorts of moral absolutes, too, and I will not argue that police deception and dishonesty is *always* wrong.

However, I will argue for what may seem like a novel and controversial thesis—namely, that good faith is the rule in policing and deception and dishonesty are the rare exceptions. My sense is that the book's thesis only seems controversial because we have become numb to the widespread, illiberal, anything-goes, dishonest, and deceptive policing that exists today. To be sure, there are times and places for dishonesty and deception in policing, but we will see that there are good reasons to think that those times and places should be much more limited than current practices suggest.

So the Police Can Officially Lie to Me? Yes.

Despite an incredulous response to Kant's conclusion about the murderer at the door, many people are equally incredulous when they think about the more basic question: *Are the police really permitted to deceive and lie to me in the course of an official investigation?* They are indeed. And the bad cases of police dishonesty can be especially bad, leading to devastating miscarriages of justice. These are not one-off cases—they're far more common than you might think. One of the most well-known examples is the Central Park Five case.

---

[9] Andreas Bergh, Christian Bjørnskov, and Kevin Vallier, "Social and Legal Trust: The Case for Africa," in *Social Trust*, ed. Kevin Vallier and Michael Weber (New York, Routledge, 2021).

[10] See, e.g., Bradford, Jackson, and Hough, "Trust in Justice."

A young woman—who had been jogging in Manhattan's Central Park—was found near death in one of the park's wooded ravines on April 19, 1989. The woman had been brutally beaten and raped but could not remember the attack when she was able to communicate weeks later. However, five teenagers confessed to the police in the days after the crime. The boys—aged fourteen through sixteen—had been in the park with a larger group of young people who had been harassing other park-goers.

By the time the teenagers had given videotaped confessions, they had been in custody and interrogated sporadically for fourteen to thirty hours.[11] They were told—individually—that the others had implicated them in the crime.[12] The US Supreme Court—in *Frazier v. Cupp* (1969)—had long before condoned this sort of dishonesty, which helped pave the way for tactics used against the Central Park Five. In the *Frazier* case, the Court allowed a confession into evidence after the police falsely told the suspect that the suspect's cousin confessed and implicated him.[13]

The police in the Central Park Five case also claimed to have physical evidence, including fingerprints, that could link the teenagers to the crime. When one of the teenagers denied being in the park on the night of the crime, a detective said he "knew" the teen was there—including because "we have fingerprints from the woman's pants, which are satiny and smooth, and if they match yours, you're going for rape." This was a blatant lie; there were no fingerprints at all, as the detective later admitted. But upon hearing of the supposedly damning evidence, the teenager "changed his story and admitted to taking part in the attack on the woman, striking her twice with a pipe and grabbing her breasts."[14] Ultimately, all five teenagers were convicted and incarcerated.

Eventually it became clear—from both the original evidence and new evidence—that the attack had not been a gang rape, but rather by a serial criminal acting alone. The intense focus on the five teenagers meant that the true criminal—Matias Reyes, who was on a rape, assault, and murder

---

[11] For an account of the police's use of deceptive, coercive interrogation tactics (including against minors), see Douglas Starr, "The Interview," *The New Yorker* (December 1, 2013).

[12] The reporting on the Central Park Five case is voluminous. See, e.g., Saul Kassin, "False Confessions and the Jogger Case," *The New York Times* (November 1, 2002); Jim Dwyer, "The True Story of How a City in Fear Brutalized the Central Park Five," *The New York Times* (March 30, 2019); Aisha Harris, "The Central Park Five: 'We Were Just Baby Boys,'" *The New York Times* (May 30, 2019); Nigel Quiroz, "Five Facts About Police Deception and Youth You Should Know," *Innocence Project* (May 13, 2021).

[13] Frazier v. Cupp, 394 U.S. 731 (1969).

[14] Ronald Sullivan, "Detective Says He Tricked Jogger Suspect," *The New York Times* (July 24, 1990).

spree—was left on the streets. In 2002, while serving time for other crimes, Reyes confessed that he alone bludgeoned and raped the jogger; his was the only DNA recovered. The Central Park Five convictions were vacated. It might seem odd for a person to confess to a crime they did not commit (assuming interrogation does not involve physical abuse), but such confessions are all too common when a person (especially a young person) is subjected to hours-long interrogation that includes deception and dishonesty, including (false) promises (e.g., that the person can go home if they say what the police want to hear). Given an extreme power imbalance, it can indeed be rational for innocent people to plead guilty.[15]

The police tactics in the Central Park Five case serve as a very limited example of the myriad deceptive and dishonest tactics at the police's disposal. These tactics fall broadly into the category of *investigative lies*: telling lies to gather evidence and make arrests in investigations. The coming chapters will consider a variety of deceptive and dishonest investigative tactics in policing, including the well-known phenomenon of undercover and sting operations. These operations often involve the construction of an elaborate, false world to induce a person to commit a crime. We will also consider cases in which the police misrepresent a person's criminal liability (telling a person they are facing forty years of prison when in fact they are eligible for ten) to get the person to do something for the police (such as collect evidence as a police informant).

Other types of police dishonesty fall under the category referred to as "testilying": the illegal practice of lying under oath in official proceedings (perjury) to get a conviction.[16] In a related way, the police might tell lies (in reports and in charging documents) about a person's conduct in order to justify an (unjustified) police encounter, or to frame a suspect.

The rise of testilying is commonly attributed to the Supreme Court's decision in *Mapp v. Ohio* (1961).[17] The Fourth Amendment to the US Constitution states that people have a right to be free from "unreasonable searches and seizures," such as searches and seizures conducted without probable cause. The *Mapp* case held that the exclusionary rule—the rule

---

[15] For a judge's perspective on related issues, see Jed S. Rakoff, "Why Innocent People Plead Guilty," *The New York Review of Books* (June 20, 2014).

[16] See, e.g., Christopher Slobogin, "Deceit, Pretext, and Trickery: Investigative Lies by the Police," *Oregon Law Review* 76, no. 4 (Winter 1997): 776; Christopher Slobogin, "Testilying: Police Perjury and What to Do About It," *University of Colorado Law Review* 67 (1996): 1040.

[17] Mapp v. Ohio, 367 U.S. 643, 660 (1961); Slobogin, "Testilying," 1040.

barring the use of unconstitutionally obtained evidence against a suspect—applied to state-level prosecutions.

In other words, after *Mapp*, if the police engage in an unconstitutional search (say, enter your house without probable cause or a warrant), then any incriminating evidence seized from your house can be excluded from being used against you.[18] One way to circumvent the exclusionary rule is to lie about the grounds for an (unreasonable and unconstitutional) search or seizure—such as when the police testify (falsely) that you dropped drugs when the police approached you ("dropsy cases"), giving the police probable cause to conduct a search or seizure.[19]

This book considers the many varieties of police deception and dishonesty—investigative lies, testilying, and everything in between—and how these varieties are intertwined. Examining the police institution holistically, we will see that there is no single case, historical event, or factor that explains police deception and dishonesty. Police deception and dishonesty has become a normative foundation of the police institution, but that means neither that the logic of lying is justified nor that the police should embrace that logic.

But I Can Lie to the Police, Right? Wrong.

It's thus clear that the police can pursue their work dishonestly and deceptively. But you might think: Sure, police make mistakes, but their heart is in the right place because, ultimately, they're simply trying catch the bad guy. Besides, the police are only leveling the playing field because there is no law that prevents the public from lying to the police, right? Wrong. Criminal justice is supposed to be about uncovering the truth. Although the police are—paradoxically—allowed to pursue truth with untruth, members of the public are generally forbidden from lying when under police investigation.

---

[18] It is worth noting the difference between a deterrence-based rationale for excluding evidence from an integrity-based rationale. A deterrence-based rationale asks if the exclusionary rule will deter the police from obtaining evidence in ways that violate citizens' rights. An integrity-based rationale asks about the effect of admitting the evidence on the court's integrity, the notion that it will undermine rule of law values by condoning lawbreaking by the police. This is good example of the line between consequentialist and nonconsequentialist rationales for honesty and nondeception in police work. See Stuart P. Green, "The Legal Enforcement of Integrity," in *Integrity, Honesty, and Truth Seeking*, ed. Christian B. Miller and Ryan West (New York: Oxford University Press, 2020), 35–62.

[19] See, e.g., Steven Zeidman, "From Dropsy to Testilying: Prosecutorial Apathy, Ennui, or Complicity?" *Ohio State Journal of Criminal Law* 16 (2019): 426.

Indeed, it is a crime to defraud and lie to the state—including law enforcement officers—but not a crime for them to lie to you. Here are some familiar examples.[20]

Conspiracy to defraud is a crime when two or more people conspire to defraud the government in any manner and for any purpose.[21] In *Hammerschmidt v. United States*, the US Supreme Court explained the nature of "defraud":

> To conspire to defraud the United States means primarily to cheat the Government out of property or money, but it also means to interfere with or obstruct one of its lawful governmental functions by deceit, craft or trickery, or at least by means that are dishonest. It is not necessary that the Government shall be subjected to property or pecuniary loss by the fraud, but only that its legitimate official action and purpose shall be defeated by misrepresentation, chicane or the overreaching of those charged with carrying out the governmental intention.[22]

So monetary or proprietary loss is not required; instead, the fraud may simply involve dishonesty, deceit, and trickery that interferes with a lawful government function. I mention this particular crime because we will see that the police can analogously defraud a person of their rights using dishonesty, deceit, and misrepresentation.[23]

Perjury is the crime of willfully stating—contrary to an oath—any material matter that a person does not believe to be true. It is also a crime to do so in a written statement made under penalty of perjury.[24] As an example,

---

[20] For the sake of uniformity, I consider four federal provisions, though there are similar laws at the state level. It's important to note that law enforcement officers themselves are of course subject to these provisions. However, unlike the general public, law enforcement officers and other government officials have the power to use these provisions as *tools* against others.

[21] 18 U.S.C. § 371.

[22] Hammerschmidt v. United States, 265 U.S. 182, 188 (1924). Note that there are a variety of laws that prohibit specific acts of fraud, including mail fraud, wire fraud, and so on.

[23] As we will see, there are many deceptive and dishonest tactics that are difficult to identify and access. Consider the many techniques that police use when conducting an interrogation: displaying a false air of confidence with the mere goal of "confirming details," disingenuously implying empathy for the suspect's unhappy childhood, disingenuously minimizing the moral seriousness of an offense in question, disingenuously blaming society for a suspect's predicament, and so on. It would be odd to say that a police officer can never pretend to be empathetic because, otherwise, only genuinely empathetic officers would be permitted to appear so. Accordingly, we will need to distinguish these sorts of cases from deceptive and dishonest policing that is on par with fraud and deviations from the rule of law. I will argue that examples of the latter would include, say, tactics such as falsely telling a suspect that his prints were found at the scene of the crime or that his co-conspirator has confessed.

[24] 18 U.S.C. § 1621. See Bronston v. United States, 409 U.S. 352 (1973), for the standard for perjury.

Grammy-award-winning ("Lady Marmalade") rapper Lil' Kim was convicted on charges of perjury for lying to investigators and to a federal grand jury about her involvement in a shooting at a New York hip-hop radio station in 2005. She served almost a year in a federal detention center for the lie.[25]

False statements are criminalized when a person knowingly and willfully makes materially false, fictitious, or fraudulent statements or representations in the course of any matter under the jurisdiction of the government. This includes falsifying, concealing, and covering up material facts through tricks and schemes.[26] The threat of a false statement is a particularly powerful tool for federal law enforcement officers (such as FBI Agents) because the violations include any lie made during an investigation. There is no requirement that the lie occur under oath or in an official proceeding. In 2004, Martha Stewart was famously convicted of lying to the FBI over the course of an insider trading investigation—as well as obstructing justice.[27]

Obstruction of justice makes a person criminally liable when they corruptly obstruct or impede (or try to influence, obstruct, or impede) the administration of law in a government proceeding. "Corruptly" means acting with an improper purpose (or influencing another to act that way), which includes making false or misleading statements and withholding, concealing, altering, or destroying documents and other information. We can thus see how obstruction of justice may converge with the false statements law.[28] Stewart's insider trading case included charges of false statements and obstruction of justice, though many considered her dishonesty relatively mild and the severity of her charges questionable. To add insult to injury, she was roundly shamed, and her public humiliation was relished by many.[29] I am no Martha Stewart apologist; certainly, there are aspects of her career and principles with which one might disagree. My point is simply that we should consider the contradiction of criminalizing and shaming citizen acts of deception and dishonesty while unquestionably condoning and normalizing most police deception and dishonesty.

James Comey—the FBI Director who was fired by Donald Trump in 2017—oversaw Stewart's case while serving as the United States Attorney for

[25] Tom Hays, "Prosecutor: Lil' Kim Lied About Shootout," *AP News* (March 1, 2005).

[26] 18 U.S.C. § 1001.

[27] Josh Saul, "What Do Michael Flynn and Martha Stewart Have in Common? A List of People Charged With Lying to the FBI," *Newsweek* (December 1, 2017).

[28] 18 U.S.C. § 1503, 1505, and 1515(b).

[29] Martha Nussbaum, *Hiding from Humanity* (Princeton: Princeton University Press, 2004), 242–244.

the Southern District of New York. He focused on the seriousness of lying in a press conference in 2003: "This criminal case is about lying—lying to the F.B.I., lying to the S.E.C., lying to investors." He then added (perhaps a bit sanctimoniously) the following assessment of the case: "It's a tragedy that could have been prevented if . . . [Stewart] had only done what parents have taught their children for eons . . . that if you are in a tight spot, lying is not the way out. Lying is an act with profound consequences."[30] Recall that Comey—who was often called a "boy scout"—wrote a book about "the toxic consequences of lying" in 2018.[31]

The irony of Comey's statement is that the police often find themselves in tight spots that could be aided by a bit of lying and deception. And when they do lie and deceive, we often just assume that such tactics are justified parts of the job. Indeed, citizens lie and break the law when they shouldn't, and it's plausible to think the police—in order to do their job and get the truth—need to be able to lie as well. But it's worth taking a moment to reflect on the presumed default justification of police deception and dishonesty—and whether norms of deception and dishonesty should be treated as more of a reciprocal, two-way street.

The Puzzle and the Plan to Solve It

If the goal of an investigation is to find the truth—and the public are legally compelled to tell the police the truth—it's rather strange that the police can lie, deceive, and misrepresent facts in ways that effect that search for truth. One idea is to level the playing field and be more lenient with the public, allowing them to lie to the police more readily. But as we will see in the coming chapters, this solution undermines the societal value of truth-telling within communities. To be sure, there are often good reasons to prohibit (and even criminalize) lying to the state. Deception, dishonesty, and fraud harm important investigations, waste public resources, and, of course, frustrate the search for the truth.

Another idea is to seek principled constraints on the police powers of deception and dishonesty. That is the idea behind the book's thesis, and I think

---

[30] Constance L. Hays, "Prosecuting Martha Stewart: The Overview; Martha Stewart Indicted by U.S. On Obstruction," *The New York Times* (June 5, 2003).

[31] Michiko Kakutani, "James Comey Has a Story to Tell. It's Very Persuasive," *The New York Times* (April 12, 2018).

there are compelling reasons in favor of the idea. Naturally, a police institution based on deception and dishonesty affects society much more significantly than Martha Stewart's lies. A police institution based on deception and dishonesty can undermine democratic self-governance (by degrading public knowledge regarding truth) and erode public faith in the police institution itself. We don't have to look hard to see these effects in society.

Ta-Nehisi Coates makes a similar point about public faith in the police institution by drawing upon the distinction between "power" and "authority."[32] The former is derived from external force and the latter is derived from cooperation (consensual and trusting relationships, reciprocation, and so on) that leads to legitimacy. The erosion of authority contributes to the police's need to rely on external force and power. Coates describes how this leaves the community skeptical of the police: Some groups simply don't trust the police because there is "a belief that the police are as likely to lie as any other citizen."[33] This is another of the book's themes—the idea that a lack of societal trust (by the police and the community) leads to preemptive defection from cooperative overtures. Both the police and the public proactively seek to lie and deceive each other.

The situation I've described suggests a puzzle about policing. Things don't have to be this way, but, as a matter of fact, the police have been entrusted to promote that facet of justice that we broadly call security. As with other state institutions, the police institution is supposed to be based on legitimacy. Legitimacy is in part a function of authority, which is in part based on reciprocal public relationships generating rights and duties.[34] Reciprocal relationships by their nature require trust and faith.[35]

---

[32] Ta-Nehisi Coates, "The Myth of Police Reform," *The Atlantic*, April 15, 2015.

[33] Ibid.

[34] A familiar account of police legitimacy is "a property of an authority or institution that leads people to feel that authority or institution is entitled to be deferred to and obeyed." Jason Sunshine and Tom R. Tyler, "The Role of Procedural Justice and Legitimacy in Shaping Public Support for Policing," *Law & Society Review* 37, no. 3 (2003), 513–548. My focus will be on *political* legitimacy, which includes a variety of theories. For example, legitimacy may be based on consent: If a person immigrates to the United States, we might say that the person has consented (perhaps tacitly) to being governed by the state. The state thus has authority to enforce the law against the person and does so legitimately as long as the state acts in accordance with the terms of the agreement with the person (in other words, the terms to which the person consented upon immigration). If the state acts outside the terms of the agreement (e.g., governs outside the rule of law), then the state acts without authority and thus illegitimately.

[35] I suppose you could argue that the police and criminals have—in a sense—a reciprocal relationship that is not based on trust and faith (the criminal breaks the law, and the police enforces the law). However, I will focus on the common way that reciprocation is tied to cooperative societal activity in moral and political philosophy: "A necessary condition of co-operative activity is trust, where this involves the willingness of one party to rely on another to act in certain ways." Bernard Williams, *Truth and Truthfulness* (Princeton: Princeton University Press, 2002), 88.

So here's the puzzle: Despite the necessity of trust and faith in reciprocal relationships, the police institution has embraced deception, dishonesty, and bad faith as tools of the trade for providing security—indeed, it seems that providing security is *impossible* without those tools. This presents a sort of paradox, which is plausibly related to the erosion of the public's faith in the police institution and the weakening of the police's legitimacy: Trust seems important to the police institution, but so do deception, dishonesty, and bad faith.

This book suggests that one way to solve the puzzle is to show that many of our assumptions about policing and security are unjustified. Specifically, they are unjustified in the way many of our assumptions about security were unjustified after 9/11, when state institutions embraced a variety of brutal rules and tactics in pursuit of perceived security enhancements.

Analogously, the police are not justified in pursuing many of the supposed security enhancements that we think are necessary, including many proactive tactics that rely upon deception, dishonesty, and bad faith. Proactive and other deceptive policing that is on par with fraud and deviations from the rule of law is illegitimate. The upshot is that the police institution should become a more reactive (legitimate)—and less proactive (illegitimate).[36] I know this sounds odd (it is intuitive to want to preemptively stop criminals before they act, for instance), but I think we will see that the widespread use of deceptive and dishonest tactics is inconsistent with fundamental norms of political morality—and can also have debilitating effects on both communities and the police institution itself.[37]

---

[36] This conclusion builds upon my earlier work regarding the liberal *limits* of policing (*The Retrieval of Liberalism in Policing*), which I discuss in the final section of this Introduction. The conclusion also builds on the excellent work of other philosophy and police scholars, such as Jake Monaghan and his idea of "legitimacy-risk profiles." Jake Monaghan, "Boundary Policing," *Philosophy & Public Affairs* 49, no. 1 (2020).

[37] There is not always a clear distinction between proactive and reactive tactics, and, as we will see, proactiveness can certainly be a justified depending on the context (such as emergency situations in which life is at stake). Or consider how a police officer walking the beat, developing personal relationships with the residents (in part to prevent crime before it happens) might be both proactive and justified; moreover, these and other proactive tactics (such as putting more officers on the street before a large public event) may not involve deception or dishonesty. It is thus important not to paint with too broad a brush, and so we will need to distinguish between nondeceptive (and/or justified) proactive policing and deceptive and dishonest proactive policing this is unjustified because it is on par with fraud and deviations from the rule of law. In any event, it is important to note that—for every advocate of proactive policing—there are critics (and empirical data supporting their criticism) of proactive policing—even when the proactive tactics are not directly based on deception and dishonesty. See, for example, Rachel Boba Santos, "Predictive Policing: Where's the Evidence?" in *Police Innovations: Contrasting Perspectives*, ed. David Weisburd and Anthony Braga (Cambridge: Cambridge University Press, 2019), 366–98.

Chapter 1 begins with the assumption that—given basic natural facts about humans—there are certain characteristics that the rules of any human society must possess. For example, law must, to some degree, account for human vulnerability (including vulnerability to fraud) in a way that permits survival. Not only would it be impossible for a society and legal system that fails this standard to be justified and legitimate, it would be impossible for such a society to exist. Chapter 1 builds on these ideas by showing how specific legal principles are grounded in universalistic positive morality (UPM). The chapter does this in part by developing the emerging field of empirical jurisprudence as it relates to areas of law relevant to a state's use of force and brutality, as well as areas of law relating to agreements that require cooperation and trust (e.g., contractual arrangements).

Chapter 2 motivates political approaches to normativity (what societies should do) and public justification (a rationale for the state's exercise of power in a way that society members can accept) by showing how *good faith* is an indispensable normative foundation of policing as a political institution given assumptions about UPM. Here, we will examine some of the core philosophical work on honesty, transparency, and fraud. Institutional bad faith is contrary to fundamental commitments of UPM, giving rise to a crisis of legitimacy. If we mostly defer to the police regarding our security—to enforce rules and sanction the rule breakers—then we must have some degree of confidence that the institution itself will act with a disposition of good faith. There would not be much point in deferring to a social institution such as the police if it does not operate in good faith—if, for instance, the police themselves enhance human vulnerability by acting with brutality and bad faith (recall the Central Park Five case), defrauding people and undermining the rule of law (issues related to UPM). It's not a stretch to think that the contemporary police institution is actually (not hypothetically) facing a related crisis of legitimacy.

Policing is of course complicated, and the book's solution will inevitably include exceptions (recall the broken-arm-boot-bashing scenario), which will be explored through case studies in Chapters 3 and 4. This part of the book follows an Interlude—which sets forth a methodology for examining the real-world problems—and draws upon the theory from Chapters 1 and 2 to address important case studies. For example, there are principled reasons why one might argue that deception and dishonesty are (sometimes) justified in emergency situations in which life is at stake (consider kidnapping, human trafficking, and so on), but not the endless cycle of illegal drug investigations that can put officers, informants, and suspects at risk of physical harm—as well as erode public trust and legitimacy. These issues will be considered in a variety of contexts, including sting operations, deceptive interrogation practices, and pretextual encounters.

Additional complicating factors arise when we consider the overlap between domestic law enforcement and national security and intelligence work (which is conducted not only by law enforcement agencies such as the FBI, but also local and state police—often as part of a "Joint Terrorism Task Force," for example). These considerations raise questions about the connections between (dis)honesty, good faith, trust, and transparency, as well as various domains of authority and democracy. For example, we will consider the idea that transparency is important to state authority, but that transparency is often in direct opposition to honesty and trust. Consider how state requirements of transparency might encourage state officials to *increase* their deception and dishonesty by telling "half-truths" to the public (thus decreasing their trustworthiness).[38] We will thus need to examine how *too much* transparency may circumvent honesty, not that transparency itself is inherently bad.

There is a lot of ground to cover, but we will take what I hope is an engaging, discursive path that draws upon a rich variety of literature and case studies. Chapter 1 begins with Dante Alighieri's fourteenth-century epic poem, *The Divine Comedy*.

Postscript: A Special Note to the Two or Three People Who Read My Prior Work on Policing

Skip this section if you are not one of the people in this category. If you do fall into this category, your patience and readership are very much appreciated. But you might be wondering: *Why does it take three books to express one's views on the legal and philosophical problems in policing?*[39] It would be disingenuous—a lie, perhaps—to say that I had not considered the fact

---

[38] See Onora O'Neill, *A Question of Trust: The BBC Reith Lectures 2002* (Cambridge: Cambridge University Press, 2002).

[39] My first book on policing was *The Retrieval of Liberalism in Policing* (New York: Oxford University Pres, 2019), which I discuss briefly in this postscript. My second book on policing was *The Police Identity Crisis: Hero, Warrior, Guardian, Algorithm* (New York: Routledge, 2021), which examines the police role and identity from within a broader philosophical context—arguing that prominent conceptions of the police are inconsistent with collective conceptions of justice.

that this book will allow me to complete a sort of trilogy on policing. But the serious answer is that the problems of policing are difficult and must be examined from multiple perspectives.

In my first book, *The Retrieval of Liberalism in Policing*, I embraced a version of nonideal theory—or, theorizing about how to address injustice in the world as it actually exists (instead of theorizing about the ideal of justice). The methodology employed in that book is based on the argument that our efforts to address injustice in the existing world should be politically possible, effective, morally permissible, and prioritize grievances given basic assumptions about the liberal ideal of justice.

Given basic assumptions about the ideal of justice, I argued that liberal personhood is a nonideal theory priority rule—meaning that our efforts to address injustice in the existing world (specifically, injustice regarding the police's use of informants, operations that might give rise to entrapment, and surveillance) are ultimately constrained by personhood. I set forth what I took to be a relatively uncontroversial account of personhood—a tripartite conception based on reciprocation, moral agency, and human dignity—steeped in liberal legal and political philosophy. This priority rule is necessarily tied to governance by rule-of-law principles because—I argued—undue police discretion (discretion that perverts the rule of law) can itself be an affront to personhood. The goal was to retrieve the aspirational ideals of liberalism.

The nonideal methodology—and the "personhood-rule-of-law" framework—are consistent with the arguments in this book. However, this book approaches the underlying issues (police deception and dishonesty) at a different level of inquiry. Why do this, especially if these issues ultimately reduce to a lower (more fundamental) level of personhood and the rule of law?

The reason is straightforward: There will be some cases and questions in which it is more appropriate (more explanatory power, in other words) to address morality in terms of lower-level (more fundamental) questions of justice broadly construed (political philosophy), while in other cases there will be higher-level (less fundamental) questions regarding specific doctrines and laws and the extent to which they are consistent with legal norms and principles (jurisprudence). For example, many of the cases that we will examine in this book cannot be explained adequately simply by reference to "personhood" or "the rule of law," even if they in some sense reduce to those concepts. The cases more specifically raise jurisprudential questions relating to narrow doctrines regarding things such as good faith and fraud (which in turn raise specific questions about honesty, transparency, trust, and so on). These cases and ideas reach beyond my earlier work.

So these "higher" and "lower" levels of inquiry are not mutually exclusive, and I will try to highlight connections between the different levels of inquiry (and my prior work) where appropriate. My hope is that this book is consistent with—not a departure from—my earlier work, while introducing new ways to examine the legal and philosophical problems in policing. The problems are complex and multifaceted, and I continue to believe that our search for answers will benefit from many different views of the cathedral, so to speak.

PART I
THE IVORY TOWER

Five Questions and Answers Explored in Chapter 1

1. **Q: What does Dante Alighieri's *Divine Comedy* have to do with police deception and dishonesty?**

   A: Quite a bit. Not only does the medieval poem identify *force* and *fraud* as the universal mechanisms of all evil acts, it identifies deceptive and dishonest acts as worse than brutal acts. Perhaps we should reconsider the justification of a police institution enmeshed in deception and dishonesty.

2. **Q: Okay, but surely funerary cannibalism and infanticide are off topic?**

   A: Fair enough, but: These sorts of examples confirm the obvious truth that different societies have different legal, political, and moral norms, while at the same confirming that universalistic values exist across societies. This includes values regarding force and fraud. For instance.

3. **Q: What, exactly, is meant by the term universalistic positive morality (UPM)?**

   A: UPM is simply a concept encapsulating the underling ideas alluded to in Q1 and Q2 above: Societal issues regarding things such as brutality (force) and dishonesty (fraud) are grounded in positive (social) morality that is universalistic in character. It should give us pause when our legal and political institutions—such as the police—depart from UPM.

4. Q: Can you be more concrete?

A: Yes. Empirical evidence suggests that societies are oriented in a universalistic direction—in other words, they tend toward universal aims given empirical generalizations about human life and society. We can see this by doing a bit of empirical jurisprudence—or looking at the law *out there, in the world.*

5. Q: Will there be cases to consider?

A: Yes. Consider a case in which the police violently pump a person's stomach to retrieve evidence of a crime, prompting the Court to ponder universalistic themes against brutality that are embedded within positive (social) law.

1

Force and Fraud in the World
(and the Nine Circles of Hell)

We can only know what a man thinks if he tells us his thoughts, and
when he undertakes to express them he must really do so, or else
there can be no society of men.

—Immanuel Kant[1]

It is not enough that we have considered what Kant said. . . . The
price of legitimizing our universalist moral posturing is that we
make a good faith attempt to address whatever reservations, doubts,
and objections there are about our positions *out there, in the world*.

—Jeremy Waldron[2]

There are nine circles of Hell in Dante Alighieri's fourteenth-century epic
poem *The Divine Comedy*. The circles are concentric, meaning that each
circle is reserved for sinners according to the nature of the sin—with each
circle increasing in severity as the sinner moves from the outer (upper)
circle to the center (lower) circle. The result is that the nine circles of
Hell are organized by three broad categories of sin, moving from least to
most evil: (1) incontinence, (2) violence and bestiality, and (3) fraud and
malice.[3]

It is somewhat surprising to learn that murderers and war-makers—those
guilty of violence, who have a reservation in the Seventh Circle—are not the

---

[1] Immanuel Kant, *Lectures on Ethics*, trans. Louis Infield (Indianapolis: Hackett Publishing,
1963), 224.

[2] Jeremy Waldron, "How to Argue for a Universal Claim," *Columbia Human Rights Law Review* 30,
no. 2 (Spring 1999): 313.

[3] Dante Alighieri, *The Divine Comedy*, trans. John Ciardi (New York: New American Library,
2003), 94 n17. John Ciardi—an esteemed translator of *The Divine Comedy*—notes that the structure
of Dante's Hell was derived from an idiosyncratic reading of Aristotle along with Christian symboli-
zation. Ibid.

Police Deception and Dishonesty. Luke William Hunt, Oxford University Press. © Oxford University Press 2024.
DOI: 10.1093/oso/9780197672167.003.0002

most wicked of Dante's sinners. The occupants of the Seventh Circle include brutal rulers Alexander the Great, Dionysius, and Atilla the Hun—along with "assassins who for many years stalked the highways, bloody and abhorred."[4] But no, it is in the Eighth and Ninth Circles—reserved for the fraudulent and the treacherous—that we find the most wicked.[5]

The worst of the worst is Judas Iscariot, who resides in the Ninth Circle for his deceptive betrayal that precipitated the crucifixion of Jesus.[6] Slightly less bad than Judas—but in the Eighth Circle and worse than the murderers—are those guilty of regular old fraud and deceit, namely the "Falsifiers of Words."[7] The point of departure in the Eighth Circle is the Greek soldier Sinon, who deceived the Trojans in Virgil's epic poem, the *Aeneid*. There, Greek warriors devise a plan to gain entry into the city of Troy's walled interior by hiding in an enormous wooden horse. The plan called for the Greeks to pretend to sail away, leaving behind a spy, Sinon, who deceived the Trojans into bringing the horse into the city. After the Trojans took the horse inside the fortified city walls, the Greeks emerged from the horse and opened the city gates— permitting the Greek army to slaughter the Trojans. In Dante's Eighth Circle of Hell, Sinon complains that he was "put down here for a single crime" of dishonesty.[8]

Why is Sinon's single act of dishonesty so bad? Is it because lying and de- ceit are intrinsically wrong, because Sinon's motivation was wrong, or be- cause of the consequences of his deception? More generally, why does Dante describe the dishonest and fraudulent as worse than the violent? And why do we care what Dante thinks in the first place? Dante's epic poem is one of the greatest works of world literature, but that is hardly a satisfying answer.

Invoking Dante is of course mostly a rhetorical move—an evocative way to illustrate the long-standing and widespread idea that fraud (and force, particularly brutality) are morally dubious, to say the least. Dante makes a compelling case, reminding us that a single act of deception can change the world forever. On the other hand, a fourteenth-century narrative poem is an idiosyncratic way to begin a book about contemporary policing. But let's continue this circuitous route—weaving in and out of legal and

---

[4] Ibid., 100–101.
[5] Ibid., 141, 248.
[6] Ibid., 266. See also the Gospel of Mark, the Gospel of John, and the Book of Acts.
[7] Ibid., 232. Also described as "the false witness."
[8] Ibid. 236.

political philosophy—as we approach the central issue of police deception and dishonesty.

Our primary objective is to begin the process of examining force and fraud in our social arrangements. The various ways that societies account for the relationship between force and fraud are important in determining the extent to which our social institutions are justified. We will jump in with a rather abstract topic: the nature of law. Admittedly, this topic can illicit yawns from even the most committed student of jurisprudence. But we will approach the topic by considering a big, controversial claim: *There are specific characteristics that the legal system of any society must possess in order for the society to exist at all.* This is presumably controversial because it is empirically true that the legal systems of different societies are vastly different. And yet we will consider how they must all converge in some very basic ways.

Other philosophers of law have made similar arguments, which I'll examine briefly. My sense is that these philosophers are mostly right—or at least gesturing toward something right—and so I won't be attacking anyone's views. Instead, I'll try to add something to the conversation that has been left out in other work. We will tie fundamental normative requirements of the law (how the law ought to be) to empirical studies regarding the way the law actually exists in the world. In other words, we will do a bit of empirical jurisprudence to show how societal issues regarding things such as brutality (force) and dishonesty (fraud) are grounded in positive (social) morality that is universalistic in character—what I call universalistic positive morality (UPM).

Despite the word *universalistic*, UPM need not depend on anything mysterious. It might be impossible to reach agreement about moral *universals* regarding force and fraud, but it is less contentious to say that all societies are oriented in a *universalistic* direction—in other words, that they *tend* toward universal aims given empirical generalizations about human life and society.[9] UPM, then, simply relies on a normative backdrop recognized by

[9] The term "universalistic" might sound like a noncommittal way of endorsing "universal" or "universalist" moral claims, but I think *universalistic* best captures the idea that the structure of human societies leads to certain common features about law and morality. There is a variety of work that helps support my account of UPM, as well as general claims about the factual importance of honesty. See, e.g., Ivar R. Hannikainen, Kevin P. Tobia, Guilherme da F. C. F. de Almeida, Raff Donelson, Vilius Dranseika, Markus Kneer, Niek Strohmaier, Piotr Bystranowski, Kristina Dolinina, Bartosz Janik, Sothie Keo, Egle Lauraityt, Alice Liefgreen, Maciej Próchnicki, and Alejandro Rosas, "Are There Cross-Cultural Legal Principles? Modal Reasoning Uncovers Procedural Constraints on Law," *Cognitive Science* 45, no. 8 (August 2021) (finding support across several languages and countries for conditions such as law's intelligibility, prospectively, and so on); John Mikhail, "Universal

the law, such as a collective positive moral conception to which institutions have some sort of obligation. The hope is that taking this path will illuminate common threads about force and fraud that are derived from empirical generalizations about people and society.

You might be thinking: How is "empirical jurisprudence" and "UPM" related to contemporary questions about police deception and dishonesty? The answer is straightforward: If the police institution is constrained by law—and if the law of all societies includes requisite characteristics of honesty and related concepts—then those characteristics of law will be relevant to the police institution in important ways. This exercise will thus allow us to consider (in the later chapters) deviations from UPM in the unique context of policing, as well as the extent to which those deviations are justified.

A few concepts will come up repeatedly in the book, and it might help to provide a preliminary account of how I will use those concepts.

- *Honesty*: The virtue of being disposed to not purposefully distort the facts as one sees them for good motivating reasons—required in cooperative relations with others.[10]
- *Good faith*: A disposition of honesty in contractual relations, including reaching agreements and the faithful adherence to the scope, purpose, and terms of agreements.[11]
- *Deception*: Intentionally misleading others so that they believe something that is false, as well as intentionally making assertions—believed

Moral Grammar: Theory, Evidence, and the Future, *TRENDS in Cognitive Sciences* 11, no. 4 (April 2007) (providing evidence in support of the relationship between legal theory and universal moral grammar, which seeks to describe the nature and origin of moral knowledge by using concepts and models similar to those used in Chomsky's program in linguistics); Tom R. Tyler, "What Is Procedural Justice: Criteria Used by Citizens to Assess the Fairness of Legal Procedures," *Law & Society Review* 22 (1988): 103–136 (indicating that procedural justice can have a significant impact on laypeople's experience with courts and police, and that honesty is an important aspect of procedural justice). With respect to theoretical work on the universal grammar of criminal law specifically, see George P. Fletcher, *Basic Concepts of Criminal Law* (New York: Oxford University Press, 1998); Stuart P. Green, "The Universal Grammar of Criminal Law," *Michigan Law Review* 98, no. 6 (2000): 2104–2125.

[10] See Christian B. Miller, *Honesty: The Philosophy and Psychology of a Neglected Virtue* (New York: Oxford University Press, 2021), 132, which will be discussed in Chapter 2.

[11] See, e.g., Daniel Markovits, "Good Faith Is Contract's Core Value," in *Philosophical Foundations of Contract Law*, ed. Gregory Klass, George Letsas, and Prince Saprai (New York: Oxford, 2014); Richard R.W. Brooks, "Good Faith in Contractual Exchanges," in *The Oxford Handbook of the New Private Law*, ed. Andrew S. Gold, John C. P. Goldberg, Daniel B. Kelly, Emily Sherwin, and Henry E. Smith (New York: Oxford, 2020); discussed in Chapter 2.

to be false—to mislead others (lying); the opposite of truth and truthfulness.[12]

- *Fraud*: Deception or dishonesty to gain an unjust advantage, injuring the rights and interests of others and leading to enmity and a lack of cooperation—the epitome of bath faith and the opposite of good faith.[13]
- *Force*: Dynamic, constraining power marked by defection, enmity, and a lack of cooperation.[14]

That is my roadmap for the chapter. We now return to a slightly more discursive discussion of force, fraud, and the law.

1. On the Nature of Law (and Cannibalism)

It is difficult to think of a more applied philosophical topic than policing. Policing is clearly a pressing concern in public life and a topic of public discourse—in the news, in academia, in the courts, and on the streets. The horrific murder of George Floyd in 2020—or Tyre Nichols in 2023—did not represent an inflection point or usher in a new era of policing. Instead, the police institution has remained the same in many respects—a reminder that we still have a long way to go.[15] Recall that the officers watched calmly as Floyd died, even while being filmed by the public in broad daylight for all to see. That is how strong the presumption is in favor of the priority of law enforcement, regardless of how petty the underlying crime might be.

---

[12] For a discussion of the moral relevance of the distinction between lying and deception, see Thomas L. Carson, "The Range of Reasonable Views about the Morality of Lying," in *Lying: Language, Knowledge, Ethics, and Politics*, ed. Eliot Michaelson and Andreas Stokke (Oxford: Oxford University Press, 2018), 145–160; Thomas L. Carson, "Lying, Deception, and Related Concepts: A Conceptual Map for Ethics," in *From Lying to Perjury*, ed. Laurence R. Horn (Berlin: De Gruyter Mouton, 2022), 15–40. I will mostly avoid this distinction, arguing more broadly that police deception and dishonesty are unjustified when they are on par with fraud. For a different (folk) concept of lying that draws on empirical studies, see Alex Wiegmann and Jörg Meibauer, "The Folk Concept of Lying," *Philosophy Compass* 14, no. 8 (2019).

[13] See Stuart P. Green, *Lying, Cheating, and Stealing: A Moral Theory of White-Collar Crime* (Oxford: Oxford University Press, 2006), which will be discussed in Chapter 2; and Stuart P. Green, *13 Ways to Steal a Bicycle* (Cambridge: Harvard University Press, 2012), 111–113, for a discussion of the meaning of the term "dishonesty" in the English law of theft. Note that Green—with whom I agree—does not equate the concepts of deception, dishonesty, and fraud, which of course have different meanings in the law.

[14] See generally the political philosophy of Thomas Hobbes and John Locke, discussed in Chapter 2.

[15] I examine Floyd's murder, the demands of justice, and what it might mean to transition toward meeting those demands in "Policing, Brutality, and the Demands of Justice, *Criminal Justice Ethics* 40, no. 1 (2021): 40–55.

Under such circumstances, it strikes me as a good thing that recent philosophical work on policing is for the most part planted firmly in the world, avoiding esoteric abstractions.[16] And when we turn to the judiciary, judges typically want (and often need) to avoid philosophical handwringing. Courts resolve real cases involving real people, not philosophical thought experiments. On the other hand, the lack of philosophical depth in judicial opinions can result in rulings that lack practical nuance: the police are simply given the benefit of the doubt based on the value of law enforcement and crime reduction—an end that justifies the means, in other words.

For example, the Supreme Court's description of police use-of-force decisions illuminates the perception that policing is inherently dangerous, and that quibbling about that point increases the danger: "police officers are often forced to make split-second judgements . . . in circumstances which are tense, uncertain, and rapidly evolving."[17] Given this backdrop, let us swim upstream and do a bit of legal and philosophical rumination—examining force and fraud as they relate to the nature of law. The payoff will include some surprising conclusions regarding how philosophical conceptions of force, fraud, and the law apply to the police.

When we talk about constraints on policing, we often talk about *the rule of law* (roughly, governance by law rather than governance by the unjustified discretion of political officials)[18] instead of *the nature of the law*. The rule of law is undoubtedly an important component of policing—and there is overlap between the rule of law and the nature of the law—but let's focus on the nature of the law itself for a moment. The police are constrained by the law and legal doctrines, and it makes sense to consider what that means on a very basic level. A fairly common understanding is that by *law* we mean

---

[16] See, e.g., Jake Monaghan, *Just Policing* (New York: Oxford University Press, 2023); Brandon del Pozo, *The Police and the State* (Cambridge: Cambridge University Press, 2023). These books are invaluable contributions to the recent philosophical literature on policing and should be read carefully.

[17] Graham v. Connor, 490 U.S. 386, 396–397 (1989). One problem with this standard is that is fails to consider officers' actions that *lead to* their being in a position that requires split-second judgments. See Ben Jones, "Police-Generated Killings: The Gap between Ethics and Law," *Political Research Quarterly* 75, no. 2 (2022).

[18] To be sure, there are good reasons to think that political discretion is justified and legitimate; this is not only because of the practical issue of limited resources, but also due to a deep background norm of discretion in liberal states. See Hunt, *The Retrieval of Liberalism in Policing*, ch. 5. Police discretion is in some sense derivative of broader state executive authority and discretion, though there are important boundaries of authority. See Monaghan, *Just Policing*; and Monaghan, "Boundary Policing." In short, the problem is not discretion itself, but rather exceeding the principled limits of discretion—which is a function of constraining rule of law principles. See Fuller, *The Morality of Law*; Raz, *The Authority of Law*. These points raise practical policy questions about how institutions can be reformed such that they operate in a way that is consistent with background norms regarding the rule of law (and mitigate unjustified and illegitimate uses of discretion).

social rules with a recognized political history and origin (or "pedigree"), including social rules that require judges to weigh moral principles given the indeterminacy of language.[19] This is one way to describe what is meant by the term *positive law*.

How is the nature of law relevant to police deception and dishonesty? Well, difficult cases regarding police deception and dishonesty should have justificatory support based upon both principles derived from appropriate sources (case precedent, legislation, and so on) and appropriate content (moral commitments regarding the rule of law, authority, discretion, and so on). Given a hard case, there will be conflicts among various principles (for instance, commitments to security versus the rule of law) that must be weighed regarding their societal appropriateness. Under this rationale, the application of the law to novel cases involving police deception and dishonesty is not only about what a relevant legal doctrine *is*, but what it *should* be.

The takeaway (my takeaway, at least) is that the law is—at bottom, notwithstanding the role moral principles may play in interpretation—*social* in nature. And yet we will examine how much of this social, positive law is also universalistic in nature. The upshot is that deviations from UPM should give us pause, especially in the case of state functions such as policing.

One worry about the idea of UPM is that it creates a puzzle: How is the law universalistic given the obvious variation in law from society to society? Consider James Rachel's classic example regarding the variety of burial practices among different cultures:

> Darius, a king of ancient Persia, was intrigued by the variety of cultures he encountered in his travels. He had found, for example, that the Callatians (a tribe of Indians) customarily ate the bodies of their dead fathers. The

---

[19] See, e.g., H. L. A. Hart, *The Concept of Law* (Oxford: Oxford University Press, 2012); Brian Bix, "H.L.A. Hart and the 'Open Texture' of Language," *Law and Philosophy* 10, no. 1 (Feb. 1991). See also Ronald Dworkin's opposing conception of the law (interpretivism), especially *Law's Empire* (Cambridge: Belknap Press, 1986). There are of course a wide range of views on these issues, and it is beyond the scope of this book to consider them in detail. Roughly, exclusive positivism maintains that a norm's legal validity is never dependent on its moral content, while, on the other hand, Dworkin maintains that the dependence of legal validity on moral considerations is an essential feature of law given the law's profoundly interpretative nature. Inclusive positivism generally maintains that legal validity's dependence upon moral considerations is a contingent proposition, thus affirming the social thesis (law is a social phenomenon) and claiming that moral considerations affect legal validity only where it is dictated by the social rules that happen to prevail in a given legal system. In other words, it might be a social rule that legal validity should be based upon moral considerations. Scott J. Shapiro, "The 'Hart-Dworkin' Debate: A Short Guide for the Perplexed," in *Ronald Dworkin*, ed. Arthur Ripstein (Cambridge: Cambridge University Press, 2007), 22–55.

Greeks, of course, did not do that—the Greeks practiced cremation and regarded the funeral pyre as the natural and fitting way to dispose of the dead.[20]

I bet you can guess what the Greeks thought about the Callatians' practice, and vice versa.

> Darius . . . summoned some Greeks who happened to be present at his court and asked them what they would take to eat the bodies of their dead fathers. They were shocked, as Darius knew they would be, and replied that no amount of money could persuade them to do such a thing. Then Darius called in some Callatians, and . . . asked them what they would take to burn their dead fathers' bodies. The Callatians were horrified and told Darius not even to mention such a dreadful thing.[21]

These sorts of examples illustrate what many people assume is a simple truth that supports a broad conception of relativism: different societies have different moral systems and "[w]hat is thought right within one group may be utterly abhorrent to the members of another group, and vice versa."[22] But perhaps it's not so simple.

As Rachels notes, if you think that eating one's dead parents sounds shocking, consider how the practice might be a gesture of respect symbolizing the desire for one's "spirit to dwell within us" (while burying or burning a corpse would be seen as a rejection of the deceased). Both those who eat their dead and those who burn their dead could thus be viewed as pursuing the same value (respect for the dead). This is true even though the societal beliefs and customs are different and even though neither custom is "objectively" right or wrong.[23]

It is one thing to consider the broad overlap between societal values, but another to think that the law itself is universalistic in character. Let's begin by considering two ways to ground UPM: viability and spirit.

---

[20] James Rachels, "The Challenge of Cultural Relativism," in *The Elements of Moral Philosophy* (1986).
[21] Ibid.
[22] Ibid.
[23] Ibid.

1.1. The Law's Viability

Like all animals, humans have unique features that set them apart from other organisms. Humans are endothermic (or "warm-blooded") mammals that must be protected in particular ways according to their biological systems. The heart must beat and pump blood for life to continue. Sooner or later, the beating action will cease, the skin will whiten and cool, and life departs the body. Both internal and external forces prompt this process—a clogged artery, an automobile accident, or the trauma inflicted by a knife or bullet piercing the body.

These obvious natural facts rarely receive a second thought, and yet they underly every facet of life because they speak to the continuation of life itself. If there is no life, then there is no human, no human society, and no human law about which to worry. It is thus a practical necessity to protect and maintain our biological systems—to eat, drink, breathe, and fend off threats to bodily integrity—if we wish to continue musing about the nature of the law.

Humans are intelligent animals who understand these platitudes—that social arrangements (whether customary rules and practices, or more contemporary conceptions of "law")—must be organized in a particular way in order to maintain life. If law is a component of those social arrangements, then law must likewise be constructed in a particular way if life is to continue. In this sense, then, one might say that the (positive) law created in our social arrangements ultimately has a necessary connection to natural facts. It is this basic point that motivates what H. L. A. Hart—perhaps the most important philosopher of law of the twentieth century—called "the minimum content of natural law."[24]

Hart was a proponent of legal positivism: the contention that "it is in no sense a necessary truth that laws reproduce or satisfy certain demands of morality."[25] In other words, unlike natural law theorists, Hart argued that morally reprehensible law can in fact still qualify as "law." How, then, does Hart square his account of legal positivism with the very idea of Natural Law

[24] Some have disagreed with Hart's characterization of this idea. S. B. Drury writes that Hart's attempt "to define 'viable' rather than 'valid' law" means that "[i]t is therefore an error to consider the minimum content theory a theory of natural law [because] [i]t fails to qualify even as a most 'attenuated' version of natural law." Drury's point is that "a legal system need have no moral content to be 'viable.'" S. B. Drury, "H. L. A. Hart's Minimum Content Theory of Natural Law," *Political Theory* 9, no. 4 (November 1981): 544. Relatedly, James Allan writes that when Hart uses the label "Minimum Content of Natural Law" he is "talking about natural law not in its core [Thomasian] sense but in a penumbral or open texture sense." James Allan, "Is You Is or Is You Ain't Hart's Baby? Epstein's Minimum Content of Natural Law," *Ratio Juris* 20, no. 2 (June 2007): 219–220.

[25] Hart, *The Concept of Law*, 184.

(the contention that "there are certain principles of human conduct, awaiting discovery by human reason, with which man-made law must conform if it is to be valid")?[26]

He distinguishes between basic truths about human beings (such as those noted above regarding the continuation of life, which are said to constitute the *minimum* content of Natural Law) from the "more grandiose and more challengeable conceptions of Natural Law."[27] In other words, unless the law has a particular sort of content to a minimum degree, humans would be unable to survive together in their social arrangements.

Indeed, Hart characterized his classic book, *The Concept of Law*, as "an essay in descriptive sociology."[28] The book examines five truisms that illuminate the relationship between natural facts and the content of legal and moral rules.[29]

   (i) Human vulnerability
  (ii) Approximate equality
 (iii) Limited altruism
 (iv) Limited resources
  (v) Limited understanding and strength of will

Let's consider each briefly, lingering on the first and the last. We will begin to see how these truisms are in fact empirical generalizations that are deeply important to both the law and the police.

If we assume that survival—simply keeping the heart beating—is a personal and societal value generally, then we have good reason to say that the content of any legal and moral code must account for *human vulnerability*. Sure, contemporary discussions of law and morality might focus on our duty to keep others alive through rescue and charity—helping the distant needy and being a "Good Samaritan," so to speak.[30] There is indeed a lot of anguish about these questions. If I can save a life in a distant land by sending $100 to a charitable organization, then perhaps I ought to send the check rather than splurge on a fancy dinner for myself—or buying a fancy pair of shoes, or a fancy bicycle, and so on. On the other hand, perhaps I have a right to live my

---

[26] Ibid., 186.
[27] Ibid., 193.
[28] Ibid., Preface.
[29] Ibid., 194–200.
[30] I consider related questions myself in "The Legitimacy and Limits of Punishing 'Bad Samaritans,'" *University of Florida Journal of Law and Public Policy* 31, no. 3 (2022).

life how I choose, instead of devoting myself to the lives of others. This debate has become a cottage industry in moral philosophy and has given rise to the controversial "effective altruism" movement.[31]

There is much less controversy regarding the extent to which people have a right to harm and use violence against others. There are good reasons to think we have no right to harm others outside a relatively narrow range of exceptions—primarily exceptions involving personal and societal defense. Almost no one seriously doubts that violence is sometimes justified (legally and morally) when the violence is necessary to stay alive due to a threat by another.[32] If my family and I are attacked in my home—or if the homeland is attacked by a foreign power—then we generally do not bat an eye when there is a proportional violent response. This simply points us back to the personal and societal value we place on survival.

Correlatively, no one seriously doubts that violence is unjustified (legally and morally) and should be restricted outside these and similar exceptions. There will always be hard cases—*Was it truly self-defense? Was it truly a just war?*—but there are many easy cases. Consider run-of-the-mill acts such as assault, rape, murder, and torture—as well as brutal acts of violence that go beyond any need or necessity. Aside from farfetched thought experiments within the ivory tower, the legal and moral impermissibility of such acts is not questioned seriously. There is near universal condemnation (legal and moral) when such acts do occur. One of the reasons for this is straightforward and uncontroversial. If we don't have rules to protect human vulnerability in these ways, then there is no point in having any rules at all because there will be no one at all to protect.

This point is supported by Hart's second, third, and fourth truisms—*approximate equality, limited altruism,* and *limited resources.* People are more or less equal; no matter how strong or cunning a person might be, they can never be free from their human vulnerability. No one has a "force field"—as children sometimes pretend in games—that keeps one safe from harm. This unique, human vulnerability is one of the things that makes us equal.[33]

---

[31] See, e.g., William MacAskill, *Doing Good Better* (New York: Avery, 2015); Amia Srinivasan, "Stop the Robot Apocalypse," *London Review of Books* 37, no. 18 (September 24, 2015) (reviewing *Doing Good Better*).

[32] Of course, an absolute pacifist might argue that violence is never justified (even in cases of self-defense and defense of others), but I will not consider such a strict view because it strikes me as extremely problematic and contrary to the basic norms of liberal (and other) political morality.

[33] The view that human beings are equal has a long history in philosophy (see, e.g., Hobbes, *Leviathan*, 94), but we need not rely on the arguments of philosophers only. Consider, say, the

Unfortunately, history and human psychology—including the human propensity for violence—have shown that people cannot account for their equal vulnerability by relying on the altruism of others. As Hart puts it, people are neither angels nor devils. So while there are some everyday saints out there, our history and evidence also suggests a strong undercurrent of human egoism and self-interest—especially given *limited resources* for survival (food, water, shelter, and so on). These descriptive claims about people show why the minimum content of any legal and moral system necessarily includes some degree of "mutual forbearance and compromise."[34]

People are still in need of the ability to predict—with some degree of confidence—that others will cooperate in such a system. Otherwise, there is no guarantee that one's forbearance will be reciprocated by others, or that one's trust and good faith reliance will not be taken advantage of by others. This leads to Hart's final truism: *limited understanding and strength of will.*

The upshot of this truism is that sanctions are necessary to ensure that one's trust and good faith cooperation will not be taken advantage of by others. This does not mean that societal rules must enforce all promises or ensure that people are always honest. The idea is not to seek some sort of human flourishing or to guide one on the path to becoming a better (moral) citizen and person (*contra* the discussion of legal scholar Richard Epstein discussed later in the chapter). No, the idea is instead that societal rules must provide some degree of sanction when people choose to defect from the rules that protect human vulnerability. We are not justified in expecting perfect compliance with the rules, but we are justified in expecting recourse when one fails to act with a basic disposition of honesty and good faith.

This is apparent at both the individual level and the institutional level. If you pay me ten dollars in exchange for my agreeing to give you ten pounds of grain after harvest, then you must have some assurance that I won't simply take the money and run—defraud you, in other words. If there is no recourse when people defect from social rules, there would be no point in having social rules because the rules would not protect people from vulnerability.

Likewise, if we defer to social institutions for recourse—to enforce rules and sanction the rule breakers—then we must have some degree of

---

scientific research of the Human Genome Project (HGP), which sought to map all the genes of the human genome. Although the genome of each individual is unique, the HGP shows that the mosaic human genome is the same in the vast majority of all humans.

[34] Hart, *The Concept of Law*, 195.

confidence that the social institution itself will act with a disposition of honesty. There would not be much point in deferring to a social institution such as the police if the police do not operate honestly—if, for instance, the police themselves enhance human vulnerability by acting with brutality and bad faith, defrauding people and undermining the rule of law.

What are the limits of these empirical generalizations? It might appear that Hart's truisms suggest a necessary connection between what is required of law and what is required of morality. Indeed, I've noted how law serves no purpose whatsoever if it does not account for Hart's minimal truisms regarding the human condition. But that does not mean there is a necessary connection between the substance of law and the substance of morality. In other words, if the minimum content of the natural law is satisfied *immorally*, it is still satisfied.[35]

Consider the history of the United States. The minimum content of the natural law—which is manifest in the protections and benefits of US law—has been extended to a wide range of the US populace. The human condition—including human vulnerability, approximate equality, limited altruism, limited resources, and limited understanding and strength of will—has been addressed through a system of mutual forbearance that is manifest in US law.

On the other hand, the protections and benefits of US law have been withheld (to varying degrees at different times) to large groups of persons—in the form of slavery, Jim Crow, contemporary policing, and beyond. And it's worth noting the police's role in enforcing slavery and Jim Crow laws.[36] The point is that the minimum content of natural law (Hart's truisms about the human condition) is necessary for there to *be* law, but that does not mean that the law is necessarily applied and distributed in a way that is consistent with morality.

The truisms about the human condition have always been addressed in US law—thus fulfilling the minimum conditions for law to exist with respect to some persons—even though the law oppressed other persons based on race, ethnicity, sex, and so on. Suppose Hart's truisms were only applied by Congress to Americans with brown and blond hair. Hart could say the United States indeed has a viable set of laws; however, they are nevertheless morally unjustified laws. This allows for there to be laws—such as the Jim

---

[35] Hart, *The Concept of Law*, 200.
[36] See, e.g., Alex S. Vitale, "The Police Are Not Here to Protect You," *Vice News*, June 1, 2020, for historic examples of the police connection to slave patrols.

Crow United States—which both meet his minimum standard yet remain immoral.

In short, the law has always reduced human vulnerability (for some) in the United States, but it obviously has not always applied morality correctly (indeed, the law has increased human vulnerability for others). It thus becomes clear that Hart's truisms about the human condition do not constitute a necessary connection between the content of law and the content of morality.

So what is minimally required of any viable legal system? It must protect (some) people from vulnerability to brutal and fraudulent behavior. A related conclusion we can draw is that people must have some degree of confidence that social institutions such as the police will act with a disposition of honesty. Again, there wouldn't be much point in deferring to the police institution if it *enhanced* human vulnerability through acts of brutality and bad faith, defrauding people and undermining the rule of law. If the police institution *is* using fraud in a way that enhances the vulnerability of some groups of people, it should give us pause.

1.2. The Law's Spirit

Consider the case of *Rochin v. California*.[37] Police entered Rochin's residence and noticed on Rochin's nightstand two capsules, which Rochin immediately swallowed. After attempting to extract the capsules from Rochin's mouth, the officers took Rochin to a hospital, strapped him to an operating table, had a tube forcibly placed in his mouth and stomach, and then gave him an emetic solution that caused him to vomit the capsules into a bucket. The officers retrieved the capsules, tested them to be morphine, and submitted them as evidence against Rochin (who was found guilty of unlawful possession of morphine). In striking down the conviction, the US Supreme Court noted that the brutality of the means used to extract the evidence "shocks the conscience" and violates the due process of law.[38]

How did the Court merge its legal conclusion with ideas of conscience? The constitutional question before the Court was about the limitations the Due Process Clause of the Fourteenth Amendment imposes on the conduct of criminal proceedings by the States. Although criminal justice is left

[37] Rochin v. California, 342 U.S. 165 (1952).
[38] Ibid., 172.

primarily to the States (e.g., defining crimes is the States' prerogative), the federal government provides oversight regarding the manner in which the state may enforce its criminal laws. To wit: The Fourteenth Amendment to the US Constitution reads: "nor shall any State deprive any person of life, liberty, or property, without due process of law." In addition to the more straightforward *procedural* protections in this language, the Fourteenth Amendment includes *substantive* due process: fundamental rights unrelated to procedure, such as rights derived from the first eight amendments to the Constitution.

Consider how the *Rochin* Court explained—with unabashedly lofty language—both its role in protecting due process and the nature of due process itself:

- *Canons of decency and fairness*: The Court's role is said to be one of determining "whether [the proceedings] offend those canons of decency and fairness which express the notions of justice."[39]
- *Traditions and conscience*: Due process of law is thus a "constitutional guarantee of respect for those personal immunities which . . . are 'so rooted in the traditions and conscience of our people as to be ranked as fundamental' or are 'implicit in the concept of ordered liberty.' "[40]
- *A fittingly imprecise sense of justice*: "Due process of law, as a historic and generative principle, precludes defining, and thereby confining, these standards of conduct more precisely than to say that convictions cannot be brought about by methods that offend 'a sense of justice.' "[41]
- *Gloss and unfixed technical content*: "The gloss of some of the verbal symbols of the Constitution does not give them a fixed technical content. It exacts a continuing process of application."[42]

The above excerpts seem clearly to be reaching beyond the law as written, but reaching for what? The Court denies that it is appealing to *natural law*, but instead suggests that the analysis of linguistic "gloss" is simply part of the judicial process.

---

[39] Ibid., 169 (quoting Malinski v. New York, 324 U. S. 416–417).
[40] Ibid. (quoting Snyder v. Massachusetts, 291 U.S. 97, 291 U. S. 105; Palko v. Connecticut, 302 U. S. 319, 302 U. S. 325).
[41] Ibid., 173 (quoting Brown v. Mississippi, 297 U. S. 278, 297 U. S. 285–286).
[42] Ibid., 170.

Drawing on this rather abstract rationale, the Court answers the specific question presented in the *Rochin* case as follows: If the police cannot forcibly extract the contents of one's mind to get a conviction, then the police cannot forcibly extract the contents of one's stomach to get a conviction. The Court's reasoning thus involves two converging lines of thought, one legal (norms of constitutional law) and one moral (norms of conscience).

There is first the legal doctrine of confessions and its relation to the Due Process Clause. The Court explains that involuntary, coerced verbal confessions are inadmissible under the Due Process Clause because they "offend the community's sense of fair play and decency."[43] Likewise, the Court reasoned, sanctioning the police's actions in the *Rochin* case (forcibly extracting physical evidence from a person's body) would amount to giving "brutality the cloak of law" and "brutalize the temper of society."[44] The concurring opinion written by Justice Douglas makes this idea more explicit: "words taken from his lips, capsules taken from his stomach, blood taken from his veins, are all inadmissible provided they are taken . . . without . . . consent. They are inadmissible because of the command of the Fifth Amendment [which protects the privilege against self-incrimination]."[45] We can thus think of the *Rochin* case both as being grounded in the prohibition of coerced confessions and coerced consent, as well as being grounded in a more abstract "conscience" regarding norms against *brutality*.

What do we make of all the legal striving regarding "conscience"? Legal scholar Sanford Levinson suggests "that there is far less of a 'common conscience' than we might wish, whatever may be the degree of our ostensible agreement on the abstract statement of the norms in question."[46] So we are left with the view that while we might in *theory* agree about abstract moral norms regarding brutality, there is actually very little "common conscious" in *practice*. This point foreshadows my conclusion that UPM must be construed in the context of empirical jurisprudence—*what we in fact do in practice*.

Before digging deeper into that idea, let's try to make better sense of the law's *conscience*—or the law's *spirit*. Jeremy Waldron does this by developing

---

[43] Ibid., 173.

[44] Ibid., 173–174.

[45] The Fifth Amendment to the US Constitution—which had not been incorporated (and so was only applicable to the federal government, not the states) at the time the *Rochin* case was decided—protects one from being "compelled in any criminal case to be a witness against himself."

[46] Sanford Levinson, "In Question of a Common Conscience: Reflections on the Current Debate about Torture," *Journal of National Security Law & Policy* 1, no. 2 (2005): 252.

the idea of a *legal archetype*: a "provision . . . which by virtue of its force, clarity, and vividness expresses the spirit that animates the whole area of law . . . a sort of emblem, token, or icon of the whole."[47] For example, a concrete rule against police brutality might express the legal system's overall spirit of conceiving of persons as moral agents, not merely objects of subjugation. And a concrete rule against fraud might express the legal system's overall spirit of conceiving of persons as moral agents deserving of honesty dealings.

These ideas echo Hart's point about the law's viability, as well as create a puzzle about the law: There are certain things that all of us need and want in society. One of those things is security, which is an important value that helps justify any political society or state. If a state cannot protect its people from each other (internal threats), there is not much point in having a state at all. No legal system is viable that fails to protect at least some of its members from human vulnerability, brutality, and fraud.

Here is the puzzle: Everyone agrees that providing security is an important state function. But how should we evaluate situations in which it seems that the state's use of repugnant tactics (torture, brutality, fraud) would *enhance* the state's ability to provide security?[48] Here is Waldron's argument in a nutshell: the state should not use such tactics because they undermine the entire spirit of the law.

Recall the earlier point that something can still be "law" even if it fails various standards of morality.[49] Jim Crow laws were deeply immoral given very basic assumptions about the moral equality of all humans, but they were still laws as long as they were enacted according to the requisite institutional processes for making law.[50] The upshot is that what we call "laws" are fundamentally social artifacts. The requisite US social institutions (US Congress, state legislatures, and so on) could make a variety of practices legal in order to enhance the state's ability to fight crime and terrorism. This might include

[47] Jeremy Waldron, *Torture, Terror, and Trade-Offs* (Oxford: Oxford University Press, 2010), 227.

[48] By "repugnant" I mean simply tactics that are contrary to the minimal legal norms for a state to be viable. As discussed earlier, all legal systems must include certain minimal content to be viable (e.g., law must protect some people from vulnerability to brutality, fraud, and so on). Because it is not true that a legal system must protect *all* people from such vulnerability in order to be viable (consider Jim Crow laws), states may embrace repugnant tactics (such as torture) that apply to a limited number of people (e.g., serious internal and external threats, such as terrorists) and still maintain a viable legal system.

[49] Hart, *The Concept of Law*, 184.

[50] The US legal system in the Jim Crow era satisfied Hart's minimum content of natural law—discussed earlier—with respect to *some* people, which is why it can be described as both a viable and an immoral legal system.

legalizing torture or police brutality—and various forms of dishonesty, deception, fraud, and corruption—in high-stakes law enforcement and intelligence cases. As was the case after 9/11, a variety of *ends justify the means* arguments were in fact used to enact similar legislation.[51] In spite of the legal validity of such laws, Waldron worries that they undermine the fundamental *spirit* of the law.

To provide a more concrete account of the law's "spirit," consider the distinction between *rules* and *principles*.[52] For instance, if I drive 65 miles-per-hour in a 60 mile-per-hour zone, then the rule (no driving over 60 miles-per-hour) conclusively resolves the underlying legal question. On the other hand, some cases cannot be resolved so easily because there aren't any applicable concrete rules. In such cases, social institutions (such as courts) must weigh and apply various *principles*—deciding cases based upon broader considerations of equity, proportion, and so on, emanating from the overall legal system.

Following this line of reasoning, one might say that certain prohibitions (such as those against brutality, torture, fraud, and corruption) are not *just* concrete rules; they also emanate background norms that undergird the entire legal system. Waldron refers to these sorts of provisions as *archetypes* because they symbolize the *spirit* of the law in question.[53]

Okay, but you probably want more of an explanation than that. Well, archetypes are housed—somewhat mysteriously—within concrete provisions of positive law; it is thus a particular provision of concrete positive law that operates as an archetype, expressing the broader spirit of the legal system. To illustrate how this works, Waldron focuses on rules against torture, asking: "What is the rule against torture archetypal *of*?"[54] His answer is relevant to policing: "The rule against torture is archetypal of a certain policy having to do with the relation between law and force, and with law's forcefulness with regard to the persons it rules."[55] By this he means that the legal system as a whole operates in a way that people are not brutalized and

---

[51] See, e.g., John Yoo and Robert Delahunty, "Application of Treaties and Laws to Al Qaeda and Taliban Detainees"; Jay Bybee, "Standards of Conduct for Interrogation under 18 U.S.C. 2340–2340A"; *Uniting and Strengthening America by Providing Appropriate Tools Required to Intercept and Obstruct Terrorism (USA PATRIOT) Act of 2001*, PUBLIC LAW 107-56—OCT. 26, 2001.

[52] Waldron, *Torture, Terror, and Trade-Offs*, 225–226; Ronald Dworkin, *Taking Rights Seriously* (Cambridge, MA: Harvard University Press, 1977), 22–32.

[53] Waldron, *Torture, Terror, and Trade-Offs*, 227.

[54] Ibid., 232.

[55] Ibid.

treated as "dumb animals, but rather as persons with human dignity."[56] We need some examples.

Here are two illustrations of how rules against torture and brutality (including police brutality) might operate as archetypes in the US legal system. First, there is the prohibition against cruel and unusual punishment in the Eighth Amendment to the US Constitution. This example is relatively straightforward, using evaluative terms ("cruel") to characterize the limits of the state's overall enforcement and punishment power.

The second example—Due Process—returns us to the *Rochin* case. The idea is not to reframe these instances of law in terms of a grand theory about torture and brutality. The idea is to show how these concrete positive rules express the overall spirit and ethos of our system of criminal law, criminal procedure, and policing (rather than merely operate on their own account). Accordingly, perhaps we can make a bit more sense of the *Rochin* Court's invocation of *cannons of decency and fairness, traditions and conscience,* and *sense of justice.*[57] The underlying idea can be explained in terms of legal archetypes.

The remaining question is this: What would it mean—philosophically and practically—to circumvent our legal archetypes? Specifically, what would it mean for the police to have the legal power to enforce the law through brutality and dishonesty—for example, beatings, kneeling on one's neck, pumping one's stomach against one's will, engaging in widespread acts of corruption, fraud, and dishonesty?

Put it this way: If we begin to loosen the rules—sanctioning the state to engage in *some* brutality and *some* fraud to promote security—then such loosening may undercut the overall spirit of the legal system (which is itself based on principles regarding the mitigation of brutality and fraud). To be sure, the legal system could still be viable assuming the state (police) mitigates the vulnerability of *some* people (indeed, the use of brutal and fraudulent tactics might *increase* security for some people), and yet the overall spirt of the legal system would be denigrated.

Ironically, then, the erosion of the law's spirit can occur through concrete legislation and legal decisions: the more we move away from prohibitions against brutal and dishonest tactics within our institutions (and sanction such tactics), the more the spirit of the legal system changes. We can no

---

[56] Ibid., 233.
[57] Rochin v. California, 342 U.S. 165, 169–173 (1952).

longer say that state-sponsored brutality and fraud are categorically wrong; instead, their prohibition would merely be based on the contingent needs and interests of some groups. Let's consider two brief examples of how the state undermines force and fraud-limiting norms through concrete policy and precedent.

In *Utah v. Strieff*, the US Supreme Court limited the scope of the Fourth Amendment's exclusionary rule—the legal rule preventing evidence collected in violation of one's constitutional rights from being used in a court of law.[58] In *Strieff*, Utah police began surveilling a suspected drug house and observed Edward Strieff leaving the house. Upon stopping and detaining Strieff on the street, officers discovered that Strieff had an outstanding warrant for a traffic violation. The officers thus conducted a search incident to his arrest and found drug paraphernalia on Strieff's person. Even though the officers lacked "reasonable suspicion" to detain Strieff (making the detention unlawful),[59] the Supreme Court ruled that the drug evidence seized during the detention was admissible because "the discovery of a valid arrest warrant was a sufficient intervening event to break the causal chain between the unlawful stop and the discovery of drug-related evidence on Strieff's person."[60] This rationale is troubling and it doesn't end with the *Strieff* case.

The Court's holding straightforwardly allows the police to undermine the spirit of the law generally and defraud a person of their rights specifically. This is because the holding bolsters (not mitigates) an opportunity for the police to abuse their authority. It increases (not decreases) the police's opportunity to unlawfully stop civilians with the goal of checking for outstanding warrants and—if a warrant exists—securing admissible evidence from the arrest.

The Court has sanctioned similar legal practices in the context of police vehicle stops, giving the police the (legal) benefit of the doubt based on the value of crime reduction (an end that justifies the means, in other words).[61]

---

[58] Utah v. Strieff, 579 U.S. ___, 136 S. Ct. 2056 (2016); see Mapp v. Ohio, 367 U.S. 643 (1961), in which the US Supreme Court held that the exclusionary rule applies to the U.S. states (in addition to the US federal government).

[59] See Terry v. Ohio, 392 U.S. 1 (1968).

[60] See Utah v. Strieff.

[61] See, e.g., Wren v. United States, 517 U.S. 806 (1996) (holding that any traffic offense committed by a driver was a legitimate legal basis for a stop); Hein v. North Carolina, 574 U.S. ___ (2014) (holding that a police officer's reasonable mistake of law can provide the individualized suspicion required by the Fourth Amendment to justify a traffic stop).

Perhaps even more troubling, we will see in the coming chapters how police are permitted to misrepresent material fact. They are permitted to lie to criminal suspects and informants in order to coerce them into engaging in dangerous and demeaning operations on behalf of the police.[62]

Now an example regarding force and brutality. When the police shot and killed Tamir Rice in 2014—a twelve-year-old Black child who made a threatened movement with a gun that turned out to be fake—the police could not be held accountable because the shooting was considered legal. This is true even if the killing was brutal, and even if the police used poor tactics that unnecessarily escalated the confrontation with Rice.[63] Recall that the courts have construed a police officer's decision to use force based on the view that policing is inherently dangerous, and that legal and philosophical handwringing increases the danger considering that officers must make "split-second judgements" in life-or-death situations.[64] The upshot is a paradox regarding the rule of law. Practices that seem contrary to the law's spirit (because they seem brutal or that they defraud one of rights) and practices that erode the idea of *governing* by law (and thus erode legitimacy) can nevertheless be *legal*.

The spirit of a legal system is based upon its social structure—the way it exists in the world, which allows it to be examined as an empirical phenomenon. From there, we can make normative claims that critique or laud the structure of our legal system, including the extent to which our concrete legal practices undermine the spirit of the overall system. And so we should ask: What in fact are the central norms of legal systems regarding force and fraud, and to what extent does the police institution depart from those norms?

2. Universalistic Positive Morality (and Infanticide)

[M]orality is not just like science or factual knowledge, and it is essential that it should not be. The point of morality is not to mirror the world [of empirical facts], but to change it. . . . But did we agree that it mirrored no facts at all?

—Bernard Williams[65]

---

[62] I discussed this point in *The Retrieval of Liberalism in Policing*, chapter 4.

[63] For astue analysis of the Rice case and the underlying problems related to police tactics, see Ben Jones, "Police-Generated Killings: The Gap between Ethics and Law," *Political Research Quarterly* 75, no. 2 (2022): 366–378.

[64] Graham v. Connor, 490 U.S. 386, 396–397 (1989).

[65] Bernard Williams, *Morality* (Cambridge: Cambridge University Press, 1993 [1972]), 33, 35.

How is the law universalistic given the vast variation from society to society? Rachels's example about the custom of eating one's dead illuminated how different burial practices may nevertheless suggest overlapping societal values: The underlying belief system may be different, but the goal of respecting the dead is the same. On the other hand, suppose the stakes are higher and the underlying concern is not the different ways that societies treat the dead but instead the different ways that societies treat the living. Here Rachels asks us to consider Eskimo culture, which was in many ways shaped by habitation in the isolated, inaccessible, and frigid extremities of the Arctic.[66]

Eskimo sexual and marriage practices seemed odd when they were first studied ("men would share their wives with guests, lending them for the night as a sign of hospitality"), but some of their practices regarding infants and the elderly seemed downright shocking. Indeed, they seemed to have less value for human life considering that mothers routinely killed their children (mostly female) at birth; they were also known to leave the elderly in the snow to die "when they became too feeble to contribute to the family."[67] Unlike customary differences among burial practices, killing infants (and leaving the old to die) seems like an irreconcilable conflict of values (and any positive law that might enshrine those values). But maybe even this is too fast. Why? Because the cultural context is important:

- Eskimo families lived in extremely harsh environments that most people cannot even imagine.
- Given the lengthy (compared to other cultures) time that Eskimo mothers nursed their children, mothers were limited in the number of children they could sustain.
- In nomadic cultures, there are physical limits to the number of children that mothers can carry in parkas while moving from place to place.
- Adult males produce food (hunt and gather), which results in premature death compared to adult females; accordingly, if male and female infants survived in equal numbers, there would be far fewer food-producing adult males in Eskimo groups.[68]

---

[66] Rachels, "The Challenge of Cultural Relativism."
[67] Ibid.
[68] Ibid. (drawing on Peter Freuchenn, *Book of the Eskimos* (New York: Fawcett, 1961); and E. Adamson Hoebel, *The Law of Primitive Man* (Cambridge, MA: Harvard University, 1954), ch. 5).

As Rachel aptly observes, then:

> [A]mong the Eskimos, infanticide does not signal a fundamentally different attitude toward children. Instead, it is a recognition that drastic measures are sometimes needed to ensure the family's survival. Even then, however, killing the baby is not the first option considered. Adoption is common; childless couples are especially happy to take a more fertile couple's "surplus." Killing is only the last resort. . . . [T]he raw data of the anthropologists can be misleading; it can make the differences in values between cultures appear greater than they are. The Eskimos' values are not all that different from our values. It is only that life forces upon them choices that we do not have to make.[69]

Could it be otherwise—in other words, could it be possible that Eskimo culture does *not* value human life? No. There are specific characteristics that the legal system of any society must possess in order for the society to exist at all. Humans (especially infants and children) are vulnerable; if we do not have rules to protect human vulnerability, then there's no point in having any rules at all because there will be no one at all to protect.

Likewise, Hart's empirical generalization regarding *limited human understanding and strength of will* is vitally important in any society. People must be able to predict—with some degree of confidence—that others will cooperate in society. The upshot is that societies need a way to ensure that one's trust and good faith cooperation will not be taken advantage of by others. Rachels echoes this point: "[C]omplex societies cannot exist without regular communication among their members. . . . It follows that in any complex society there must be a presumption in favor of truthfulness." Even if there are exceptions to the rule, then, societal rules against dishonesty and deception are necessary for societies to exist.

Our discussion of the law's viability and spirit provided an important foundation to the question by illuminating how the law is oriented in a universalistic direction. Let's try to build on that foundation in this concluding section. We will see that one way to understand UPM is through commonality. For

---

[69] Ibid.

example, commonality is the core of the concept of *the law of nations*, with Waldron putting it this way:

> The ius gentium [the law of nations] . . . is a body of positive law [law established by human institutions] regulating relations within states particularly between citizen and government but also sometimes between private individuals. Its distinguishing feature is its commonality: the law of nations represents a sort of overlap between the positive laws of particular states, something they have in common. The idea is that it has a claim on us by virtue of that commonality.[70]

Likewise, our goal is to build on the prior sections by highlighting the ways that societal positive law has a common, universalistic orientation given empirical generalizations about human life and society among various states.

2.1. Intuitions and Functions

If you are at all like me, you are probably suspicious of newfangled academic terms that go by acronyms—case in point: UPM. Let me try to ease your suspicion by motivating UPM with an appeal to intuition and function.

Philosophers indeed have a habit of making their point with exotic thought experiments that appeal to intuition. The trolley problem—and its many variations—is a good example: A runaway trolley is racing toward five people who are tied to the track; there is a lever you can pull that will divert the trolley to another track (saving the five people), but the problem is that one person is tied to the second set of tracks. Would you pull the lever—saving five people and killing one—or would you do nothing?[71] These sorts of abstract thought experiments are supposed to tell us something about ethics based in part on our intuitions.[72]

---

[70] Jeremy Waldron, *"Partly Laws Common to Mankind": Foreign Law in American Courts* (New Haven: Yale University Press, 2012), 28.

[71] For a recent, accessible discussion, see David Edmonds, *Would You Kill the Fat Man?: The Trolley Problem and What Your Answer Tells Us about Right and Wrong* (Princeton, NJ: Princeton University Press, 2014).

[72] Likewise, when it comes to arguing about the nature of the law, philosophers generally rely on conceptual analysis and appeals to intuition. Brian Leiter writes that jurisprudence "relies on two central argumentative devices—analyses of concepts and appeals to intuition." Brian Leiter, "Beyond the Hart/Dworkin Debate: The Methodology Problem in Jurisprudence," *The American Journal of Jurisprudence* 48, no. 1 (June 2003): 17, 43–44.

As vague as "intuition" might sound, it has a lot to be said for it. Thomas Nagel aptly noted the following: "Given a knockdown argument for an intuitively unacceptable conclusion, one should assume there is probably something wrong with the argument that one cannot detect—though it is also possible that the source of the intuition has been misidentified."[73] The goal, then, is to think in terms of reaching some sort of "reflective equilibrium" with respect to our abstract theories, our intuitions, and the way the world actually is.[74]

UPM is motivated by the idea that we should not merely talk about force, fraud, and the law in the context of abstract musings in the history of philosophy (such as Kant's conception of lying) or exotic thought experiments (such as the trolley problem). Our inquiry should also have one foot planted squarely in the world as it exists.[75] It stands to reason that we should consider empirical data regarding the nature of law and how that data harmonizes with the more theoretical claims made by philosophers.

A different but related motivation for UPM is *functionalism*, which stands for the idea that the vast differences among various legal systems are more about the forms law takes rather that the functions that law performs.[76] If we start with some basic points about the functions of law (settling disputes, co-ordinating and altering behavior, determining authority and how decisions are to be made, and implementing the institutions to perform these tasks), those points can help illuminate the universalistic characteristics regarding law's general functions.[77] A step toward saying how the law is universalistic, then, is to focus on function over form.[78]

Of course, there will always be disagreement about the precise details of the law's function. We saw how Hart's idea of the minimum content of the natural law is ultimately about the law promoting human survival in order

---

[73] Thomas Nagel, *Mortal Questions* (Cambridge: Cambridge University Press, 1979), x.

[74] Reflective equilibrium is a methodology that involves working back and forth among judgments (or intuitions) regarding cases and the principles and theoretical considerations that govern those judgements—and then revising as needed to reach coherence among the various considerations. See John Rawls, *A Theory of Justice*.

[75] For related methodological ideas, see William L. Twining, *General Jurisprudence: Understanding Law from a Global Perspective* (Cambridge: Cambridge University Press, 2009); Nicola Lacey, "Analytical Jurisprudence Versus Descriptive Sociology Revisited," *Texas Law Review* 84, no. 4 (2006).

[76] See Kenneth M. Ehrenberg, *The Functions of Law* (Oxford: Oxford University Press, 2016), 145.

[77] Ibid.; K. N. Llewellyn, "The Normative, the Legal, and the Law-Jobs: The Problem of Juristic Method," *Yale Law Journal* 49, no. 8 (June 1940).

[78] See generally Felix S. Cohen, "Transcendental Nonsense and the Functional Approach," *Columbia Law Review* 35, no. 6 (June 1935): 809–849 ("A thing is what it does.").

to be viable. However, one might construe (*contra* Hart's meaning) the "minimum" content of the law more expansively—or "not so minimum," as legal scholar Richard Epstein puts it.[79]

Epstein argues that the *function* of the law is instead to "maximize some overall measure of social happiness or welfare."[80] Although this might be a controversial interpretation,[81] his general point about the relationship between force and fraud is well taken. He writes that the arrangement of human affairs entails a general prohibition ("as a matter of natural law") against using force, and, on the other side of the coin, a general commitment to keeping promises.[82]

But why stop there? Why not think of the nature and function of the law as promoting much more than mere viability and survival? Epstein thinks that Hart's "minimum" content of natural law can be naturally extended to social rules that lead to "*maximum* flourishing."[83]

For example, we cannot think of the concept "contract" without thinking of a great many other, related concepts that expand our normative commitments. The concept of a contract naturally entails considerations regarding when something *cannot* be an enforceable contract.[84] We are thus required to consider other concepts, such as *fraud*. And we cannot think of concepts such as fraud without thinking about values such as "honesty" and "good faith" in our societal arrangements. One can thus make the case that the minimum content of the law naturally expands such that it precludes things such as fraud and includes things such as honesty.

[79] Richard A. Epstein, "The Not So Minimum Content of Natural Law," *Oxford Journal of Legal Studies* 25, no. 2 (Summer 2005): 219–255.

[80] Ibid., 221.

[81] See, e.g., James Allan, "Is You Is or Is You Ain't Hart's Baby?," 228, concluding that "the strongest reason for resisting Epstein's call to inflate Hart is that it would undermine the latter's core level demand that we distinguish between 'law as it is' and 'law as it ought to be.'"

[82] Epstein, "The Not So Minimum Content of Natural Law," 227. This idea is reminiscent of the Hobbesian dilemma we will consider in Chapter 2. In the state of nature (or the absence of political society), one may pursue survival by either cooperating (keeping one's promises, despite the risk of being defrauded) or defecting (primitively breaking promises, leading to enmity). When we shift to societal arrangements—rather than the state of nature—there is reason to think that behaving honestly and keeping one's promises is the rational choice given the presence of law. This is because the law—in order to be viable—must protect against fraud, force, and defection to some degree. Otherwise, we are in a sense back in a state of nature because there's no guarantee that one's forbearance will be reciprocated by others, or that one's trust and reliance will not be taken advantage of by others.

[83] Ibid., 228.

[84] Ibid., 234–39, discussing Hart's "The Ascription of Responsibility and Rights."

We are one step closer to thinking about justice (including the nature and function of basic social institutions) as requiring a broader range of values than is obvious. It starts with the viability of the law and human survival and leads to commitments related to honesty (for instance). Sanctions—precluding things such as force and fraud and promoting things such as honesty and good faith—are necessary to ensure that one's trust and cooperation will not be taken advantage of by others.

As Epstein notes, this idea is not merely relevant to traditional business and commercial transactions, but also social institutions and *relational contracts* "that posit long term co-operation under some general rubric of good faith." And good faith—to which we turn in the next chapter—stands for the idea of "honesty in dealings."[85]

So we can begin to see how one of the police institution's normative foundations might be derived from the principles of relational contract. And this means that if we want the police institution to at least be viable—and perhaps promote more than minimal societal wellbeing—it's plausible to think that the police must generally commit to honesty in societal dealings.

2.2. Empirical Jurisprudence

With these motivations for UPM in place, all that is left to do is examine empirical data about institutions and the law—law *out there, in the world.* This will allow us to see how the more abstract philosophical theories discussed earlier converge with empirical-sociological analysis regarding the universalistic character of the law.[86]

A brief word about what to call this sort of methodology. It might be tempting to associate the underlying idea with methodologies such as

---

[85] Ibid., 250.

[86] Law is not the only social means of solving coordination problems, but sociologists of law have aptly noted that "[a]ll law aims at solving social problems that consist of repetitive patterns of social behaviors characterized by law-makers as undesirable. Law constitutes government's principal tool for channeling behaviors in desired ways." Ann Seidman, Robert B. Seidman, and Michael McCord, "Theory and Methodology for Investigating the Function of law in Relation to Governmental Institutions: The Case of the Development Bank of Southern Africa," *Acta Juridica* 1993 (1993): 264. See also Joseph Raz, "The Functions of Law" in *The Authority of Law* (Oxford: Oxford University Press, 2009), 163–179.

experimental philosophy (X-phi),[87] or, more specifically, experimental jurisprudence (you guessed it: X-jur).[88] Legal scholar Kevin Tobia helpfully describes X-jur this way:

> There are complementarities between traditional and experimental jurisprudence. Traditional jurisprudence often proposes "shared" intuitions, claims about a universal response to a thought experiment. Experimental jurisprudence can help assess the robustness of that claim—by seeking responses from a larger set of persons, including those who may have less at stake in the theoretical debate.[89]

I am not proposing that we go out and collect data by surveying people about their views on force, fraud, and the law; instead, the goal is simply to address jurisprudential questions in a way that is at least in part *informed by* empirical evidence.[90] *Empirical jurisprudence*, then, is the better name for what we're doing.[91]

This brings us to the crux of the matter: How do abstract ideas regarding the viability and spirit of the law relate to empirical data? Let's begin by examining commitments against force and brutality relevant to policing generally.

There is no agreement about the exact number of sovereign states (countries) in the world given disputes about sovereignty, but most people agree that there are approximately 200 states. (For instance, the United Nations [UN] has 193 member-states.) With this in mind, consider the following table.[92]

Upon ratification by a state, the above treaties are binding on the state's government and laws (the above three treaties have been ratified by the United States). To be sure, some of the states who ratified and signed these agreements did so for self-serving political reasons; they had no intention

---

[87] See Joshua Knobe and Shaun Nichols, "Experimental Philosophy," *The Stanford Encyclopedia of Philosophy*, ed. Edward N. Zalta (Winter 2017), https://plato.stanford.edu/archives/win2017/entries/experimental-philosophy/

[88] See Lawrence B. Solum, "The Positive Foundations of Formalism: False Necessity and American Legal Realism," *Harvard Law Review* 127, no. 8 (2014): 2464–2465.

[89] Kevin Tobia, "Experimental Jurisprudence," *Chicago Law Review* 89 (2022).

[90] Ibid. It is in part for this reasons that Tobia accepts the term "empirical jurisprudence."

[91] Consider as an analogy the difference between economics that uses empirical data (not pure theory) and experimental economics.

[92] The data in this table comes the Office of the High Commissioner for Human Rights (UN Human Rights), https://www.ohchr.org/EN/Pages/Home.aspx.

Table 1.1 International Constraints on Force

Some international treaties constraining the use of force	State parties (ratified)	States signed but not ratified	No signature or ratification
International Covenant on Civil and Political Rights ("ICCPR")	173	6	18
Convention against Torture and Other Cruel, Inhuman or Degrading Treatment or Punishment ("Torture Convention")	173	4	20[a]
International Convention on the Elimination of All Forms of Racial Discrimination ("CERD")	182	3	12

[a]Note that—as with the ICCPR—the "Torture Convention" includes an "optional protocol" establishing a system of regular visits by international and national bodies to places of detention to prevent torture and other cruel, inhuman or degrading treatment or punishment. Fewer states have agreed to these protocols. Torture Convention. Note also that the United States, for example, ratified these treaties with various reservations that carve out some of the expanded protections.

of following the underlying provisions of the agreements. Moreover, the states that signed the agreements with sincerity fulfill their commitments imperfectly.[93] Be that as it may, the states that did sign the agreements sincerely come from a wide range of political, legal, social, religious, and moral traditions. And yet they all agreed to the same, basic principles that relate to force generally and policing specifically. To what did they commit?

Article 6 of the ICCPR beings with a basic commitment to human survival, stating that all humans have an inherent right to life that shall be protected by law—and that no one shall be arbitrarily deprived of life.[94] Beyond mere survival, Article 7 constrains the kind of force that may be used on persons: "No one shall be subjected to torture or to cruel, inhuman or degrading treatment or punishment."[95] Article 10 and 26 frame these commitments in terms of each person's equal humanity, stating that "[a]ll persons deprived of their

---

[93] If empirical jurisprudence is what we in fact do in practice, then both committing to refrain from various practices (e.g., international commitments to refrain from brutality) and actually refraining from those practices are facts about practices within the scope of empirical jurisprudence. Naturally, most people will be more concerned with the latter (whether states actually do what they say they will do), as well as the fact that, say, human rights treaties often seem to be ineffective. See Oona Hathaway, "Do Human Rights Treaties Make a Difference?" *Yale Law Journal* 111, no. 8 (June 2002): 1935–2042. Regardless, both sorts of facts about practices are relevant to our understanding of the way the world is.

[94] ICCPR.

[95] ICCPR.

liberty should be treated with humanity and with respect for the inherent dignity of the human person" (Article 10), and that "all persons are equal before the law and are entitled without any discrimination to the equal protection of the law" (Article 26).

Likewise, the Torture Convention is relevant to constraints on the police's use of force around the world. It not only prohibits torture, but also requires states to prevent acts of cruel, inhuman, or degrading treatment or punishment within its territories.[96] Turning to the third agreement on the chart, CERD, we see a commitment to prohibit racial discrimination and discrimination under law, as well as a commitment to end discriminatory effects of the law.[97]

In addition to these legally binding treaties, consider three other international standards relating to police use of force specifically:

The CCLEO provides that law enforcement officials shall respect and protect human dignity, uphold the human rights of all persons, and use force only when strictly necessary in accordance with their duty.[98] Article 5 adds that no law enforcement official may tolerate any act of torture or other cruel, inhuman, or degrading treatment or punishment.[99] Similarly, the BPUFF outlines international human rights standards that are central to policing, including the principle that police officers shall "as far as possible, apply non-violent means before resorting to the use of force and firearms."[100] The BPUFF also emphasizes proportionality regarding the amount of force used, while the Victim Declaration compels states to proscribe abuses of power and provide remedies to victims of such abuses.[101]

Now let us turn briefly to international commitments related to honesty in the context of contractual relations. The table provides a snapshot of these commitments from a diverse array of states around the world.

We should first acknowledge that these provisions are about commercial transactions and relations. One worry, then, is that such provisions are not relevant to broader social agreements and relations within states that are based upon more nebulous principles of fairness and reciprocation. This is undoubtedly a valid concern because not all facets of commercial transactions are relevant outside the commercial context. That said, it

---

[96] Torture Convention.
[97] CERD.
[98] CCLEO, Article 2 and Article 3.
[99] Ibid., Article 5.
[100] BPUFF.
[101] Ibid.; Victim Declaration.

Table 1.2 International Constraints on Policing

Some international agreements relating to law enforcement specifically	Adoption
Code of Conduct for Law Enforcement Officials ("CCLEO")	Adopted by UN General Assembly resolution 34/169 of 17 December 1979
Basic Principles on the Use of Force and Firearms by Law Enforcement Officials ("BPUFF")	Adopted by the Eighth UN Congress on the Prevention of Crime and the Treatment of Offenders, 27 August to 7 September 1990
Declaration of Basic Principles of Justice for Victims of Crime and Abuse of Power ("Victim Declaration")	Adopted by UN General Assembly resolution 40/34 of 29 November 1985

is plausible to think—for reasons regarding political cooperation versus defection—that the underlying contractual norms of honesty are important in all manner of bilateral and multilateral agreements.

The analogy to commercial law is particularly apt when we consider commercial concepts such as "relational" agreements noted earlier. Although English law promotes honesty (and prohibits dishonesty) in a variety of ways, it does not include a universal implied duty on contracting parties to perform their obligations in good faith. However, there is support in English caselaw for obligations of good faith in some commercial contracts, and that a general duty of good faith should be implied in long-term, "relational" agreements.[102]

These sorts of long-term relationships are based on an intention that the respective roles of the parties will be performed with collaboration, communication, cooperation, integrity, mutual trust, and fidelity.[103] Such considerations are especially important considering that the spirit and objective of relational agreements include ventures that may not be capable of being expressed exhaustively in a written contract.[104]

These are the exact sorts of values and concerns that undergird long-term political and institutional relations between communities and institutions such as the police. In other words, societal arrangements modeled on the ideal of a social contract—agreements between the government and the governed—are relational in nature and cannot be captured in a literal, explicit

---

[102] See, e.g., the High Court's opinion in *Yam Seng Pte Ltd v. International Trade Corp Ltd.*

[103] Bates v Post Office Ltd (No 3) [2019] EWHC 606 (QB). These elements are different from those involved in a fiduciary relationship.

[104] Ibid.

Table 1.3 International Constraints on Bad Faith

State	Commitments relating to honesty in contractual relations
China	• General Principles of the Civil Law, Article 4 (honesty in civil activities) • Chinese Contract Law, Article 6 (good faith in rights and obligations)
Egypt	• Egyptian Civil Code, Article 148 (contracts must be performed in good faith)
England	• *Yam Seng Pte Ltd v International Trade Corporation Ltd* [2013] EWHC 111 (holding that there is a duty of honesty in English law and that good faith may be an implied contract term)
France	• French Civil Code, article 1104 (good faith in the negotiation, formation, and performance of contracts)
Iran	• Iranian Civil Code, Article 439 (providing the option to terminate contracts founded on dishonesty)
United States	• Uniform Commercial Code, sections 1-304 and 2-103 (requiring contracts and duties to be performed with good faith, honesty, and fair dealing)

contract. They are instead derived from long-term relationships based on roles requiring communication, cooperation, and mutual trust steeped in honesty.

The more basic point is that there is wide-ranging support for a general commitment to honesty in contractual relations from a variety of political, legal, social, religious, and moral traditions around the world. We see this in Chinese law, which states that "civil activities" must be conducted with "the principles of voluntariness, fairness, compensation for equal value, honesty, and credibility."[105] When we turn to Iran—as well as Middle East and North African (MENA) states—legal scholars describe how "Islamic contractual good faith is of a religious nature and can be derived from some general rules dealing with Muslims' internal beliefs and ethical behavior."[106] The legal tradition in MENA states thus converges with Chinese, US, and European law with respect to honest relations—even if the basis for such principles is more explicitly religious.

These scholars point to Egyptian law's requirement (which was influenced by French law and serves as a model for many Arab states) that contracts be executed in good faith—an approach that "has been adopted by other

---

[105] General Principles of the Civil Law ("GPCL"), Article 4.

[106] Ebrahim Shoarian and Mahsa Jafari, "Good Faith Principle in Contract Law: A Comparative Study under Sharī'ah, Islamic Law Jurisdictions with Emphasis on Iranian Law," *Arab Law Quarterly* 35 (2021): 4.

Islamic–Arabic countries, including Iraq, Palestine, Libya, United Arab Emirates, Lebanon, Jordan, Qatar, Syria, Kuwait, and Sudan, which recognize the duty to act in good faith at the performance stage."[107] More generally, Islamic Law is based on concepts such as (1) *talaqqī al-rukbān*: "attempt[ing] to trade with merchants at an unfair price"; (2) *naǧš*: "when a third party without a genuine intention to buy colludes with a seller to offer higher bids for the goods in order to induce a prospective buyer to purchase at the proposed price"; (3) *tadlīs*: prohibitions regarding "fraudulent misrepresentation"; and (4) *ġiš*: prohibitions regarding "deception."[108] These concepts stand for the broad principle that parties should disclose essential information relating to agreements, as well as avoid fraudulent activities such as taking advantage of one's ignorance.[109]

Despite the obvious differences between states such as Iran and the United States (and the fact that what many states agree to do is far from what they do in practice), we can at least find common ground when it comes to basic commitments of honesty—and commitments against fraud—in our contractual relations. The United States is not unique in its requirement that contractual relations—whether commercial or political—be based on good faith, honesty, and fair dealing.[110] Far from it, as we see commonalities regarding force and fraud around the world.

The upshot is that normative questions about brutality (force) and dishonesty (fraud) are grounded in positive (social) morality that is universalistic in character—hence, UPM. This allows us to make reasonable assumptions regarding normative constraints on force and fraud given their basis in universal social concerns—including the assumption that deviations from UPM should raise red flags, especially in the case of state functions such as policing.

2.3. Outlaws and Relativists

We close this chapter by reconsidering a central objection to UPM: Notwithstanding our analysis of eating the dead and infanticide, you might reasonably object that a more fine-grained analysis would reveal significant

---

[107] Ibid., 17.
[108] Ibid., 5–7.
[109] Ibid., 27.
[110] See Uniform Commercial Code, sections 1–304 and 2–103 (requiring contracts and duties to be performed with good faith, honesty, and fair dealing).

disparities among various legal traditions—disparities suggesting a more relativistic stance regarding positive morality. Afterall, we know there are states that engage in egregious lies and violations of human rights against both their own citizens and citizens of other states.

We need not name names but can simply refer to such regimes as—following John Rawls—*outlaw states.*[111] According to Rawls, such states "refuse to comply with a reasonable Law of Peoples," failing to uphold "universal rights . . . [that] are binding on all peoples and societies."[112] No one denies that such states exist; nor is it debatable that vast legal and moral differences exist among almost all states.

There will always be "conceptual relativity" because—as we have discussed—legal concepts are social in origin.[113] Joseph Raz fittingly puts it like this: "all concepts are parochial" because they are "the product of a specific culture."[114] Such truisms about concepts need not lead one to deny truth claims about positive (social) morality. This is because claims about truth can be made coherently provided the claims are relative to a background system of concepts.[115] We can thus say (based in part on our analysis of empirical data in the prior section) that it is true that persons and institutions ought to deal with others with a disposition of honesty provided that good faith is a normative backdrop recognized by the law—a collective positive moral conception to which institutions have some sort of obligation.

As shown in the charts, definitions of evaluative terms relating to force and fraud vary from society to society. Although it is impossible to reach agreement about moral *universals* regarding force and fraud, it is much less contentious to say that all societies are oriented in a *universalistic* direction—in other words, that they *tend* toward universal aims given empirical generalizations about human life and society that have been discussed. .

The concept of a "contract" has served as a good example. Is it possible to identify a "general" or "universal" theory of contract given

---

[111] John Rawls, *The Law of Peoples* (Cambridge: Harvard University Press, 1999), 4–5.

[112] Ibid., 4–5, 80–81.

[113] John Searle puts it this way: "Because any true description of the world will always be made within some vocabulary, some system of concepts, conceptual relativity has the consequence that any true description is always made relative to some system of concepts that we have more or less arbitrarily selected for describing the world." John R Searle, *The Construction of Social Reality* (New York: Free Press, 1995), 161.

[114] Joseph Raz, "On The Nature of Law," *ARSP: Archiv Für Rechts- Und Sozialphilosophie* 82, no. 1 (1996): 5.

[115] Brian Tamanaha, "What Is General Jurisprudence: A Critique of Universalistic Claims by Philosophical Concepts of Law," *Transnational Legal Theory* 2, no. 3 (2011): 291.

conceptual similarities and dissimilarities that have been noted among different societies? If there is one truth of the matter about the nature of a contract (must contracts necessarily entail good faith, honesty, fairness, and so on?), why do societal manifestations of contracts (and scholarly theories about contracts) diverge regarding what that truth is?[116] The straightforward answer is that we can't agree upon a moral universal regarding the concept of a contract given conceptual relativism. However, we can at least agree that people from different societies are able to speak to one another about "contracts" in the abstract, despite the difference among their particular conceptions of a contract.[117]

There is a common understanding of what it means to be deceived, defrauded, and treated with dishonesty in private and political contractual relations whether one is in the United States, Iran, China, or England—even if the precise meanings of those terms vary widely from one society to another. As Epstein notes, there are many forms that a contract might take in various societies (handshake, writing, and so on), but "[a]ll societies establish forms of contractual exchange . . . beneath them lay certain regularities as to the importance of voluntary exchange and the prohibition against the use of force."[118] There will always be questions about whether borderline cases satisfy purist definitions of "contract," but such questions can belie other pressing issues regarding rights and responsibilities:[119] Did one breach a duty not to deceive or defraud? Was one's right to be treated honestly and in good faith respected?

* * *

Let me close on a bit of a downer. The world is not one big happy family in which everyone agrees (obviously). To be clear, my emphasis on UPM does not mean that persons in one society cannot (or should not) disagree morally with the practices of another society.[120] There is certainly a distinction between science and facts (the way the world is) and values (the way the world ought to be). So we will of course find aspects of various legal traditions with

---

[116] Brian Bix, "The Promise and Problems of Universal, General Theories of Contract Law," *Ratio Juris* 30, no. 4 (December 2017).

[117] This point notwithstanding, Bix discusses several weaknesses of universal, general theories. Ibid.

[118] Epstein, "The Not So Minimum Content of Natural Law," 227.

[119] Ibid., 235.

[120] To draw this conclusion—that we must accept practices of other societies—is what Bernard Williams refers to as "vulgar relativism." Bernard Williams, *Morality*, 25.

which we disagree (vehemently) on moral and legal ground. But these inevitable disagreements are not inconsistent with the view that positive law among various states has a common, universalistic orientation based on empirical generalizations about human life and society.

Consider the excerpt from Williams at the beginning of the section: "[M]orality is not just like science or factual knowledge . . . The point of morality is not to mirror the world, but to change it."[121] Even though morality is not in the business of *mirroring* the world of empirical facts, that does not mean that morality relies on *no* facts about the world.[122] As Williams adds, "moral thinking *feels* as though it mirrored something, as though it were constrained to follow"[123] (rather than merely being a choice one makes) *given the way the world is.* This has been the underlying idea of the chapter: we are not simply looking to empirical facts as a way to tell us what we ought to do; we are seeking moral answers about what we ought to do given the way the world is.

The point to remember is that all obligations and duties—whether recognized as legal or moral rules—vary in some degree from society to society, but all societies include obligations and duties that require persons and institutions to sacrifice their individual goals and interests for societal survival.[124]

We see this most clearly in the case of rules constraining the use of force and brutality, as well as in the case of rules requiring honesty and good faith in dealings with others.[125] Without the latter, persons would be compelled to pursue their interests with force. As Hart writes, "If conformity with these most elementary rules were not thought a matter of course among any group of individuals, living in close proximity to each other, we should be doubtful of the description of the group as a society, and certain that it would not endure for long."[126] So it is not *just* commonalities regarding the law's function that we see in one society to the next; we also find commonalities regarding content. The aspects of society regarding brutality (force) and dishonesty (fraud) are grounded in positive (social) morality that is universalistic in character.

Chapter 2 looks more closely at how universalistic positive morality is relevant in the unique context of relations between the police institution and the broader political community.

---

[121] Ibid., 33.
[122] Ibid., 35.
[123] Ibid., 36.
[124] See Hart, *The Concept of Law*, ch. VII.
[125] Ibid., 172.
[126] Ibid.

Five Questions and Answers Explored in Chapter 2

1. Q: The police are supposed to promote security—isn't it naïve to think they can do that without relying on deception and dishonesty?

   A: A lot of people thought it would be naïve for military and intelligence agents to promote (national) security without torture after 9/11, but there were good reasons to think government agents shouldn't torture suspected terrorists. Likewise, there are good reasons to think the police's pursuit of (domestic) security is not the end of the story. It's plausible to think the police should also be concerned with things such as truth, trust, and legitimacy.

2. Q: Okay, but why do we need a baroque theory based on contract law?

   A: Because this is a philosophy book, but hear me out because the point about contracts is straightforward. Suppose I'm charged with a crime, and subsequently agree to do something for the police (gather evidence, testify, confess) in exchange for a (potentially) reduced sentence. If my agreement is based on a material misrepresentation by the police, then it sounds like I was subjected to a fraudulent bargaining process. The norms of contract law illuminate that point.

3. Q: Fair enough, but we're talking about the police institution, not just isolated examples, right?

   A: Right. Societal arrangements modeled on the ideal of a social contract—agreements between the government and the governed regarding security—are relational in nature even if they cannot be captured exhaustively in a literal contract. Persons are conceived as entrusting certain tasks (governing, judging, policing) to agents of the state, and it is through this entrustment that persons can be thought of as having a right to be secured in good faith.

4. Q: That's all well and good, but a lot of people—namely, criminals—
    don't hold up their end of the social contract, so why are they owed
    good faith, honesty, transparency, and so on?

    A: Good point, but we will need to consider the possibility that
    some criminal "deviance" is a (reasonable) *response* to preemptive
    bad-faith policing that imposes an unfair distribution of security on
    communities.

5. Q: Still, it would be a fool's errand to try to account for every white
    lie told by the police, right?

    A: Right. And that's why we will focus on deceptive and dishonest po-
    licing that is on par with fraud and deviations from the rule of law.

2

Good Faith Policing

> When regard for truth has been broken down or even slightly weakened, all things will remain doubtful.
>
> —Saint Augustine[1]

The police ask a woman—who is facing a drug charge that gives the police leverage over the woman—to engage in oral sex with the target of a police investigation. The police's goal is to gather evidence against the target and charge the target with soliciting a prostitute. The woman agrees to assist given the prison sentence she is facing. The police provide the woman with a recording device and a napkin. The recording device is for documenting the sex act. The napkin is for gathering physical evidence: the woman is instructed by the police to spit the target's semen into the napkin.

There is one more detail to consider: The leverage the police have over the woman is based in part on the police's claim that the woman is facing a forty-year prison sentence for the drug charge; the woman could receive a potential reduction from the lengthy sentence by assisting the police. In fact, however, the charge the woman is facing would have made her guilty of a crime for which the sentence range was only six to ten years.

We don't have to concoct fanciful thought experiments in which these scenarios occur because they occur in real life.[2] It might be tempting to think that the woman simply relied on her bargaining freedom to gain a benefit (the chance for a sentence reduction). But upon reflection, it seems clear that the woman's bargaining freedom was *undermined* by the false claim made by the police. Indeed, the police used *untruth* to enhance their leverage over the woman—denying her the right to make an informed choice about whether to work with the police. To be sure, the police often make false claims to further

---

[1] Augustine, "Lying," in *Treatises on Various Subjects*, ed. R.J. Deferrari (New York: Catholic University of America Press, 1952).

[2] *Alexander v. DeAngelo*, 329 F.3d 912 (2003). The court ruled against the informant's subsequent legal claim based in part on the informant's supposed bargaining freedom.

Police Deception and Dishonesty. Luke William Hunt, Oxford University Press. © Oxford University Press 2024.
DOI: 10.1093/oso/9780197672167.003.0003

their law enforcement goals. If these false claims constitute bad faith, then the police's conduct is on par with fraud.

Although this case is characteristic of detectives and other investigators (rather than patrol officers), the scenario raises issues that are familiar at all levels of policing. Federal agents, city detectives, and patrol officers are often faced with situations in which they need (or want) a person to do something. It is often the case that a ruse (or some form of deception and dishonesty) is an effective way to get the person to do the thing. This is more or less how it's always been. Law and policing scholar Jerome Skolnick aptly noted—four decades ago—that the police consider deception "as natural to detecting as pouncing is to a cat."[3] Given this convention, Chapter 2 argues in favor of what may seem like a counterintuitive claim: Good faith is a normative foundation for the police as a political institution.[4]

I'll try to show that this is a plausible claim based on two considerations: (1) good faith is a core value of contracts, and (2) justified policing is contractual in nature.[5] This leads to the preliminary conclusion that good faith is a normative foundation for the police as a justified political institution. The first premise is relatively uncontroversial in the philosophy of contract law, and I'll sketch briefly why that is so. The second premise raises a host of objections—both theoretical and practical—and will need to be explained and qualified in more detail. One objection is that policing (whether justified or not) is simply not something that is "contractual in nature." We thus need to consider why it is plausible to think of policing broadly as contract-like (in the context of social contract theory), as well as narrowly (in the context of concrete encounters between law enforcement officers and the public).

A second objection can be raised by the practical concerns noted in the case: Perhaps good faith cannot be a normative foundation for the police given that the practical nature of the police role entails enforcing the law through dishonesty and deception (which is inconsistent with good faith). We will consider this objection more fully in the next part of the book, which posits that dishonesty and deception are justified only as a narrowly circumscribed investigative tool constrained by institutional commitments

---

[3] Jerome H. Skolnick, "Deception by Police," *Criminal Justice Ethics* 1, no. 2 (1982): 40.

[4] This chapter is based on my paper, "Good Faith as a Normative Foundation of Policing," *Criminal Law and Philosophy* (2023).

[5] I have included the term "justified" simply to distinguish unjustified policing from activity that is not policing at all: A constantly deceptive, fraudulent police force that governs outside the rule of law is, strictly speaking, still a police force.

to the fair distribution of security and the rule of law. The practical upshot is the preclusion of dishonest and deceptive police tactics on par with fraud— leading to a police institution that is less proactive and more reactive.

First, though, let's consider the idea of honest (and dishonest) institutions. As the informant-sex-act case illustrates, saying that a disposition of good faith is relevant to the police institution is not merely a theoretical claim. A lack of good faith in police–community dealings can have real and profound consequences on those being policed.

1. Truth

The pursuit of *security* is without a doubt one of the central goals of policing. We thus need to say quite a bit about the police obligation to provide security—as well as any constraints on that obligation. But we should also consider another important aspect of policing that is often (and oddly) overlooked: *Truth*. We don't merely want security; we want the truth. (Consider organizations such as Innocence Project, which seeks to exonerate people who have been wrongfully convicted.) We want to know who *in fact* is a threat to security, who *in fact* broke the law and is criminally responsible, who *in fact* should have their rights and liberty curtailed (and what those rights and liberties are), and who *in fact* should be subject to punishment.[6] We want the truth about these matters, and we want questions about these matters to be answered by the police truthfully.

More generally, we want the police to be truthful as a public institution. It is difficult to imagine putting trust in a public institution that is not truthful with the public. To put it another way, the police don't have a blank check in their pursuit of security. Public institutions must do the job the public pays them to do; we feel we are *owed* truthfulness given the nature of democratic institutions. This creates a paradox given the police's reliance on *untruth*. To address the puzzle, it makes sense to first say something about truth generally.

---

[6] These concerns are naturally relevant to any system committed—at least in part—to retributive justice and deontological constraint. A retributive system of law depends on an accurate determination of blameworthiness, and, ultimately, on its ability to determine what is true. So truth and truthfulness in policing and other government functions are not merely free-standing values in a liberal system but also important elements in a liberal system of retributive justice.

In *Truth and Truthfulness*, Bernard Williams frames things rather starkly: "[T]o the extent that we lose a sense of the value of truth, we shall certainly lose something and may well lose everything."[7] This sort of strong case regarding the importance of truth is exactly in line with the thesis of the previous chapter. We considered how there are specific characteristics that the legal system of any society must possess for the society to exist at all; societal norms regarding things such as brutality (force) and dishonesty (fraud) are grounded in positive (social) morality that is universalistic in character— what I called universalistic positive morality (UPM). Williams puts his claim about truth similarly, arguing that there can be no societal cooperation without trust between members of the community—and there can be no societal trust without the truth-based virtues of sincerity and accuracy.[8] In other words, to think of a society based on untruth—a society based on dishonesty, deception, and lying—is to think of a society without reciprocation and mutual forbearance. Williams's point is that it's not plausible to think of such a society (and the social institutions within such a society) as existing at all.

Williams relies upon a familiar device in political philosophy to defend the value of truthfulness, namely, the thought experiment known as *the state of nature*. Roughly, the state of nature is a hypothetical condition in which persons live without political society and political authority. We will examine some of the famous accounts of the state of nature later in the chapter, where we will see how Enlightenment-era philosophers such as Thomas Hobbes and John Locke (as well as contemporary philosophers such as Tommie Shelby) rely on the device to motivate and justify their conception of political society. Williams's point is that even in a state of nature—in the absence of political society—people would need truth-based virtues such as sincerity and accuracy. Given limitations of knowledge and resources, people couldn't survive without some degree of trust, truthfulness, and cooperation. Accordingly, the values of truthfulness are presumed to be pre-political and pre-institutional (given that they would be necessary in a state of nature). Departing from those values should thus give us pause.[9]

What, specifically, is the role of the truth-based virtues of accuracy and sincerity? Williams says the former is the careful disposition of acquiring beliefs that are based upon the best available evidence. We should do our best

---

[7] Bernard Williams, *Truth and Truthfulness* (Princeton, NJ: Princeton University Press, 2002), 7.
[8] Ibid., 84, 123.
[9] Ibid., chs. 2–3.

to ensure that our beliefs are consistent with the truth. On this point, we can already see how the police might fall short: policing that is brutal, biased, or simply sloppy, is not sensitive to the disposition of accuracy, and it's plausible to think that deceptive and dishonest tactics can in some cases be a shortcut that circumvents accuracy.

With respect to sincerity, Williams is interested in the way people communicate—quite simply, speaking truthfully instead of relying on things such as dishonesty and deception.[10] Here again, we can see a direct connection between (un)truth and the police institution. As an institution seeking to enforce the law and reduce crime, there are myriad factors compelling the police to act deceptively and dishonestly—not least of these is the fact that law-breakers are often not honest themselves. But if insincerity can be a wrong, then the police must contend with Socrates's mandate in Plato's *Crito*: It's wrong to return a wrong with a wrong.[11] The police's adherence to a disposition of sincerity—in the face of insincerity—would thus count as a significant virtue. On the other side of the coin, we need to consider whether untruth and deviance by the community is—if not justified—*reasonable*. We will return to that issue later in the chapter when we examine Tommie Shelby's analysis of social deviance in the ghetto—which is interestingly relevant to Williams's analysis of truth.

Despite his strong stance on the value of truthfulness, Williams takes an equally strong stance in support of the idea that lying can be justified. Recall the cases I raised in the introduction: The fictional undercover police officer who lies about being a cop in order to stop a crime boss from beating his broken arm with a boot, as well as Kant's "murderer at the door" example (Is it morally defensible to lie to someone about your friend's location if you think the person is trying to harm your friend?). Williams argues that such persons—the crime boss and the murderer at the door—have given up their right to the truth because they themselves have turned their backs on trust and mutual respect.[12] This is a compelling view that we should take very

[10] Ibid., ch. 5.

[11] See Plato, "Crito," in *Plato: Complete Works*, ed. John M. Cooper (Indianapolis: Hackett, 1997), 49a–c. On the other hand, one might argue that if, say, I use violence as a last resort to protect myself against another person's violence, then I am not returning a wrong with the wrong; instead, there is nothing wrong with the necessary violence I use to protect myself because self-defense is not a case of returning a wrong with the wrong. But note how this argument often does not apply to police deception and dishonesty because the police do not reserve deception and dishonesty for situations in which it is necessary (or use deception and dishonesty as a last resort).

[12] Williams, *Truth and Truthfulness*, 114–122.

seriously. Indeed, I think Williams is correct inasmuch as police untruth *is* justified in some cases, such as when deception and dishonesty are clearly necessary to protect people. This is in many ways the crux of the matter, and we will spend Chapters 2 and 3 trying to sort out the details through a careful analysis of case studies. Nevertheless, I hope to illustrate how the police have taken untruth too far in their widespread, default reliance on deception and dishonesty.

For present purposes, one of the more interesting aspects of Williams's argument is the connection he makes between, on the one hand, deception, dishonesty, and untruth, and, on the other hand, *power* and *resentment*. He writes that when one deceives a person one is simply exerting one's will (instead of a disposition of accuracy regarding the world) on the person:

> The victim recognizes the bare-faced lie as a pure and direct exercise of power over him, with nothing at all to be said for it from his point of view, and this is an archetypal cause of resentment: not just disappointment and rage, but humiliation and the recognition that in the most literal sense he has been made a fool of.[13]

It is not difficult to imagine how this point about power and resentment is deeply relevant to the relationship between the police and communities being policed. Truthfulness is indicative of a commitment to cooperation, while deception and dishonesty are indicative of using power to impose one's will on another with power. The former is a path to cooperation and mutual trust, while the latter is a path to defection, enmity, and distrust. Problems regarding power and resentment will be highlighted in the coming discussion of Hobbes, Locke, and Shelby, especially with respect to their views on the state of nature and the social contract.

The final point to make about Williams' conception of the value of truthfulness is simply the idea that truth is inextricably intertwined with liberal, democratic institutions. It should go without saying that this point is deeply relevant to policing. The police paradox I have described is plausibly related to the erosion of the public's faith in the police institution and the weakening of the police's legitimacy. Deceptive, dishonest, and bad-faith tactics can undermine the fair distribution of security (and thus legitimacy), as when such tactics enhance the security of some at the expense of others. This can lead to

---

[13] Ibid., 119.

community distrust and resentment, and, ultimately, the need for the police to rely on power.

With these points about truth in mind, we can sketch an answer to the puzzle by reconsidering some of our assumptions about policing and security. Let's begin by examining the novel idea that the police institution is contractual in nature and deeply connected to good faith, which in turn raises questions of honesty and transparency.

2. Good Faith

Suppose I want to purchase a rare baseball card valued at $2,000. And suppose I have a friend who owns the card—and who would strongly prefer to keep the card—but who is in desperate need of cash. If I leverage the situation, drive a hard bargain, and purchase the card from my friend for $1,000, then there is no obvious way that I acted in bad faith. Why is this so?

If there was something wrong with the substance or terms of the agreement with my friend—or the procedures through which the agreement with my friend were entered—there are separate legal doctrines to deal with those concerns (such as the doctrine of unconscionability, which can make a contract unenforceable when it is based on unfair bargaining and oppressive terms).[14] But as long as I dealt with my friend with a disposition of honesty—such that my friend could make a decision freely—then I have acted in good faith.

I use "freely" simply in the sense that I did not disguise my intentions or manipulate my friend's expectations regarding the terms of the agreement in a way that affected my friend's ability to make an informed decision to close the deal. In other words, good faith does not require me to *look out* for my friend as if I were acting as his *fiduciary* (which is often said to require one "to treat his principal as if the principal were he").[15] Instead of some sort of

---

[14] I examined unconscionability as it relates to policing in my book, *The Retrieval of Liberalism in Policing* (New York: Oxford), ch. 4, arguing that agreements between the police and informants are unjustified to the extent that they deviate from the bargaining norms that underpin the doctrine of unconscionability.

[15] On these points, see Daniel Markovits, "Good Faith Is Contract's Core," in *Philosophical Foundations of Contract Law*, eds. Gregory Klass, George Letsas, and Prince Saprai (New York: Oxford, 2014), 277 (quoting *Mkt. St. Assocs. Ltd. P'ship v. Frey*, 941 F.2d 588, 593 (7th Cir. 1991), arguing that "[g]ood faith . . . does not require contracting parties to display substantive other-regard or altruism, preferring their partners' interests over their own, or even weighting the two interests equally, within their contract"). For a broader analysis of fiduciary law as it relates to political theory, see Stephen R.

loyalty to my friend, good faith requires *a disposition of honesty in contrac-tual dealings, including reaching agreements and the faithful adherence to the scope, purpose, and terms of agreements.*[16]

So good faith does not require contractors to be altruistic Good Samaritans. We can glean from this simple example that good faith precludes bad faith (obviously), with bad faith calling into question whether the parties to a contract deal with each other honestly. Honesty thus plays a central role in the concept of good faith. Let's briefly consider the role good faith—and thus honesty—play in contract law.

A familiar claim in the philosophy of contract law is—as legal scholar Daniel Markovits puts it—that "good faith [is] contract's core value."[17] Claiming that something is a "core value" in the law need not depend on anything particularly mysterious. There need only be a normative back-drop recognized by the law, such as a collective moral conception to which institutions have some sort of obligation. We saw this in the discussion of UPM in Chapter 1: societal issues regarding things such as brutality (force) and dishonesty (fraud) are grounded in positive (social) morality that is uni-versalistic in character. With respect to good faith, there is indeed a long his-tory of practical, legal, and philosophical thought—including various social contract theories—based upon a disposition of good faith in our covenants and reciprocal dealings with others.

This normative backdrop has been codified widely. Legal scholar Richard R. W. Brooks has described the contractual duty of good faith as an "ancient doctrine" that was "[a]lready timeworn when it first appeared in the formal rules governing sales in Roman antiquity" and is now "broadly incorpo-rated in national regimes, international law, and transnational legal orders."[18] Contemporary formalizations in the United States include the *Restatement*

Galoob and Ethan J. Leib, "The core of fiduciary political theory," in *Research Handbook on Fiduciary Law*, eds. D. Gordon Smith and Andrew Gold (Northampton: Edward Elgar Publishing, 2018), 401–417.

[16] For example, Book 5, Title I, Section 1375 of the Civil Code of Quebec states that "[t]he parties shall conduct themselves in good faith both at the time the obligation arises and at the time it is performed or extinguished." See also *ASB Allegiance Real Estate Fund v. Scion Breckenridge Managing Member, L.L.C.,* 50 A.3d 434, 440–441(Del. Ch. 2012) *aff'd in part, rev'd in part on other grounds,* 68 A.3d 665 (Del. 2013).

[17] Markovits, "Good Faith is Contract's Core Value," 272.

[18] Richard R.W. Brooks, "Good Faith in Contractual Exchanges," in *The Oxford Handbook of the New Private Law*, eds. Andrew S. Gold, John C. P. Goldberg, Daniel B. Kelly, Emily Sherwin, and Henry E. Smith (New York: Oxford, 2020), 497–512.

(Second) of the Law of Contracts, stating that "[e]very contract imposes upon each party a duty of good faith and fair dealing in its performance and its enforcement," and the *Uniform Commercial Code* (UCC), stating that "[e]very contract or duty within the Uniform Commercial Code imposes an obligation of good faith in its performance and enforcement."[19] More broadly, the *United Nations Convention on Contracts for the International Sale of Goods* reads: "In the interpretation of this Convention, regard is to be had to . . . the observance of good faith in international trade."[20] Even where good faith has not been incorporated explicitly, similar principles have been adopted to exclude bad faith.[21]

How might the norms of good faith apply to policing? A familiar account of *legitimate* political power is based on the idea that the political entity wielding the power must have *authority* to do so.[22] Receiving explicit consent might be a surefire way to receive authority, but we know that receiving such consent from everyone governed in a community is a practical impossibility. As a practical matter, then, one might say that the police institution has authority inasmuch as there is reciprocity between the police and the community through honest communication and agreements—conducted in good faith—regarding the enforcement of applicable laws, regulations, and policies. So one important point is that good faith is fundamental to the legitimacy of reciprocal relationships within the polity, framing the correlative rights and duties forged by those relationships.

Although the state may in principle demand that persons do their part in law enforcement, persons are conceived as entrusting certain tasks (governing, judging, policing) to agents of the state in order to permit a mutually beneficial division of labor. And it is through this *entrustment* that persons can be thought of as having a right to be secured in good faith. It is thus

---

[19] *Restatement (Second) of Contracts* § 205 (Am. Law Inst. 1981); U.C.C. § 1–304.

[20] *United Nations Convention on Contracts for the International Sale of Goods*, S. Treaty Doc. No. 98–99, art. 7 (1983).

[21] In England, Lord Mansfield claimed that good faith underscores all contractual dealings, though generally "English common law is said to rely on other devices, particularly principles of estoppel and interpretation, to exclude bad faith in exchange settings." Brooks, "Good Faith in Contractual Exchanges" (citing See Boone v. Eyre [1789] 126 Eng. Rep. 148 (K.B.); Carter v. Boehm [1766] 97 Eng. Rep. 1162, 1164 (K.B.)).

[22] See, e.g., A. John Simmons, *Justification and Legitimacy—Essays on Rights and Obligations* (Cambridge: Cambridge University Press, 2001). For a descriptive (rather than normative) account of police legitimacy, see Jason Sunshine and Tom R. Tyler, "The Role of Procedural Justice and Legitimacy in Shaping Public Support for Policing," *Law & Society Review* 37, no. 3 (2003): 513–548 ("a property of an authority or institution that leads people to feel that authority or institution is entitled to be deferred to and obeyed").

plausible to think that good faith is a fundamental component of modes of political deliberation and agreement through which persons entrust the state with (legitimate) authority. Entrustment is thus important to the police's obligation to promote security (and the corelative right of persons to be secured by the state) in good faith.[23]

In sum, good faith entails a disposition of honesty in contractual dealings, including reaching agreements and the faithful adherence to the scope, purpose, and terms of agreements. Although I've been using the words *honest* and *honesty* quite a bit, we have yet to examine honesty as a value specifically. The next step, then, is to consider how the concept of good faith requires an account of honesty—as well an account of transparency and trust. For there can be no good faith without a commitment to these values.

2.1. Honesty

An undercover police officer approaches a person on a street corner and asks to buy heroin (or a street name for heroin). The person responds: "You're not a cop are you?" The undercover officer replies: "No" (or a more colorful version of "no"). This seems to be a straightforward example of dishonesty, and yet most people probably think it would be absurd for the undercover officer to be truthful in this case. How else would the police do their job? As with the concept of truth, let's try to make sense of honesty in its own right before applying it to police case studies in the next two chapters.

As the example illustrates, the concept of honesty seems pretty simple. But appearances can be, well, deceiving. Philosopher Christian Miller has taken on the task of explicating honesty as a *virtue*. Importantly, he makes clear that his project is not one of *virtue ethics* (a moral theory often construed as competing with Kantian deontology and other rival theories), but instead *virtue theory* (or "understanding the nature of virtue").[24] Accordingly,

---

[23] Hunt, *The Retrieval of Liberalism in Policing*, 107–109.
[24] Christian B. Miller, *Honesty—The Philosophy and Psychology of a Neglected Virtue* (New York: Oxford University Press, 2021), 145. For a different account of honesty as a virtue, see Thomas Carson, *Lying and Deception: Theory and Practice* (Oxford: Oxford University Press, 2008), ch. 14. Carson distinguishes between what he calls *honesty in a negative sense* ("having a strong principled disinclination to tell lies or deceive others") and *honesty in the positive sense* ("being candid, open, and willing to reveal information"). He argues that honesty in the former sense is a cardinal virtue in ordinary circumstances, but honesty in the latter sense is often not a virtue. Ibid., 257.

Miller's approach may be coherently embraced by Kantian, consequential, and other moral theories.

With this in mind, perhaps the undercover police officer *acted* dishonestly, but is otherwise an honest person. Despite the dishonest act, then, we might be able to ascribe the virtue of honesty to the officer. As Miller puts it, *acting from honesty* entails that one is an honest person—though "the honest action is distinct from, and metaphysically dependent upon, the virtue of honesty."[25] Likewise, mental activities such as judgments may be honest or dishonest, but such judgments are distinct from the *virtue* of honesty itself (though the virtue of honesty may *shape* an honest judgment). The *virtue* of honesty is illustrated straightforwardly in statements that reflect a disposition, such as: *The police officer is an honest person.*[26]

Another important question about honesty is its scope. On this point, I'll follow Miller and approach the issue negatively, listing a few police behaviors that would not be compatible with honesty.[27]

- *Lying*: An officer says something to you that she believes is false, intending to deceive you.[28] Example: "No, I'm not a cop" (when she is in fact a cop).
- *Misleading*: An officer withholds information in order to mislead you without telling a lie. Example: An officer tells a suspect: "We have fingerprints" (when the police have fingerprint evidence belonging to someone other than the suspect).
- *Stealing*: Example: An officer arrests a person in their home for selling drugs; the person has $1,000 on their kitchen table, and the officer takes $100 for himself knowing that someone else has a right to the property (e.g., the person, the government).
- *Cheating*: An officer purposefully violates the rules governing their job. Example: An officer going through a divorce uses a police database for personal reasons, gaining an unfair advantage in a custody hearing.

---

[25] Miller, *Honesty*, 4.

[26] Ibid., 4–5.

[27] Ibid., 8–18. As Miller notes, in each category there may be exceptions regarding acts of dishonesty that are justified by competing moral concerns and obligations.

[28] Ibid., 8. Miller cites Jennifer Mather Saul, *Lying, Misleading, and What Is Said: An Exploration in Philosophy of Language and in Ethics* (Oxford: Oxford University Press, 2012), 3–8; and Don Fallis, "What is Deceptive Lying?" in *Lying: Language, Knowledge, Ethics, and Politics*, eds. Eliot Michaelson and Andreas Stokke (Oxford: Oxford University Press, 2018), 26 fn. 2, for this "traditional account of lying" but notes that there is considerable disagreement about how to characterize lying. I will not consider technical problems related to the traditional account of lying.

- *Promise-breaking*: Example: An officer tells a criminal suspect in custody: "I promise I'll help you go home if you just confess to the crime." The suspect confesses and the officer purposefully does nothing to help the suspect go home.

There may be cases when such acts of dishonesty are justified; we'll get there. But, here, if the acts are broadly incompatible with honesty, what are the correlative virtues of honesty? Here are some police examples that correspond with Miller's list.[29]

- *Truthfulness*: Example: An officer disposed to tell the truth for good moral reasons.
- *Forthrightness*: Example: An officer or institution disposed to avoid misleading others of relevant facts for good moral reasons.
- *Being respectful of property*: Example: An officer or institution disposed to respect the property of others for good moral reasons.
- *Proper compliance*: Example: An officer or institution disposed to comply with institutional rules for good moral reasons.
- *Fidelity to promises*: Example: An officer disposed to keep promises for good moral reasons.

The idea is that these narrower virtues are subsumed under the broader virtue of honesty. This is an important and interesting approach that strikes me as quite plausible. But given the context of this book, I want to mention a question that Miller touches on only briefly, namely, whether the virtue of honesty itself may be subsumed under a broader virtue.

A prominent answer to this question is that honesty falls under (or is a species of) the cardinal virtue of *justice*.[30] Of course, justice is central to policing. Indeed, John Rawls opens his massively influential book, *A Theory of Justice*, with the following: "Justice is the first virtue of social institutions."[31] Rawls isn't focused on policing specifically, though he does explain that he is interested in the way "the major social institutions distribute fundamental

---

[29] Miller, *Honesty*, 20–22.

[30] Ibid. 22–23 (citing Aquinas, *Summa Theologiae* II-II, Question 109, Article 3, as a "historically prominent example of this taxonomy"). It is worth noting that Miller's more nuanced taxonomy includes a middle category of virtues (between honesty and the five narrow virtues), which includes *veracity* and *trustworthiness*; the latter will be discussed in the Interlude.

[31] John Rawls, *A Theory of Justice* (Cambridge, MA: Harvard University Press, 1999 [1971]), 3.

rights and duties and determine the division of advantages from social co-operation."[32] The police qualify as such an institution (and it's worth noting that Rawls writes about nonideal theory, or how we should transition from the existing world of injustice toward the ideal of justice), and questions of justice are naturally tied to questions about policing. It is thus important to highlight the traditional idea that honesty is a facet of justice.

With this background in mind, we're in a position to consider a firmer account of the necessary conditions for honesty. Here is Miller's final account:

> The virtue of honesty is the virtue of being disposed, centrally and reliably and as dictated by the capacities associated with practical wisdom, to not intentionally distort the facts as the agent sees them, and primarily for good or virtuous motivating reasons of one or more kinds K_1 through K_n of sufficient motivating strength and modal robustness and scope to encompass all human beings, along with the absence of significant nonvirtuous motivation to distort the facts as the agent sees them.[33]

Although you wouldn't call this account succinct, it is a compelling theory of honesty that addresses some of the central issues that have been raised—including the idea that honesty is a *virtue* marked by a *disposition*. Importantly, it is a disposition based on *intention*. In other words, one purposely does not distort facts. Relatedly, the phrase "as the agent sees them" accounts for honest mistakes of fact. Suppose a police officer tells a criminal suspect that the police obtained the suspect's fingerprints from the crime scene. Miller's theory of honesty accounts for the officer's statement if it is untrue but he believes it to be true (for instance, if the officer obtained fingerprints believed to be the suspect's, but a subsequent test reveals that the fingerprints in fact belong to a different person).

We need not dwell on all the technical details of Miller's complex account, though it's worth explaining some of the more esoteric points. The

---

[32] Ibid., 7.

[33] Miller, *Honesty*, 132. After considering several counterexamples to refine the account, he labels this version "H10." It is a rich and rewarding discussion, but the details are beyond the scope of this book. Regardless, keeping with this book's ecumenicism, it is important to note that one need not embrace Miller's account of honesty to embrace honesty's importance to policing. One might think that it is enough that the police are honest (regardless of whether they have the *virtue* of honesty), which might be understood as simply telling the truth and not misrepresenting facts (whatever their reasons for doing so). Relatedly, one might think that it is not very important for the police to have a *disposition* of honesty given cases (discussed in the Interlude and second half of the book) in which it is justified for the police to act dishonestly.

phrase "primarily for good or virtuous motivating reasons of one or more kinds K_1 through K_n" would account for cases in which, say, a police officer is motivated to tell the truth in order to *harm* someone—or only to avoid getting in trouble. Such cases of truth-telling would not be indicative of the *virtue* of honesty. For one's behavior to arise from the virtue of honesty, one must be motivated by good reasons "K_1 through K_n," which is simply a place-holder for motivating reasons such as *justice*.[34] Honesty is again tied to per-haps the fundamental virtue of policing: justice.

The phrase "sufficient motivating strength and modal robustness and scope to encompass all human beings" accounts for motivations that seem virtuous (at least with respect to some groups of people) but are in fact dis-honest (because the motivation does not apply to other groups of people). Consider, say, a police officer who is thoroughly honest with fellow officers because he wants to help and respect (not harm) the police; however, the of-ficer is readily dishonest when it comes to dealing with people who do not work in law enforcement.

In a similar way, "modal robustness" accounts for situations in which, say, a police officer stops behaving honestly to a person who ceases being a police officer (for instance, the other person quits the police and decides to become an advocate of "police abolition."). The officer's motivation is not "modally robust" because it cannot "survive changes in . . . circumstances such that if one kind of motivation is no longer applicable, another kind can be brought to bear."[35] Finally, "practical wisdom" (*phronesis*) is derived from Aristotle's *Nicomachean Ethics*, and Miller concludes that practical wisdom may simply be treated as "a shorthand way to refer to those capacities required for the proper functioning of the virtue of honesty."[36] All in all, this comprehensive account of honesty will provide a helpful baseline as we move to policing applications and exceptions in Chapters 2 and 3.

Before we move ahead, we should at least introduce how the virtue of hon-esty might be affected by cases in which intentional distortions of fact are (or are believed to be) morally permissible. The examples we have been working with include the undercover officer who lies about his identity to stop a crime

---

[34] Ibid., 101.

[35] Ibid., 106–107.

[36] Ibid., 132. On the idea that one can be honest or dishonest without being an honest or dishonest person, we might consider the well-known Aristotelian idea that "one swallow does not make a summer." In a similar vein, consider the distinction between being hypocritical and being a hypo-crite. See Paul Bloomfield, "The Character of the Hypocrite," *Journal of Philosophical Research* 43 (2018): 69–82.

boss from beating his broken arm with a boot. We have also considered Kant's "murderer at the door" example (lying to the murderer about the location of his intended victim).

Miller suggests two ways to think about these sorts of cases: (1) "The virtue of honesty does not apply" to these kinds of cases, or (2) lying in these kinds of cases "is still a failure of honesty, but it is all things considered morally permissible."[37] He prefers the second option, which strikes me as the best choice, too. As Miller put it, "it seems intuitively obvious . . . that the person would be telling a genuine lie in intentionally giving a false location to [a murderer] at the door." Under this conception, one can do things that are not honest (dishonest) but that are "justified overall" (and thus not representative of the *vice* of dishonesty).[38] We can sum up this section with the tentative conclusion that it is coherent to reconcile honesty as a virtue with dishonest and deceptive acts that are morally permissible.

With this account of honesty in mind, we turn to a preliminary analysis of *transparency*—which, like honesty, is an important facet of good faith. And like honesty, we will see that *complete* transparency is neither required nor justified. Absolutist positions rarely are.

2.2. Transparency

President Barack Obama signed and sent a memorandum to the heads of executive departments and agencies on his first day in office, titled "Transparency and Open Government." The memorandum describes the Administration's goal "to ensure the public trust and establish a system of transparency, participation, and collaboration," which "will strengthen our democracy."[39] The memorandum thus focuses on three related points:

(1) Government should be transparent.
(2) Government should be participatory.
(3) Government should be collaborative.

---

[37] Ibid., 74.

[38] Ibid., 76. This sort of view has support from a variety of fronts—including Thomas Carson's work describing how there are cases of "morally permissible lying that violate[] someone's right to know the truth." Carson, *Lying and Deception*, 19–20.

[39] The White House, *Transparency and Open Government: Memorandum for the Heads of Executive Departments and Agencies* (Jan. 21, 2009), https://obamawhitehouse.archives.gov/the-press-office/transparency-and-open-government.

There is no limit to my cynicism about politics, but the memorandum plausibly links transparency to accountability. Simply put, transparency allows the public to hold the Government accountable for its actions. And by giving the public this power of accountability, we can participate and collaborate with the government. In other words, transparency allows the social contract to work—it allows the public and the government to engage with each other. Unsurprisingly, the memorandum doesn't get very philosophical about transparency. Let's do that now.

Although transparency is not typically discussed in the context of the legal doctrine of good faith, we will see that transparency is a central facet of the normative content of good faith. There are indeed compelling reasons to think that transparency is a facet of honesty, with honesty being one of the central facets of good faith. The term transparency is used in different ways in different contexts and thus can have different meanings. It is helpful to begin—as we did with honesty—with a stand-alone account of transparency, namely: transparency as a virtue that individual people may possess. Then we can consider how the trait may be relevant to institutions such as the police.

Philosopher T. Ryan Byerly conceives of intellectual transparency as a character trait—one falling within "the domain of sharing one's perspective with others" to promote "others' epistemic goods."[40] A person with this trait wants others to attain goods such as knowledge and truth belief, and faithfully communicates their perspective (their "take" on a matter) to promote those goods in others.

Right away, then, a link to policing is foreshadowed—especially as it relates to communication with others. When a police officer interrogates a criminal suspect, she might raise the topic of the prison sentence the perpetrator of the crime will face. If the officer fails to be transparent—say, fails to share her perspective regarding the true length of the prison sentence the perpetrator will face—then the officer may obtain an advantage over the suspect.

To be sure, this may very well be a beneficial law enforcement advantage, but it comes at the expense of the suspect's knowledge of the case's stakes—preventing the suspect from making an informed decision based on true belief. We should reserve judgment on such cases at this point—they are of

---

[40] T. Ryan Byerly, "Group Intellectual Transparency: A Novel Case for Non-Summativism," *Synthese* 200, no. 69 (2022): 2. Conversely, a lack of transparency could mean, say, a person's reliance on hidden, undisclosed intentions to misrepresent or alter the person's outward, objective words and actions. See, e.g., Lucy v. Zehmer, 196 Va. 493; 84 S.E.2d 516 (1954).

course fact-specific—but it's important to highlight the competing interests we will encounter. In any event, Byerly's analysis makes it clear that we need not *always* be intellectually transparent—as when displaying such transparency is not possible and would not promote one's epistemic goods.[41] As we move forward, I'll consider how opacity can be justified when transparency would fail to promote epistemic goods such as knowledge and true belief overall (not just with respect to a person from whom transparency is withheld).

Here, though, the point is simply that it's plausible to think of institutions (not just individuals or individual police officers) as likewise being transparent (or not). The idea is straightforward, especially considering the intuition that institutions often are *not* transparent. For example, philosopher Jennifer Lackey describes how *groups* of people can cause epistemic harm by lying, bullshitting, and misleading others—harm that naturally leads us to view such groups contemptuously.[42] This sentiment seems to be a pretty accurate picture regarding the contemporary police institution.

When we turn to the way the police figure into the idea of the *social contract*—and breaches of the social contract—we will see that there are strong reasons to think many communities distrust the police institution in part due to dishonesty, deception, and a lack of transparency. Indeed, as a state institution that affects the distribution of rights, communities *need* the police to be transparent if community members are to enjoy their rights. Tentatively, then, we can say that there is at least a prima facie case supporting transparency in the police institution.

On the other hand, it is often suggested that transparency must be "balanced" against security—particularly national security. The presumption is straightforward: If our state institutions (especially law enforcement institutions) are too transparent, the public's security will be compromised. The idea is reminiscent of American World War II propaganda slogans and posters such as *Loose Lips Sink Ships*. The general sentiment is simply that the state should keep security-related information close to the chest. To be sure, there is a time and a place for state opacity—a topic we'll consider further in Chapter 4. But that's not the whole story.

---

[41] Ibid., fn 1. Byerly's overall point is to show that group intellectual transparency "involves something beyond the intellectual transparency of individual group members." This view is called "non-summativism" (contrasted with "summativism," the view that group intellectual transparency is simply a function of individual group members themselves having intellectual transparency). Ibid., 6.

[42] See Jennifer Lackey, *The Epistemology of Groups* (Oxford: Oxford University Press, 2020).

For instance, it was ironically a lack of transparency that led to the inability to stop one of the most significant breaches of national security in US history. Congressional hearings after the 9/11 terrorist attacks revealed that excessive secrecy and a lack of transparency among law enforcement and intelligence agencies hampered the ability of those agencies to prevent the attacks. In many cases, there was simply a lack of communication and knowledge sharing among law enforcement and intelligence agencies. Knowledge meant status and *power* for such agencies, meaning that part of the problem was simply bureaucratic competition.[43]

The failure of transparency was not only between law enforcement and intelligence agencies; it was also a failure with respect to those agencies and the public. In testimony before the joint House and Senate select intelligence committee investigating the September 11 attacks, the staff director of the inquiry summarized investigative findings as follows:

> [T]he record suggests that prior to September 11th, the U.S. intelligence and law enforcement communities were fighting a war against terrorism largely without the benefit of what some would call their most potent weapon in that effort—an alert and a committed American public. One need look no further for proof of the latter point than the heroics of the passengers on Flight 93 or the quick action of the flight attendant who identified shoe-bomber Richard Reid.[44]

The broader point is that it's worth rethinking the standard presumption that transparency is always outweighed by security. As a practical matter, opacity can lead to catastrophic breaches of security. Philosophically, the public cannot hold the state accountable for its policies and processes if they are opaque—a point learned all too well following the 9/11 attacks. It thus stands to reason that transparency plays a significant role in promoting honest institutions and honest policies that are based on democratic support: Transparency can empower the public and facilitate effective law enforcement, all while keeping the police institution honest.

---

[43] These issues were covered extensively in the media following the 9/11 attacks. See, e.g., "Lost Chance on Terrorists Cited: INS, FAA Might Have Found 2 of 19 Hijackers, Officials Say," *The Washington Post*, October 2, 2002; Vernon Loeb, "When Hoarding Secrets Threaten National Security," *The Washington Post*, January 26, 2003.

[44] "Testimony from the Joint Intelligence Committee," *The New York Times*, October 17, 2002.

2.3. The Spectrum of Good Faith

Here is where our analysis stands: Good faith entails a disposition of honesty in contractual dealings, including reaching agreements and the faithful adherence to the scope, purpose, and terms of agreements. Such a disposition is vitally important to the police institution assuming that we care about fulfilling social obligations in a way that protects reasonable expectations. Naturally, dishonesty, deception, and opacity discourage a good faith disposition.

Moving forward, we will examine counterexamples in which the police *seem* to be justified in their departure from a good faith disposition, suggesting that good faith is not a binary concept inasmuch as there is a spectrum of good faith (a party may more or less have a disposition of good faith given that good faith is multifaceted). Considering each end of the spectrum, we can safely say that good faith requires more than simply not engaging in fraud, but it requires less than fiduciary loyalty.[45]

Given the range and complexity of good faith, I want to home in on a clear case of bad faith in the proceeding sections: *fraudulent* dealings.[46] The term "fraudulent" is ubiquitous, making it difficult to pin down exactly what a person means when using the term. The term certainly isn't limited to the legal context, but that's a good place start. Legal scholar Stuart Green's incisive analysis of fraud is situated within the context of white-collar criminal law.[47] He explains that fraud is traditionally associated with the requirement of *deceit*, though deceit is not necessary for fraud under modern criminal codes.[48] The judicial opinion in *Hammerschmidt v. United States*—the Supreme Court case that I raised in the book's Introduction—sets forth the principle that the

---

[45] See Markovits, "Good Faith is Contract's Core Value," 272 (citing Mkt. St. Assocs. Ltd. P'ship v. Frey, 941 F.2d 588, 594–595 (7th Cir. 1991)).

[46] Recall the many deceptive and dishonest tactics that are difficult to identify and access, such as interrogation techniques in which police display false empathy so that a suspect is more likely to talk and confess. It would of course be odd and impractical to say that only genuinely empathetic officers are permitted to appear so. This is in part why we must distinguish these sorts of tactics and other deceptive and dishonest tactics that are on par with fraud and deviations from the rule of law. Examples of the latter will include tactics such as falsely telling a suspect that his prints were found at the scene of the crime or that his co-conspirator has confessed.

[47] Stuart P. Green, *Lying, Cheating, and Stealing—A Moral Theory of White-Collar Crime* (Oxford: Oxford University Press, 2006), 148–149 (citing *Hammerschmidt v. United States*, 265 U.S. 182, 188 (1924)).

[48] Green's general point is about how the concept of fraud has been used in legal practice, not that he endorses such a broad (often confusing) understanding of the term (an understanding that is an artifact of how the relevant fraud statutes have been constructed and interpreted).

means of nondeceptive fraud is simply *dishonesty*. Therefore: *Deception and dishonesty—the two concepts in this book's title—give fraud its character.*

The point is that—as discussed in the book's Introduction—monetary or proprietary loss is not required in the federal crime of conspiring to defraud. Instead, such frauds may simply involve dishonesty, deceit, and trickery that interferes with a lawful government function. From a more general perspective, Green's explanation of the *object* of fraud is especially illuminating: fraud "is used more broadly to refer to schemes not just to obtain money or property, but also to achieve any 'unjust advantage' or to 'injure the rights or interests of another.'"[49] He illustrates this point with 18 U.S. Code §1346, the federal statutory provision defining "scheme or artifice to defraud" as one that "deprive[s] another of the intangible right of honest services."[50] *Intangible* is important here because it highlights the breadth of fraud.

Green explains that the goal of fraud in the public sector can be "to deny the public its rights to honest governmental services," and in the private sector "to deny an employer its right to the honest services of its employee."[51] Although the analogy is not perfect, we will see that government agents such as the police can similarly defraud a person of their rights using dishonesty, deceit, and misrepresentation.

In short, the most important point to note about the concept of fraud is its varying moral content. Although "deception and stealing" constitute the traditional understanding of fraud's moral wrongfulness, Green shows that the moral content of fraud is far more expansive. Fraud may be carried out by way of "dishonesty" (e.g., exploitation, promise-breaking), not just traditional acts of deception. In this light, the analogy to police deception and dishonesty in no way stretches the limits of credulity. Indeed, if there are cases (and there are) in which the police use deception or dishonesty to secure an unjust advantage through, say, exploitation or coercion (injuring the rights and interests of others) then we are squarely in the realm of fraudulent behavior.

It is thus a good time to examine how policing is contractual, which raises the issue of concrete tactics that are deceptive, dishonest, and fraudulent (and potentially illegitimate), as well as the more abstract issue of institutional dishonesty and illegitimacy in the context of breaches to the *social contract*.

---

[49] Ibid., 150 (quoting the *Oxford English Dictionary*).
[50] 18 U.S.C §1346.
[51] Green, *Lying, Cheating, and Stealing*, 150.

3. Concrete Agreements and Fraud

Issues of good faith are straightforwardly raised in exchanges between citizens and government agents. For example, arrangements between prosecutors and cooperators and between police and informants are in many ways like a contract in that both sides voluntarily enter into an agreement with the intent that each side will assume certain obligations under the agreement. If this is accurate, then certain background norms and principles of contract law—including good faith—might have weight with respect to such agreements in addition to the more familiar sources of law.[52] We can see this by examining different conditions—including both procedural and substantive context—under which people agree to bargain with state agents. Here is a sketch of how it might work:

(1) The police indicate that they have evidence that a woman—Jane—committed a crime that exposes Jane to potential punishment (incarceration).

(2) The police make Jane an offer: If Jane acquires evidence or information for the police (including through conduct that would otherwise be illegal) then the police will consider advising the prosecutor (responsible for prosecuting Jane's alleged crime) of Jane's assistance so the prosecutor can consider recommending that Jane receive a downward departure from the punishment for which she is eligible.

(3) Jane accepts the offer and performs according to the terms of the bargain.

Under this common formulation, it is plausible to think that broad principles of contract law have weight with respect to the underlying agreement between Jane and the police.

For example, (2) expresses the police's willingness to enter into an agreement with Jane and an invitation to Jane to conclude the agreement by expressing her assent to the deal in (3). If this is like an offer (and acceptance), then it is plausible to think that various norms of offers and acceptances are relevant here—such that Jane and the police knowingly and willingly agree to the overall arrangement and its specific terms. The example also seems to suggest that something is bargained for by Jane and the police ("consideration"),

---

[52] See Hunt, *The Retrieval of Liberalism in Policing*, ch. 4.

namely: Jane will engage in certain activities to acquire evidence for the police in exchange for the police advising the prosecutor of her assistance. We can thus see how the scenario is different from a scenario in which Jane or the police simply make a gratuitous promise without consideration (without a bargained-for exchange).

The point is simply to suggest that the bargaining process raises the normative principles underpinning contractual relations and give those principles weight with respect to questions about the justification of the agreement between the police and the informant. This is especially relevant with respect to a contractual disposition of good faith that entails honesty and transparency. Indeed, legal philosophers such as Seana Shiffrin have taken the position that contracts raise moral obligations based upon promissory elements (in addition to legal obligations). In other words, parties cannot remove the promissory element of contracts—and any underlying moral elements—by simply declaring that one has done so (such as when the police state that they do not make promises to informants).[53] Irrespective of that line of reasoning, if one construes the agreement between Jane and the police as *contract-like*, then it raises bargaining principles of contract law such as good faith.[54]

Suppose you are skeptical and think the connection between Jane's scenario and a background norm of good faith is tenuous. Drawing on the last section, let's thus try to make the modest case that agreements such as Jane's require a disposition of good faith that minimally precludes acts by the police that are on par with *fraud*. Instead of a legal claim of fraud, I simply have in mind a normative backdrop associated with the sort of universalistic positive morality (UPM) regarding force and fraud discussed in Chapter 1. With respect to fraud, then, one might say that the police institution is constrained by a background norm that precludes intentional or negligent misrepresentations of fact on which the police intend for a person

---

[53] Seana Valentine Shiffrin, "Is a Contract a Promise?" in *The Routledge Companion to Philosophy of Law*, ed. Andrei Marmor (New York: Routledge, 2012), 241–257.

[54] These issues are not limited to the use of informants at the investigation phase; they're also relevant at the prosecution phase, as philosopher Adina Schwartz's has argued regarding the injustice of plea agreements and cooperation agreements (a cooperation agreement is an agreement under which a person agrees to plead guilty and testify for the government in exchange for leniency). See Adina Schwartz, "A Market in Liberty: Corruption, Cooperation, and the Federal Criminal Justice System," in *Private and Public Corruption*, eds. John Kleinig and William C. Hefferman (Lanham: Rowman & Littlefield, 2004), 177. And it is worth noting that courts have construed "cooperation agreements" as contracts. United States. Khan, 920 F.2d 1100, 1105 (2d Cir. 1990), cert. denied, 499 U.S. 969 (1991); United States v. Hon, 17 F.3d 21, 26 (2d. Cir. 1994); see also United States v. Ganz, 806 F.Supp. 1567, 1570 (S.D.Fla. 1992) ("The contract between the parties required Mr. Ganz to provide information, truthful testimony, and to work under the direction of Customs in an undercover capacity").

(such as Jane) to rely (such that Jane in fact relies on the misrepresentation and is harmed).

Indeed, in the case with which this chaptered opened, *Alexander v. DeAngelo*, the court raised the issue of fraud explicitly, stating that "the threat [of a 40-year prison sentence] may have been fraudulent" given that the woman was facing only a six-to-ten-year sentence.[55] Recall that the police in the *Alexander* case asked a woman—who was facing a drug charge that gave the police leverage over the woman—to engage in oral sex with the target of a police investigation. The police's goal was to gather evidence against the target and charge the target with soliciting a prostitute. Based on the facts, the court said that "[i]t thus appears . . . that the police may have obtained [the informant's] consent to sex by fraud, and if so that was a battery."[56] The court emphasized "that the use of trickery is an accepted tool of criminal law enforcement and does not in itself give rise to liability," though there are legal limits to the police's use of deception.[57]

Ultimately, the court held that the police were not liable because they had qualified immunity (even though the elements of fraud were potentially present in the case). The court reasoned that they "cannot say that it would have been obvious to the average officer that the deceit employed in this case rose to the level of a constitutional violation" of the woman's rights.[58] Here is the crux of the court's analysis:

> The police did not rape [the woman] in the ordinary sense of the term "rape," or for that matter cause [the police target] to rape her in the ordinary sense in which one would speak of A having caused B to rape C—nor have we found any "third party" rape cases. Characterization of [the police target's] action as rape and hence battery required us to engage in a close and perhaps not entirely intuitive analysis leading to a conclusion likely to startle many police officers.[59]

Whatever one might think about the court's ruling on the issue of qualified immunity (an important topic beyond the scope of this book), it is clear that

---

[55] Alexander v. DeAngelo, 329 F.3d 912 (2003).

[56] Ibid.

[57] For example, the court noted that the police may "actively mislead" a person to obtain a confession if a rational decision by the person remains possible. Ibid. (citing United States v. Ceballos, 302 F.3d 679, 695 (7th Cir. 2002)).

[58] Ibid.

[59] Ibid.

the prospect of a concrete case of fraud was a live issue in this case. And even if such frauds aren't always actionable, it's reasonable to think that the police ought to act in good faith (which precludes fraudulent tactics) inasmuch as we care about the universalistic positive morality (UPM) discussed in this chapter and the last. We will return to these issues in the second part of the book, but now let's consider the more abstract issue of institutional illegitimacy and breaches of the social contract.

4. Social Contracts and Institutional Good Faith

> It would be wishful thinking . . . to expect individuals to bring about major changes in the collective practices of deceit by themselves. Public and private institutions, with their enormous power to affect personal choice, must help alter the existing pressures and incentives.
>
> —Sissela Bok[60]

The 2023 Pulitzer in Local Reporting was awarded to a team of journalists in Alabama—the state in which I live and work—who uncovered a small-town (Brookside, Alabama) police department's practice of preying on residents to inflate revenue through the abusive use of citations, fines, and forfeitures (seizing property allegedly connected to criminality).[61] One of the winning journalists—John Archibald—desribed how "Brookside revenues from fines and forfeitures soared more than 640 percent and now make up half the city's total income," with "poorer residents or passersby fall[ing] into patterns of debt they cannot easily escape."[62] This is the epitome of "policing for profit."[63] It is also an egregious breach of the social contract and institutional good faith.

Policing for profit might involve tactics that are strictly speaking legal (e.g., it might be legal for the police to enforce—by issuing a citation—*every*

---

[60] Sissela Bok, *Lying: Moral Choice in Public and Private Life* (New York: Vintage Books, 1999 [1978]), 244.

[61] See "The 2023 Pulitzer Prize Winner in Local Reporting" (John Archibald, Ashley Remkus, Ramsey Archibald and Challen Stephens of AL.com, Birmingham), available at pulitzer.org.

[62] John Archibald, "Police in This Tiny Alabama Town Suck Drivers into Legal 'Black Hole,'" *AL. com*, January 19, 2022. The reporting ultimately prompted the resignation of the police chief, four new laws, and a state audit.

[63] See, e.g., Chris W. Surprenant, "Policing and Punishment for Profit," *Journal of Business Ethics* 159 (2019): 119–131.

violation of a jay walking law), but that does not mean the police are *governing* by the rule of law.[64] The Brookside police force used their discretionary power (to enforce the law) in a way that perverted the law: The police as an institution relied upon discretionary law enforcement power to dishonestly generate revuenue instead of policing the community in good faith.

We should, then, take a step back from specific (deceptive and dishonest) law enforcement tactics to consider how good faith—and its constituent parts, honesty, and transparency—is important to the police as a political institution. If honesty and transparency promote healthy, trusting interpersonal relationships, then it is plausible to think they promote and strengthen trust and legitimacy at the societal and institutional levels.

This is an especially timely issue given recent fractures in police–community relationships, requiring us to think about broader cultural factors within policing that encourage dishonesty at the group level and shape its development in the police institution. Examples of institutional bad faith unfortunately go far beyond policing for profit. Consider the phenomenon known as the "blue wall of silence," the informal code among some police officers not to report on a colleague's misconduct but instead plead ignorance of another officer's wrongdoing or claim to have not seen anything. The code is motivated by the view that (some) institutional dishonesty is honorable and is justified by the larger goal of promoting security and reducing crime in society.

But there is an even more basic sense in which policing is both contractual and tied to good faith, honesty, and transparency. We often hear people say things such, "You can't trust the government." Or, "The entire police department is dishonest." They are not referring to a particular member of the government or a particular police officer, but rather the government or the institution as a whole. In one sense, this seems perfectly natural because people say such things all the time. But on closer inspection, these sentiments can seem odd given our discussion of honesty as a *virtue*—a disposition based upon concrete beliefs, intentions, and motivations—that *persons* may possess. Now we are talking about *governments* and *institutions*.[65] We raised the notion of honest and transparent *institutions* in the last section. In this

---

[64] On this point, see *The Retrieval of Liberalism in Policing*, 93–100.

[65] On these points, see, e.g., Kenneth Silver, "Group Action Without Group Minds," *Philosophy and Phenomenological Research* 104, no. 2 (2022): 321–342; Kyle G. Fritz, "Hypocrisy, Inconsistency, and the Moral Standing of the State," *Criminal Law and Philosophy* 13, no. 2 (2019): 309–327.

section, we'll further develop the idea by showing the connections between *social contracts* and good faith.[66]

In short, societal arrangements modeled on the ideal of a social contract—agreements between the government and the governed regarding security—are relational in nature even if they cannot be captured exhaustively in a literal, explicit contract.[67] They are instead derived from long-term relationships based on roles requiring communication, cooperation, and mutual trust steeped in honesty and transparency.

4.1. Security

We considered the prospect of framing questions about "honest institutions" in light of the idea that honesty is a facet of justice (justice being a central virtue of social institutions). We also considered how the police have been entrusted to promote that facet of justice that we call *security*. State institutions such as the police are supposed provide security legitimately, which is in part based on authority. Suppose you take it upon yourself to mow my lawn and then demand $100 as payment. Your demand lacks legitimacy

---

[66] We should note that there can be a distinction between the virtues of agents of the state (e.g., police officers), and the virtues of the rules and systems that justify the institutions of which agents of the state are a part. For example, it is in principle possible for people to contract honestly, in good faith, into arrangements in which the state creates an institution that will sometimes deceive them; accordingly, if honesty is a virtue of individual police officers, it can be distinct from the contractual nature of policing. To put it differently, if the police as a whole should be honest and act in good faith, it does not follow that each agent of the state must *always* act in good faith because there may be additional values (beyond the values inherent in a contract) that should be expressed by those involved in executing a contract. Regardless, even if we construe social contract theory in terms of simple metaphor (given that contracts between communities and the police are not enforceable in the way that they are between individuals), it is plausible to think there are (social contract) values and norms that we can draw upon to understand the relationship between communities and state institutions such as the police. The point is that one facet of understanding the relationship between communities and the police is to think about the role good faith plays in that relationship. See generally Jeremy Waldron, *Political Political Theory* (Cambridge, MA: Harvard University Press, 2016), regarding the relationship between the contract model, state institutions, and the character and political virtue required of those who inhabit those institutions. See also Cristina Bicchieri's important work on social norms, e.g., *The Grammar of Society: The Nature and Dynamics of Social Norms* (Cambridge: Cambridge University Press, 2006).

[67] Markovits's account of good faith illustrates the connection to the social contract: "Good faith . . . connects the solidarity of the contract relation . . . to the broader formal equality that lies at the bottom of the democratic . . . societies in which contract typically flourishes." Markovits, "Good Faith Is Contract's Core Value," 292. It is also worth considering doctrinal analogues to the social contract, including Chapter 1's discussion of *relational contracts* consisting of long-term relationships and intentions that the respective roles of the parties will be performed with collaboration, communication, cooperation, integrity, mutual trust, and fidelity.

because you had no authority to mow my lawn. But had I consented to the arrangement, you would have been a legitimate lawncare provider because you had authority to mow my lawn.

Of course, in the political context, receiving consent from everyone in a political community regarding the provision of security is impractical. One way (not the only way) to think realistically about political authority is in terms of reciprocity: public relationships generating rights and duties between state institutions and communities. Such relationships by their nature require good faith—which in term requires some degree of honesty and transparency—inasmuch as they are based on mutual understanding regarding the enforcement of applicable laws, regulations, and policies. Recall President Obama's executive order on *transparency and open government* and the claim that government should be both "participatory" and "collaborative." It is difficult to conceive of a "social contract" without participation and collaboration. Good faith is thus a fundamental criterion of the legitimacy of reciprocal political relationships, governing the correlative rights and duties forged by those relationships. To what extent does the police institution adhere to these norms in providing security?

First, I assume that the security of all persons by social institutions is a basic component of justice and determining the extent to which a polity is justified. On this point, we can draw from canonical thinkers such as Thomas Hobbes and John Locke (below) regarding life with (and without) a centralized security apparatus. This helps motivate the idea of state institutions such as the police—in other words, the idea of collectively providing for security by centralizing the right to punish in order to eliminate bias, personal incapacity, and arbitrariness.

Second, we should also point out that security is a multifaceted concept. It means much more than simply one's basic *safety*. For example, security raises questions of *depth*: security is not just about staying alive, but also about comprehensive ways people want to live their lives. Security also raises questions of *breadth*; in other words, the distribution of security across various groups.[68] Law enforcement and crime reduction are related to the facets of security that justify the polity over the state of nature: People often need protection from others (who do not reciprocate), and one important way to provide security is through a centralized enforcer (the police, for

---

[68] Jeremy Waldron, *Torture, Terror, and Trade-Offs* (Oxford: Oxford University Press, 2010), 116–122.

example) who can reduce and stop harm and violence by other members of the polity.

Third, we should acknowledge a presumption that failed reciprocation is dealt with in accordance with the rule of law and respect for one's equal personhood.[69] For instance, Locke claimed that political power and authority are limited—meaning that persons have a right to be secured legitimately within the bounds of authority. This suggests a moral foundation for limitations on the ways that enforcement may occur (security from enforcers, in other words).[70] The upshot is that state institutions can act illegitimately when they act in bad faith, imposing measures (including those that rely on deception, dishonesty, and bad faith) that unfairly enhance the safety and security of some groups at the expense of other groups.[71] So it is in part the reciprocal political relationship—and how the state deals with breakdowns in the relationship—that highlights the role of good faith.

A final point about the provision of security: Dishonestly and deceptively defecting from cooperative relations—taking advantage of another's trust—can be a correlative of force inasmuch as defecting from cooperative relations leads to enmity. This illuminates a central facet of contemporary policing: *proactive* policing, which often relies on dishonesty and deception to preemptively stop crime. Proactive policing is a form of *preemptive* defection (albeit defection that is in some cases justified) from cooperative relations—and a source of enmity between the police and the community when proactive policing enhances the security of some groups at the expense of other groups.[72] This enmity between police and community may be observed in each side's posture of anticipation and distrust.

Contemporary police and communities are thus faced with a dilemma that can lead to a so-called *state of war*: each side anticipates wrongdoing and

---

[69] See Lon L. Fuller, *The Morality of Law* (New Haven, CT: Yale University Press, 1969); Joseph Raz, *The Authority of Law* (Oxford: Oxford University Press, 2009 [1979]).

[70] See generally John Locke, *Two Treatises*.

[71] These points are a clear example of the tension with consequentialist reasoning: The state cannot legitimately reduce the security of some in order to maximize the security of others—for example, through widespread deception and dishonesty that focuses on certain groups and crimes.

[72] As noted earlier, there is not always a clear distinction between proactive and reactive. An officer walking the beat, developing personal relationships with the residents (in part to prevent crime before it happens) might be both proactive and justified, as would putting more officers on the street before a large public (which is proactive and does not involve deception or dishonesty). Again, our focus is on deceptive and dishonest policing (which is *often* proactive) that is on par with fraud and deviations from the rule of law.

chooses bad faith and preemptive action to take advantage of the other side. Let's consider the historical context of these ideas before moving to contemporary questions.

4.2. The Hobbesian Dilemma: Cooperate or Defect?

It is interesting to consider how the relationship between force and fraud grounds some of the most fundamental principles of modern political and legal philosophy. Thomas Hobbes—one of the founders of modern political philosophy—wrote his famous book, *Leviathan*, three-hundred years after Dante's *Divine Comedy* was completed. And yet it picks up with some familiar themes regarding force and fraud—themes that underpin the contemporary legal philosophy we examined in Chapter 1. Hobbes is known for his description of life without political (and legal) society—the hypothetical condition we have been calling the *state of nature*. Let's consider the idea more carefully, as it will illuminate the relationship between force and fraud.

Hobbes famously described the state of nature as a condition of war that is "solitary, poor, nasty, brutish, and short."[73] Why? The basic idea is that such a condition would be tantamount to war—all against all—and the two cardinal virtues of war are indeed *force* and *fraud*.[74] The reason people would be enemies in the state of nature is that they naturally desire the same things necessary for survival. But if there is competition for a scarcity of resources (coupled with rational fear of attack from others and no common power to keep one safe), then the result is war. One of Hobbes's central ideas is to motivate the justification of political society based upon a few natural, empirical generalizations about people.[75] Consider how these generalizations illuminate the relationship between force and fraud.

The Hobbesian state of war presents a paradox given the assumption that most people would in fact prefer the exact opposite, namely: a state of peace. For Hobbes, the problem is that the state of nature permits no individually rational path to obtain the peace we all desire. It doesn't appear prudent to

---

[73] Thomas Hobbes, *Leviathan*, intro. W. G. Pogson Smith (Oxford: Clarendon Press, 1909 [1651]), 97 (chapter 13). For an incisive synopsis of Hobbesian political philosophy, see A. John Simmons, *Political Philosophy* (New York: Oxford University Press, 2007), 24–32. I am grateful to have worked with Professor Simmons during my doctoral work at the University of Virginia; his work continues to inform my understanding of Hobbes (and certainly Locke), as expressed in these pages.

[74] Hobbes, *Leviathan*, 98 (ch. 13).

[75] Hobbes, *Leviathan*, 94–96 (ch. 13).

peacefully cooperate with others when there is no political authority to enforce reciprocation. We would all have to blindly trust others in the absence of an enforcer who can ensure that our trust is not taken advantage of by others. This leads to what we describe today as a *prisoners' dilemma*—the opportunity to take advantage of another's cooperative behavior, coupled with the need to guard against being taken advantage of oneself. The result is that the pursuit of the mutually preferred outcome (peace and cooperation) is irrational.[76] As we will see, contemporary police and communities are in a sort of prisoner's dilemma. Consider a classic example illustrating the form of the dilemma.

Jane and John are suspected of burglary and are taken into custody by the police.[77] The police do not have enough evidence to convict them of burglary, only to convict them on the charge of possession of stolen property. If neither Jane nor John confesses to the police (instead cooperating with each other by not talking to the police), they will both be charged with the lesser sentence of possession of stolen property: one year of prison each. The police will question Jane and John in separate interrogation rooms, which means that they cannot communicate. The police will also try to convince Jane and John to confess to the crime by offering them an enticing deal (zero years in prison), while the other suspect will be sentenced to a ten-year term. If both Jane and John confess (and therefore they defect, failing to cooperate with each other), each will be sentenced to eight years. Both Jane and John are offered the same deal and know the consequences of each action, and they are aware that the other has been offered the exact same deal.

Here's the kicker. If Jane confesses, she knows she will get either *eight* or *zero* years in prison, and she knows she will get either *ten* or *one* year in prison if she doesn't confess to the police. Jane will thus rationally choose to confess, since she will be better off either way (and thus it would be rational for John to confess, too). Accordingly, Jane and John each get *eight* years in prison. The problem is that their rational strategy is not optimal. If Jane and John cooperated with each other (not confessing to the police), then each would get *one* year in prison. So by acting rationally and confessing, Jane and John are worse off than they would be if they both had acted irrationally.

---

[76] As Simmons notes, the situation could perhaps be altered slightly so that the mutually preferred outcome could be reached, such as when the players had good reasons to trust each other (e.g., if they were friends), or if both were known to keep promises. Moreover, motivations of sociability and sympathy might also help resolve the prisoner's dilemma. Simmons, *Political Philosophy*, 28.

[77] See Simmons, *Political Philosophy*, 26–32, for discussion of similar scenarios.

By analogy, this is also the Hobbesian dilemma in the state of nature: If two people are rational in the state of nature, neither will do as they agreed to do—and the mutually desired exchange (some sort of mutually beneficial forbearance) will not take place. The opportunity to take advantage of another's cooperative behavior along with the need to guard against being taken advantage of oneself combine to make pursuit of the mutually preferred outcome irrational.

We can thus see that the Hobbesian argument is straightforward: You have a few options in the absence of political and legal society. You can hide and avoid contact with others. You can lay down arms and come to some kind of understanding—in other words, cooperate. Or you can anticipate, thinking about what others will do and then taking preemptive action. Hobbes thinks anticipation is the best option for one's preservation in the state of nature, though it leads to war. He gets to this point by relying on three empirical generalizations: Humans are largely egoistic (self-interested, death-adverse, forward-looking). Humans are largely equal, and even those who are more advantaged can be taken advantage of (we all sleep, for example). Finally, there exists a moderate scarcity of goods, resulting in competition to get what we want.

The point is that the empirical generalizations lead Hobbes to the conclusion that we would inevitably get war in the state of nature, even if we behave rationally.[78] Understandably, you might at this point be thinking: But we *do* live in political society—not a state of nature—so how does all this esoteric political philosophy relate to contemporary police deception and dishonesty?[79]

---

[78] Hobbes concludes that an enforcer (sovereign) is needed, but how would people come together in the state of nature to establish an enforcer if that means acting cooperatively (irrationally)? Hobbes ultimately alludes to a way out of the paradox. There is a character in the *Leviathan* (Hobbes's "fool") who says there is no such thing as justice—only one's contentment—and there is no reason to keep covenants if they are not to one's benefit. Hobbes, *Leviathan*, 110–111 (ch. 15). However, in the state of nature, persons in a "prisoner's dilemma" would confront each other repeatedly. One might succeed in taking advantage of another once or twice but would be excluded from dealings with others at some point. So it seems irrational—over the *long-term*—to base one's chances of happiness on the gullibility of others. This means that the potential payoff for cooperation in the state of nature is a lot higher than *single-play* advantage; it's not irrational to perform one's part of an agreement if the other person has already performed their part. Hobbes's final position thus seems to be—as Simmons puts it—that it is "prudentially rational to join with others to create states where none exist and to behave cooperatively so as to preserve states where they do exist." Offensive violations of agreements—with those trying to cooperate with you—are irrational because they are not conducive to one's long-term well-being. Simmons, *Political Philosophy*, 29–32.

[79] For one response to this question, see Raff Donelson's excellent paper, "Blacks, Cops, and the State of Nature," *Ohio State Journal of Criminal Law* 15, no. 1 (2017): 193–210. Although we take somewhat different paths to get to Hobbes—and reach somewhat different conclusions—my

The Hobbesian argument illustrates one way that fraud (which includes dishonestly taking advantage of another's trust in contractual relations) is a correlative to force (defecting and failing to cooperate, which leads to enmity and what Hobbes calls a state of war). Likewise, what may seem rational and in our best interest (defrauding others and defecting from agreements) within society can in fact prevent us from obtaining our desired outcome (peace, through cooperative relations that require honesty and trust).

More to the point, the Hobbesian argument—especially its empirical generalizations about people and society—have important resonances in contemporary understandings of the nature of law and the law's connection to social institutions such as the police. We saw this in Chapter 1 when considering Hart's philosophy of law, especially the idea that any legal system must—at a minimum—address human vulnerability (regarding force and fraud, for example). So it is not farfetched to think that contemporary police can be in a similar "state of war" with communities. Indeed, the police have thoroughly embraced a "warrior" ethos given the view that they are in a "war" against drugs, terror, crime, and so on.[80] This is related to the rise of proactive policing—anticipating community wrongdoing and taking preemptive law enforcement action.

We could describe the situation as a contemporary prisoner's dilemma within political society. Of course, such dilemmas involve two sides, and we should consider how and why the other side (the community) defects, too.

4.3. The Lockean Reply: Trust, Authority, and Resistance

Consider again the essay by Ta-Nehisi Coates mentioned in the book's Introduction.[81] Coates drew upon the distinction between "power" and "authority," specifically how the former is derived from external force and the latter is derived from cooperation (consensual relationships, reciprocation, and so on). To put it a bit differently, with the erosion of authority comes the default need for external force. Authority erodes when there are no longer

---

argument is largely consistent with Donelson's, especially with respect to his emphasis on the breakdown of trust between the police and the community.

[80] I have written about this sort of warrior policing in Luke William Hunt, *The Police Identity Crisis—Hero, Warrior, Guardian, Algorithm* (New York: Routledge, 2021), ch. 2.

[81] Ta-Nehisi Coates, "The Myth of Police Reform," *The Atlantic*, April 15, 2015.

societal relations based on reciprocation and mutual forbearance (the parties have defected, so to speak), leading to enmity.

Coates argues that the central relationship between some groups—specifically, African Americans and the police—is based on power, not authority. He describes how the breakdown of authority has led to the police's reliance on power, which naturally (given that power is not based on mutual cooperation) leaves the community skeptical of the police. Hence some groups simply don't trust the police—there is "a belief that the police are as likely to lie as any other citizen," and that belief leads to preemptive defection from cooperative overtures.[82]

We can consider the idea of a philosophical breakdown of authority by drawing upon the so-called "father of liberalism," John Locke.[83] Whatever issues one might have with Locke, his work undeniably influenced modern thinking about political power and authority. We begin with what has become a platitude of Lockean philosophy—the idea that a state's power is *limited* by its authority. The unpleasantness of the state of nature led Hobbes to the conclusion that we need an *absolute* (no limits) sovereign. This seems anathema to liberal thought, so why would Hobbes reach such a conclusion? The reason he thought an absolute state was necessary is because, otherwise, it would not be clear who is the actual authority. We would disagree about the law and disagree about who's really in charge, leading to some of the unpleasantness of the state of nature (where there is no political authority). Locke sees things much differently.

The first four chapters of Locke's *Second Treatise* can be viewed as a reply to Hobbesian absolute sovereignty.[84] The rough contours of Locke's political thought are well-known and relatively straightforward. Locke thinks we are born free of political authority and with a set of rights that allow us to govern ourselves. Accordingly, it is only through our free choice (consent) that we are under the authority of another entity.[85] This means a *legitimate* political

---

[82] Ibid.

[83] See Nancy J. Hirschmann, *Gender, Class, and Freedom in Modern Political Theory* (Princeton, NJ: Princeton University Press, 2009), 79, 112.

[84] On this point, see generally Felix Waldmann, "John Locke as a Reader of Thomas Hobbes's Leviathan: A New Manuscript," *The Journal of Modern History* 93, no. 2 (June 2021).

[85] The Lockean state of nature is a state of perfect freedom within the bounds of the law of nature—or reason. It is also a state of perfect equality because all are born with the same advantages of nature, using the same faculties. Reason is said to show us that (being equal and independent) no one ought to harm another's life health, liberty, or possessions. Accordingly, we are not talking about a state of license, but instead a state of liberty promoting preservation (given that one doesn't have the liberty to destroy oneself or others). John Locke, *Two Treatises of Government*, ed. Peter Laslett (Cambridge: Cambridge University Press, 1988), 269–272 (*Second Treatise*, sect. 6–8). See also A.

society is one in which everyone has given up some of their rights (consensually) in exchange for something else. We thus have cooperation based upon mutual forbearance, or a social contract.

It follows that the state cannot do certain things, namely, it cannot infringe upon the rights we have retained. Such infringement would be a use of external *force* outside the bounds of the *cooperative* agreement. This sort of infringement would mean that the state *defects* and acts outside the bounds of legitimate *authority*. For Locke, then, people have a (natural) right to resist government when it oversteps its bounds and tries to infringe upon the rights people have retained.

Importantly, though, Locke says that one can also *forfeit* one's rights: the nonvoluntary loss of rights through wrongdoing. For example, if a person deviates from (natural or legal) duties or proscriptions—if one, say, assaults or kills another—then one forfeits one's rights and is subject to punishment.[86] Accordingly, one might argue that some people—say, contemporary criminals or criminal suspects—have defected through wrongdoing and are subject to the loss of rights through force. This of course seems true in many cases. We can think of straightforward crimes against persons—assault, rape, murder, and so on—which justify a response from the state. On the other hand, we can also imagine *preemptive* or *proactive* state force (relying on deception and dishonesty) that is only ostensibly a reaction to wrongdoing. In some cases, such force *may* (it's yet to be determined) be illegitimate inasmuch as the force qualifies as anticipatory defection that departs from principled limits of political authority. We are thus in the realm of state-of-nature-like *power*, not *authority*.

The problem is that some states might in a sense be a continuation of the state of nature—or, for some groups under the state's power, worse than the state of nature. For example, states in which a person or a group are bound to submit to the unjust will of another—or made a political slave—is tantamount to a state that is at war with (some of) its people. It's not difficult to think of historic and contemporary groups of people who have been in just this sort of position—especially with respect to their relations with the police. We can look back to pre–Civil War slave patrols in the United States as

John Simmons, *The Lockean Theory of Rights* (Princeton, NJ: Princeton University Press, 1992), chs. 1–3; Simmons, *Political Philosophy*, ch. 2, on which my account draws.

[86] Simmons, *The Lockean Theory of Rights*.

well as subsequent enforcement of Jim Crow law and present-day enforcement discrepancies that fall along ethnic and socioeconomic lines.

Such state power can be conceived as illegitimate with respect to oppressed groups because the state lacks authority over the group: persons have
of course not *consented* to a state of political "slavery" and "war." Accordingly,
this point requires us to reevaluate the nature and extent of an oppressed
group's obligations with respect to the state and the state's governing
institutions (even if all persons continue to have obligations to each other
given the law of nature).

As with Hobbes, then, we can see a contemporary analogue in the context of a breakdown in police authority. The upshot is a "state of war" and
enmity driven by power.[87] Rather than operating under a common law of
reason, each side views the other with a lack of trust and resorts to unjustified
uses of fraud and force. Indeed, Locke describes one's liberty in society as a
being under no legislative power except that established by consent in the
commonwealth and enacted according to *trust* put in it. This is similar to the
way Coates describes the contemporary relationship between the police and
some communities—there is an expectation of dishonesty and thus a lack of
trust. Avoiding enmity, force, and fraud in our relations is supposed to be one
of the central reasons of joining society and leaving the state of nature in the
first place.

4.4. Contemporary Dilemmas: Gangsters, Hustlers, and Reasonable Resistance

Despite the benefits of society, there is a (Lockean) presumption of a natural
right to resistance when one is subjected to force and fraud that lacks authority. This raises the question of when such force and fraud rise to a level of
injustice that triggers a right to resist.

With respect to the state imposing unjust law on people, contemporary political philosophers such as John Rawls put it this way: "When the
basic structure of society is reasonably just, as estimated by what the current state of things allows, we are to recognize unjust law as binding provided they do not exceed certain limits of injustice."[88] Of course, the tricky

---

[87] Locke, *Second Treatise*, ch. 3.
[88] Rawls, *A Theory of Justice*, 308.

part is explaining "certain limits of injustice," especially considering that contemporary laws are not typically unjustified on the surface (but instead in their application). Philosophers such as Tommie Shelby have developed the Rawlsian position in ways that are particularly illuminating with respect to contemporary policing.[89]

We can begin with the idea of the police's moral standing (and authority) and the extent to which that standing and authority is undermined by hypocrisy, complicity, and dishonesty. In the book's Introduction, for example, we considered double standards in which the police can lie but citizens cannot. And in the next chapter we will consider cases in which the police seem complicit in crimes when they perform undercover sting operations (such as using individuals to initiate terrorist schemes). These and other examples point to the more general idea that injustice can undermine the standing and authority states have to condemn criminal offenders.

If the police lack the moral standing to hold individuals accountable for their crimes, then the fact that the police tell citizens to do something may provide no additional (moral) reason for citizens to do those things given a lack of (moral) authority. As we will see, the point is that even if there are cases in which the police *should* lie and deceive (emergency situations to save life, for instance), routine dishonesty and deception is often a serious cost for police that can undermine their moral authority to enforce certain laws.[90]

This framing of the issue leads to the idea of *resistance*. When thinking about resistance, we should first acknowledge the distinction between the *civic* obligations of citizens and the *natural* duties persons have to each other as moral agents. This idea has roots in the Lockean position we just

---

[89] Tommie Shelby, *Dark Ghettos: Injustice, Dissent, and Reform* (Cambridge: Belknap Press, 2016); Tommie Shelby, "Justice, Deviance, and the Dark Ghetto," *Philosophy & Public Affairs* 35, no. 2 (2007).

[90] On these points, see Shelby, *Dark Ghettos*; Göran Duus-Otterström and Erin I. Kelly, "Injustice and the Right to Punish," *Philosophy Compass* 14, no. 2 (February 2019); Kyle G. Fritz, "Hypocrisy, Inconsistency, and the Moral Standing of the State," *Criminal Law and Philosophy* 13, no. 2 (2019): 309–327; Erin I. Kelly, "The Ethics of Law's Authority: On Tommie Shelby's, *Dark Ghettos: Injustice, Dissent, and Reform*," *Criminal Law and Philosophy* 16 (2022). Here it is worth recalling the three distinct (but related) categories of concern mentioned in the book's Preface: (1) the legitimacy and authority of the police institution, (2) the practicality, effectiveness, and consequences of police deception and lying; and (3) the extent to which honesty as a virtue is relevant to both individuals and institutions. The first category is about how deception and dishonesty can be problematic even if it does not lead to negative consequences (because deception and dishonesty can undermine police authority in the first place). The second category is about how lying and acting in bad faith make the police less effective at their jobs because it erodes public trust and makes people less likely to cooperate with police. The third category is about the extent to which we should seek to understand virtues (moral character) instead of consequences and deontological duties.

considered: Irrespective of whether we have civic obligations to each other because we're all citizens under a common authority, we still (even in a state of nature) have natural duties to preserve and not harm others—as well as uphold just institutions. Whether I have a legitimate civic obligation to pay my taxes or an obligation to not commit the crime of murder (because a law prohibits murder) is a contingent political-legal matter. But I have an unconditional natural duty not to kill innocent persons, irrespective of whether there exists a law prohibiting murder. The idea, then, is to keep these different obligations in mind when considering community *resistance*.[91]

Shelby is interested in how we should characterize particular kinds of resistance to the state (namely: *deviance* by groups such as the *ghetto* poor) given certain assumptions about the state's major economic, social, and political institutions (including the police institution), as well as how the state distributes the benefits and burdens of social cooperation. We are to understand *deviance* as crime and contempt for authority.[92] Our characterization of this sort of resistance will naturally differ in institutionally unjust (racist, economically stratified, and so on) societies from institutionally just societies.

By *ghetto* Shelby means areas defined by race and poverty in inner city areas.[93] Beyond a general contempt for authority, deviance in the ghetto is based on a "criminal ethics" exemplified by "gangsters" and "hustlers." Gangsters are said to be fighters who use violence, threats, and intimidation (*force*, in other words) to get what they want from others. Getting what they want typically takes the form of robbery and other criminal violations. On the other hand, hustlers rely on *deception* (lying, treachery, and so on) to get what they want from others. For hustlers, getting what they want typically means crimes such as *fraud* and theft. In both cases, then, we see instances in which the community has "defected" from cooperative, societal agreements to follow the law.[94]

So is such deviance *justified*? No—at least not to the extent that such deviance is inconsistent with one's natural duties.[95] So we cannot justify much of

---

[91] "Justice, Deviance, and the Dark Ghetto," 144 (following a similar distinction made by Rawls in *A Theory of Justice*).

[92] Ibid., 128.

[93] Ibid., 134–143. Shelby acknowledges that while many of the ghetto poor are deeply alienated from society, a substantial segment is not. Ibid., 136.

[94] Ibid., 137.

[95] Ibid., 152.

what we think of as resistance that takes the form of deviant force and fraud. But Shelby wants us to reevaluate the way we characterize this sort of preemptive community defection from societal obligations—to think beyond simple *disregard for authority*. Recall the distinction between power and authority, as well as the presumed breakdown of the police's authority and inevitable reliance on power. If we couple this with institutional injustice, we are led to an entirely different characterization of political resistance and deviance in the ghetto.[96] Although deviance may not be justified, it can be construed as a *reasonable* response given that, say, the police have preemptively defected from *their* societal obligations regarding authority.[97]

Consider the well-documented reliance on surveillance and racial profiling in ghetto communities. The police's use of "stop and frisk" tactics may be constitutional when they have reasonable suspicion ("specific and articulable facts") that crime is afoot. However, routinely stopping and frisking community members is not constitutional when it is based simply on skin color, ethnicity, clothing style, and so on.[98] Or consider the history of enforcing the law for minor legal violations that result in major penalties (e.g., possession crimes, parole violations, and so on) in some communities but not others. I have lived in college towns all my adult life, and it is apparent that laws against drug use are enforced more strictly in some areas ("ghetto") rather than others (the so-called "student ghetto" where more affluent university members live). Shelby adds felony disenfranchisement laws and the general harassment of young urban Blacks to the list of institutional injustice, and it's not difficult to think of injustices that are unique to other groups of people.

If we can agree that such institutional injustice occurs, and if those living in the ghetto are thus governed by biased power that lacks authority, then perhaps we can say that deviant resistance within the ghetto is a *reasonable*

---

[96] Shelby provides a detailed discussion of a variety of institutional injustice relating to employment, housing, and the criminal justice system broadly. Ibid., 140.

[97] Ibid., 143–152.

[98] A police stop and frisk is constitutional only if the police have reasonable suspicion (based upon "specific and articulable facts") that a person has committed, is committing, or is about to commit a crime and has a reasonable belief that the person "may be armed and presently dangerous." Terry v. Ohio, 392 U.S. 1, 21–30 (1968). But consider, for instance, that the New York Police Department documented 685,724 stops (and 381,704 frisks) in 2011, and, of those frisked, a weapon was found only 1.9% of the time; moreover, over 70% of those stopped and frisked in the ten precincts with the lowest Black and Latino populations were Black and Latino. New York Civil Liberties Union, *2012 Stop and Frisk Report* (2012).

response to the state's failure to uphold its end of the deal (even if gangster and hustler deviance is neither prudent nor justified).

Look at it this way: Suppose you come home after a long day of work to find your partner having sex with your best friend. If—in the heat of the moment—you fly off the handle and begin inflicting verbal abuse on your partner and best friend, then we wouldn't describe such abuse as prudent or justified. However, we might think your response is understandable—in other words, it's not *unreasonable* under the circumstances of such a deceptive betrayal. Likewise, Shelby suggests that the reasonableness of societal deviance depends on the institutional justice (or lack thereof) within society. We must imagine (if it isn't happening to us in fact) what it would be like to live under conditions in which the rules are not applied fairly. Perhaps you would remain compliant under such conditions—or calm and collected upon walking in on a cheating partner—but most of us would not be surprised if you weren't.

Here is where the distinction between civic obligations and natural duties (obligations to others qua fellow citizen versus duties to others qua fellow human beings) becomes important. As Shelby notes, the former is grounded in the *reciprocity* of liberal societies. As I've written elsewhere, the concept of a liberal society *just is* a concept based on reciprocal arrangements between members of the society.[99] From the discussion of Hobbes and Locke—up through contemporary liberal thought—it is apparent that the ideal of liberal societies is based on reciprocal arrangements that aim for fairness. When the arrangements aren't fair, they're not just. And when the arrangements entail power wielded without authority, then they are not legitimate.

We have thus come full circle—back to the history of political philosophy and the Lockean right to resist illegitimate institutions that wield power without authority. Now, all things considered, perhaps the injustice and illegitimacy in a place such as the United States has not reached a tipping point that justifies resistance. After all, there are quite a few good things we can say about democratic societies such at the United States. Notwithstanding the faults, everyone enjoys protection from external invasion, a high degree of free speech, and many other democratic freedoms. But, again, we're not arguing about whether deviant resistance is justified, but instead whether it's

---

[99] Hunt, *The Retrieval of Liberalism in Policing*, 54–56.

a *reasonable* response to injustice. As Shelby notes, constitutional essentials (such as free speech, and so on) are not an adequate threshold for tolerable injustice because they do not guarantee (fair) reciprocity and equality of opportunity.[100] A young person in the ghetto who is arrested and put in the "system" (unfairly) is probably not impressed by the fact that he continues to enjoy the protection of, say, the US military.

What does all this mean for the police? First, we see that societal deviance is a correlative of institutional force and fraud. Rather than focusing exclusively on those who are social deviants, we might turn our attention to the institutions that motivate some of that (reasonable) deviance. Indeed, there is an important way that Shelby's analysis may be flipped, focusing on the institutional actors (e.g., the police) instead of the community: The use of preemptive defection in the form of fraud and force (including some forms of proactive policing, for example) may not always be not *justified*, even if it sometimes seems reasonable. The point is that Shelby's work cuts both ways: "A climate of fear and suspicion erodes any chance of developing mutual trust."[101] Good faith can promote trust by mitigating the breakdown of reciprocal political relations.

* * *

In this chapter, we have considered (1) how good faith is a core value of contracts, and (2) how justified policing is contractual in nature—broadly (in the context of social contract theory), as well as narrowly (in the context of concrete encounters between law enforcement officers and the public).

We then examined how good faith entails honesty and transparency and precludes fraud. Of course, the issue lurking in the background is breach of the social contract by members of the public through criminality. Given criminality—so the argument goes—perhaps the state (police) may cancel any duties of good faith with respect to members of the public. In other words, when people commit crimes they are no longer entitled to be treated with honesty and good faith by the police. Let me conclude this chapter with two analogies to contract law.

The doctrine of *rescission* stands for the position that a contracting party may rescind a contract if subjected to things such as misrepresentation—thus

---

[100] Shelby, "Justice, Deviance, and the Dark Ghetto," 145.
[101] Ibid., 159.

bringing the parties back to their original positions (before entering the contract).[102] Analogously, when members of the public engage in criminality over the course of fulfilling social contractual obligations, we might say the police have the right to rescind their end of the deal—bringing the police and the public back to a pre-contract *state of nature* (and state of war), so to speak. Indeed, that's how things tend to look in the real-world. But this line of argument is deficient in two related ways, as illustrated by the next analogy to contract law.

The police have what we might call a *preexisting duty* to engage with the public in good faith. The preexisting duty rule simply means that performance of a preexisting duty is not a valid basis of the bargain in a contract. Suppose there is a murder and a $10,000 reward for anyone providing information leading to the arrest of the murderer. Now suppose the lead detective on the case finds a key piece of evidence; he promptly schedules a press conference and offers the evidence in exchange for the reward. This would of course be absurd, and the doctrine of preexisting duties establishes that public officers such as the police, whose efforts were made in the performance of official duty, are not entitled to share in rewards.[103] There is no "consideration" (basis of the bargain) for the offeror's promise of a reward because the police had a duty to do the work anyway.

The analogy is not perfect, but it's reasonable to think that the state's duty of good faith is not contingent upon the public's criminality (which is of course inevitable given human nature). As we saw in the last chapter, the nature and existence of political society is based upon reciprocation that necessitates good faith; this suggests that good faith reciprocation is a sort of preexisting duty. More concretely, we just saw from Shelby how societal deviance can be a correlative of institutional force and fraud. Instead of focusing exclusively on those who are so-called social deviants, we can turn our attention to the institutions that motivate some of that (reasonable) deviance.

If the police foster an environment of deception, dishonesty, and bad faith, they exacerbate fear, distrust, and deviance. So when we think of public deviance and criminality as a "breach" of the social contract, we should pause to consider the possibility of a prior failure by the state to fulfill its

---

[102] See, e.g., Abdallah, Inc. v. Martin, 242 Minn. 416, 420, 65 N.W.2d 641, 644 (1954).
[103] See, e.g., McNeil v. Board of Supervisors, 114 App. Div. 761, 764 (N.Y. App. Div. 1906); Atwood v. Armstrong, 102 App. Div. 601 (N.Y. App. Div. 1905).

preexisting duties. Naturally, there will be exceptions and caveats, but the central point will remain: Good faith is necessary to mitigate police deception and dishonesty that is fraudulent and illegitimate. Moving forward—in the Interlude and Part II—we will face the difficult task of determining when it makes sense to say that the police are justified in deviating from the norms of good faith.

INTERLUDE

FROM THE IVORY TOWER TO THE STREET

Five Questions and Answers Explored in the Interlude

1. **Q: Is the Interlude the part of the book that moves from theoretical concerns to more practical concerns and case studies?**

   A: Not quite. The Interlude is where we consider *how* to move from theoretical concerns to practical concerns. That may sound overly fussy, but the goal is simply to distill the theory from Part I in a way that it's applicable to a principled framework for examining the case studies in Part II.

2. **Q: I assume that the Interlude's proposed framework will necessarily affect conclusions about the case studies in Part II, so won't the framework inevitably be controversial?**

   A: Perhaps, but: If we want to talk about addressing police injustice in the existing world, we should probably say something about our ideal of justice so that our efforts to address real-world injustice have a target for which to aim. Now, it would be naïve to think everyone will agree on a theory of justice, but there will likely be a few uncontroversial things on which most people can agree. I hope this includes some of the values discussed in Part I such as a good faith, honesty, transparency, legitimacy, personhood, and their normative backdrop in universalistic positive morality (UPM).

3. **Q: How will we ever reach any practical conclusions given so many different values in play?**

   A: It's reasonable to try to evaluate practical concerns about existing policing strategies in light of the values and assumptions discussed in Part I. For example, when thinking about strategies to address real-world police deception and dishonesty, we should keep in mind practical issues such as political possibility and efficacy—as well as more philosophical issues regarding the moral permissibility of strategies given the priorities of justice discussed in Part I.

4. **Q: Can you give me a specific example of how this approach allows us to evaluate the justification of police deception and dishonesty that is on par with fraud?**

    A: I concede that it would be impossible to discern a bright-line rule, but I propose a framework that I call the *prerogative power test*. The test is grounded in well-established principles of legal and political philosophy, allowing us to evaluate when the police may deviate from rule-of-law principles to engage in deception, dishonesty, and bad faith that are on par with fraud.

5. **Q: If I don't like this approach, can you give me some other options to consider?**

    A: Absolutely. We will consider some of the excellent ideas proposed by others.

Quantico

Here is the deadly force policy I learned while training to be a special agent at the FBI Academy at Quantico:

> Special agents may use deadly force only when necessary—when the agent has a reasonable belief that the subject of such force poses an imminent danger of death or serious physical injury to the agent or another person.[1]

The Fourth Amendment to the US Constitution protects the "right of the people to be secure in their persons . . . against unreasonable . . . seizures." A police officer's use of force (deadly, or otherwise) constitutes a seizure and must be reasonable. Courts have construed the "reasonableness" of force based upon "the perspective of a reasonable officer on the scene, rather than with the 20/20 vision of hindsight."[2] The upshot is that questions regarding the police's use of deadly force are construed permissively.

We can see how the FBI policy language tracks the broad "reasonableness" of the Constitution and case law: The use of deadly force is based upon (1) necessity, which is defined as (2) a reasonable belief that (3) serious harm will occur (4) imminently.

Although force (and deadly force specifically) is not the central topic of this book, it is correlatively related—as described in Chapters 1 and 2—to the police's use of deception, dishonesty, and bad faith. First, let's assume that some uses of police force and violence are clearly justified, with an easy example being an active shooter in a school. Can we thus say that whenever force would be justified to make an arrest, dishonesty and deception would be as well? And if so, then is good faith a foundation of policing similar to how principles constraining the use of force are? I think something like this is right, but how do we move from questions about philosophical foundations to questions about real-world applications? In this brief Interlude, I'll sketch some options for transitioning from discussions of theory to discussions of practice.

---

[1] The FBI's policy on the use of deadly force by its special agents is available at: https://www.fbi.gov/about/faqs/what-is-the-fbis-policy-on-the-use-of-deadly-force-by-its-special-agents. One note about this conception of necessity is that it makes no reference to it being the case that there is no way to prevent the threat without carrying out the harmful action. On this point, see Seth Lazar, "Necessity in Self-Defense and War," *Philosophy & Public Affairs*, 40, no. 3 (2012): 44; Christopher Nathan, *The Ethics of Undercover Policing* (New York: Routledge, 2022).

[2] Graham v. Connor, 490 U.S. 386 (1989).

Police Deception and Dishonesty. Luke William Hunt, Oxford University Press. © Oxford University Press 2024.
DOI: 10.1093/oso/9780197672167.003.0004

1. Values

If we want to talk about addressing injustice in the existing world—instead of the philosopher's abstract possible world(s)—then we first need to say something about our ideals and goals. Otherwise, our efforts to address injustice will lack an aim. In other words, without some sort of rough ideal, we won't have anything to reference when seeking answers to our real-world questions about injustice.[3]

Naturally, we typically set our sights on the ideal of *justice*. Plato attributes the virtue of justice to the state, arguing that a particular harmony of the parts of the state is required for the state to be just. In Plato's *Republic*, Socrates puts it this way: "[L]et's first find out what sort of thing justice is in a city . . . [i]f we could watch a city coming to be in theory, wouldn't we also see its justice coming to be, and its injustice as well?"[4] Relatedly, we have already considered the traditional idea that honesty falls under (or is a species of) the cardinal virtue of justice,[5] as well as the more contemporary idea that "justice is the first virtue of social institutions."[6] So we are on pretty solid ground when we use an ideal of justice as a reference for questions about how to address policing problems in the existing world.

Of course, any conception of justice will be based on a set of values and articulating those values (and how they work together) is quite controversial. Some people are focused on values that are prominent in egalitarian conceptions of justice, while others embrace more libertarian or Marxian theories—and still others argue in favor of strict utilitarian theories of justice, and so on and so on. Let's try to mitigate these complications by narrowing our context to values that are commonly ascribed to what people call "liberal" and "democratic" societies (understanding that those terms themselves can be controversial).

For our purposes, I simply mean societies that embrace pluralism and diversity by promoting the common good through the protection of basic liberties (think of, say, the US Constitution's Bill of Rights), as well as

---

[3] See John Rawls, *The Law of Peoples* (Cambridge, MA: Harvard University Press, 1999), 90.

[4] Plato, "Republic," in *Plato: Complete Works*, ed. John M. Cooper (Indianapolis: Hackett, 1997), 1008 (369a).

[5] Christian B. Miller, *Honesty: The Philosophy and Psychology of a Neglected Virtue* (New York: Oxford University Press, 2021), 22–23 (citing Aquinas, *Summa Theologiae* II–II, Question 109, Article 3, as a "historically prominent example of this taxonomy").

[6] John Rawls, *A Theory of Justice* (Cambridge, MA: Harvard University Press, 1999) (1971), 3.

commitments to more procedural values such as the rule of law.[7] These are broad strokes, and I certainly do not mean to suggest that I have some sort of privileged ability to identify an exhaustive, definitive set of values. The modest goal is simply to make some reasonable assumptions about the values that would be necessary for any broadly liberal, democratic ideal of justice.[8] But we should also keep in mind the argument in Chapter 1 regarding how some values are necessary for *any* society to be viable. To be sure, the values we have been discussing are important to nonliberal, nondemocratic societies, though beginning with a frame of reference such as "liberal" and "democratic" societies helps keep things manageable.

We have already discussed in detail many of these values that are important to justice, such as *good faith* in our dealings with others: A disposition of honesty in contractual relations, including reaching agreements and the faithful adherence to the scope, purpose, and terms of agreements. We considered how good faith entails some degree of **honesty**, the virtue of being disposed to not purposefully distort the facts as one sees them for good motivating reasons (required in cooperative relations with others). Good faith also entails some degree of *transparency*: sharing one's perspective with others to promote epistemic goods (rather than relying on hidden, undisclosed intentions to misrepresent or alter one's outward, objective words and actions).

Commitments to good faith, honesty, and transparency necessarily preclude things such as *fraud*: deception or dishonesty to gain an unjust advantage, injuring the rights and interests of others and leading to enmity and a lack of cooperation. Without good faith and other commitments against fraud, persons and groups would have to rely upon *force* (dynamic, constraining power marked by defection, enmity, and a lack of cooperation) to meet needs.

Borrowing from norms underpinning legal standards against fraud,[9] we can identify a few key elements:

- *Knowing and willful*: Police are human, and the police institution is a human institution. It stands to reason that we should focus on

---

[7] Kevin Vallier puts it well in *Trust in a Polarized Age* (New York: Oxford University Press), 210, where he writes: "Democratic constitutionalism holds both that the legislative process should appeal to extensive citizen input (democratic), and that government officials should convert citizen input into policy via processes that are predictable, effective, and neutral between citizens (constitutionalism)."

[8] It's worth noting that Plato was not a fan of democracy, which I discussed in Chapter 3 of my *The Police Identity Crisis: Hero, Warrior, Guardian, Algorithm* (New York: Routledge, 2021).

[9] See 18 U.S. Code § 1343 (fraud by wire, radio, or television).

more egregious cases involving so-called guilty minds, not "honest mistakes."[10]

- *Materiality*: The deception, dishonesty, and bad faith on which we focus should be material.[11] This encompasses misrepresentations as well as the omission or concealment of material information, as long as such omissions can induce false beliefs.[12] We can limit the scope of materiality by requiring that a person's reliance on deception and dishonesty is relevant to a material (not collateral) component of an agreement. And we can add that the deception and dishonesty is not mere prediction or "puffery" (such as vague statements that are not easily ascertainable) by the police (discussed in Chapter 3).

- *Harm*: The police deception, dishonesty, and bad faith must injure the rights and interests of others by seeking an unjust advantage.

There is of course a fair amount of gray area with respect to these elements. But we can tentatively say that the police are precluded from intentionally devising any scheme or artifice to obtain evidence (including incriminating statements that affect one's rights) by means of false or fraudulent pretenses, representations, or promises.

One reason to emphasize these norms against fraud is the value of the **rule of law**. There are a variety of ways to conceive of the rule of law, including *formal* conceptions (the form that legal norms take, such as consistency and congruency), *procedural* conceptions (legal procedures—such as hearings—within institutions such as courts), and *substantive* conceptions (substantive commitments such as judicial review and a presumption of liberty).[13]

For example, government officials—such as the police—might be (legally) exempt from following the law, as when the police are sanctioned to deceptively purchase drugs in sting operations. But the existence of such power does not mean that the police are exempt from exercising the power in accordance with rule-of-law principles. If the police's power to break the law

---

[10] Analogously, there is a "good faith exception" that allows evidence collected by the police in violation of the Constitution to be admissible if the police relied upon a defective search warrant *in good faith* (i.e., they reasonably believed their actions were legal). This means that courts must consider the mental state of the police officers. See United States v. Leon, 468 U.S. 897 (1984); Massachusetts v. Sheppard, 468 U.S. 981 (1984).

[11] Neder v. United States, 527 U.S. 1, 25 (1999).

[12] United States v. Morris, 80 F.3d 1151, 1161 (7th Cir. 1996).

[13] Jeremy Waldron, "The Rule of Law and the Importance of Procedure," in *NOMOS: Getting to the Rule of Law*, ed. J.E. Fleming (New York: New York University Press, 2011), 3–7.

is unduly incongruent with the law as stated (a formal problem)—or if the police's law enforcement discretion perverts procedural safeguards (such as rights against self-incrimination or unreasonable searches and seizures)—then the police would no longer be governing in accordance with rule of law principles (even if their tactics are strictly speaking legal).

In a similar way, if the police possess vast, blanket authority (general authority to act lacking adequate oversight of specific actions) to engage in deception and dishonesty, then such "authority" would raise questions regarding whether they are *governing* by law in a nonsuperficial way. If not, then they are governing with power under "color of law" (or the pretense of law), which lacks authority and *legitimacy*.

A particular conception of **personhood** emanates from these values, namely, a conception of persons as *reciprocators* with the capacity for (and right to) cooperative relations that involve mutual forbearance; a conception of persons as *moral agents* who are free and responsible given a capacity for reason and a sense of justice and the good;[14] and a conception of persons as having *human dignity*, in terms of a high-ranking legal status expressing human equality and in terms of having a nonfungible, intrinsic value.[15] Without this sort of conception of personhood, there wouldn't be any (or much) reason to worry about things such as the rule of law and legitimacy.

Here is the problem: Sometimes these values are in tension with other important values, such as security and law enforcement. This brings us to the crux of the matter. What sort of methodology should we use to address this tension between values in the existing world?

2. Methods

In terms of methods, when we talk about addressing injustice in the existing world we are typically talking about **nonideal theory**. By nonideal theory I simply mean theorizing about justice in the context of existing, imperfect institutions. Nonideal theory may be contrasted with ideal theory—or theorizing about justice in the context of idealized assumptions about society and institutions. How should nonideal theory approach the pressing

---

[14] John Rawls, *Political Liberalism* (New York: Columbia University Press, 2005), 19.
[15] I developed this tripartite conception of liberal personhood in chapter 3 of my *The Retrieval of Liberalism in Policing* (New York: Oxford University Press, 2019).

problems of the police institution? There are many promising ways to construe nonideal theory, but let's try to balance practical concerns about existing policing strategies *in light* of the values and assumptions sketched in
the first part of the book and summarized above.

This approach requires consideration of policing strategies in terms of practical issues such as *political possibility* and *efficacy*, as well as more philosophical issues regarding the *moral permissibility* of strategies given the *priorities*
of justice above.[16]

With respect to political possibility, policing and the pursuit of security
should be consistent with the distribution of security discussed in Chapter 2.
In other words, policing should be committed to inclusive security so that
coercive power is not used unfairly to impose conformity within a diverse society. With respect to efficacy, policing and police reform must in fact accomplish the goal of security—including law enforcement and crime reduction.
This raises the use of deceptive, dishonest, and bad faith tactics, which may
in fact be an effective way to enforce the law. Beyond empirical questions of
political possibility and efficacy, nonideal theory must address philosophical questions regarding whether policing policies are morally permissible. It
must also prioritize injustices.

If security consists of components beyond law enforcement and crime
reduction—such as legitimacy and authority to wield power—then the police
obligation to enforce the law and reduce crime must be consistent with those
components to be consistent with justice. In other words, what are morally permissible strategies for pursuing security and crime reduction through law enforcement, and how do we balance other components of a holistic conception
of security (e.g., a conception attuned to values beyond personal safety, such as
legitimacy and the distribution of security among community members)?

This question returns us to our values and ideals, asking us to stipulate
ideals for which the policies of nonideal theory may aim. As discussed in
Chapter 1, *empirical jurisprudence* can help us make sense of the relationship between descriptive accounts of the way the world *is* and normative

---

[16] The methodology sketched here—a form of transitional nonideal theory—is derived from
Rawls. See A. John Simmons, "Ideal and Nonideal Theory," *Philosophy and Public Affairs* 38, no. 1
(Winter 2010), for a comprehensive account of the method, and my work (e.g., Hunt, *The Retrieval
of Liberalism*, ch. 2; *The Police Identity Crisis*, Introduction; "Policing, Brutality, and the Demands of
Justice," *Criminal Justice Ethics* 40, no. 1 (2021): 40–55) for accounts of how the method might be applied to policing. This book proceeds based on the assumption that we know enough about a broad
outline of an ideal theory of justice to permit coherent nonideal theorizing (i.e., we know enough
about the target ideal such that we have something for which to aim in our nonideal theorizing).

accounts of the way the world *should* be. Normative questions about evaluative predicates such as brutality (force) and dishonesty (fraud) are grounded in positive (social) morality that is universalistic in character—hence, universalistic positive morality (UPM).

UPM allows us to make reasonable assumptions regarding normative constraints on force and fraud given their basis in universal social concerns. This includes the assumption that deviations from UPM should give us pause, especially in the case of state functions such as policing. Any broad outline of an ideal theory of justice will (whatever else it may or may not do) prioritize persons and respect for personhood given the normative backdrop of UPM discussed in Chapter 1. What sort of framework helps ensure respect for personhood?

As the introduction to this Interlude suggests, there are certainly instances in which it seems clearly justified for the police to use (deadly) force. So it seems absurd to think deception, dishonesty, and bad faith are unjustified when such force is justified. Indeed, complete honesty and transparency are not even legally required in contractual relations. For example, a general commitment to the values of honesty and transparency does not mean that party 1 must disclose the highest they are willing to pay for something that party 2 is selling. However, transparency does mean that the parties cannot rely on their hidden, undisclosed intentions to misrepresent or alter their outward, objective words and actions.[17]

Likewise, it may not be legally wrong to dishonestly tell someone the maximum one is willing to pay for something (though such lies may be morally wrong). However, it would be legally wrong to use deception or dishonesty to seek or obtain an unjust advantage—or to injure the rights or interests of others—that rises to the level of fraud.[18] The point is that while good faith

---

[17] A classic example is the case of *Lucy v. Zehmer*—a staple in legal education—Lucy and Zehmer were drinking alcohol in a bar when Lucy offered to purchase a farm owned by Zehmer for $50,000— inviting Zehmer to write out a contract for sale. Zehmer drafted an agreement on the back of a bar receipt stating his intention to sell the farm to Lucy for $50,000. Lucy requested that Zehmer's wife sign it, too, though she initially refused. Zehmer whispered to her that the whole thing was merely a joke; his wife signed the agreement, though neither communicated to Lucy that they intended it to be a joke. When Zehmer realized Lucy was serious, Zehmer then stated that he was just joking. Lucy left the bar and ultimately sued Zehmer in order to have the agreement enforced. Lucy prevailed based on the principle that the objective, outward expression of one's intent to be bound in an agreement (as opposed to one's secret, subjective mental assent to the agreement) is what matters when determining the existence of a valid and enforceable agreement. So while contractual norms certainly do not require perfect transparency, those norms do protect parties from secret intentions that undercut outward expressions. Lucy v. Zehmer, 196 Va. 493; 84 S.E.2d 516 (1954).

[18] See Stuart P. Green, *Lying, Cheating, and Stealing* (Oxford: Oxford University Press, 2006), 150.

and fraud are distinct doctrines, they raise overlapping issues that help define the outer limits of contractual relations. As with the police's use of force, we know there must be some police uses of deception and dishonesty that are justified. Again, we can avoid some of the gray areas by focusing on clear cases of bad faith that are unjustified (fraud).

But here is the more difficult question: Are there cases in which the police are justified in engaging in dishonesty, deception, and bad faith that are on par with *fraud*—in other words, engage in a deliberate dishonest disposition ("DDD") that is *fraudulent*? Yes. Although it would be impossible to discern a bright-line rule, I suggest a framework that I refer to as the ***prerogative power test*** for determining when the police may deviate from rule of law of principles and engage in deception, dishonesty, and bad faith that are on par with fraud.[19] The test draws on John Locke's theory of prerogative power (in other words, a prerogative to use one's judgment about how to make a practical determination), coupled with jurisprudential doctrines of executive emergency power (exceptional cases in which the executive is justified in using its prerogative power to deviate from rule-of-law principles).

I certainly do not want to sound dogmatic about the test or suggest that is the only way to proceed; my point is simply that the test is based on familiar, vetted principles of political morality within so-called liberal and democratic societies. Although the test is steeped in liberal, democratic norms (primarily relating to the rule of law), it reaches beyond liberalism (and is thus tied to the underlying ideas behind UPM discussed in Chapter 1) given that various facets of liberal personhood reach beyond liberalism (e.g., moral agency, human dignity) and given that protecting (at least some) persons from vulnerability is a necessity for any human society (as discussed in Chapter 1).[20] So while one need not commit to liberalism to follow the test, these parameters will help keep our discussion from becoming too unwieldy.

In the present context, the test allows us to consider how engaging in deception and dishonesty on par with fraud (in concrete cases, and abstractly

---

[19] I first invoked this framework as a model for addressing questions regarding the police's power to engage in "Otherwise Illegal Activity" (breaking the law as a way of enforcing the law), a power that is strictly speaking legal but that involves breaking what would otherwise be an array of substantive laws in an array of non-emergency situations. See Hunt, *The Retrieval of Liberalism in Policing*, 189–200.

[20] By this I simply mean that there is overlap between the liberal character of the prerogative power test and the universalistic character of UPM. Because UPM is universalistic, it is in a sense "thinner" (less demanding) than specific theories of governance such as liberalism (meaning that non-liberal societies may count as evidence for UPM). We can thus see how liberal and non-liberal theories may intersect at the level of UPM.

in terms so social contract theory) might be a justified deviation from governance by law. The test[21] suggests that the police may use their prerogative power to deviate from the rule of law in accordance with the following constraints:

(1) *Purpose constraint*: The power must be wielded for public good / national security;

(2) *Prudential constraint*: A legislative action is not viable;

(3) *Personhood constraint*: The power must not be an affront to liberal personhood;

(4) *Emergency constraint*: The power must be reserved for emergencies that involve:

    (a) An acute threat of death or serious bodily harm,[22] and

    (b) The threat cannot be averted without wielding the power.[23]

A few notes for clarification: Regarding the prudential constraint, the legislature could of course enact a broad law that, say, makes all police deception and dishonesty legal against all "suspected criminals." However, this sort of broad, blanket authority would be inconsistent with rule-of-law principles considering the tenets of limited authority. For example, consider the implications of a law permitting the police to "break any law in order to enforce the law." Such blanket authority can be contrasted with more narrowly tailored legislation permitting dishonesty and deception against specific persons or groups of persons who pose serious threats of harm. On the other hand, such legislation would likely be too slow and cumbersome to be useful (especially in countries such as the United States, though it is possible to imagine states with more nimble, efficient legislative processes), not to mention that it would alert specific suspect groups of the police's planned tactics.

---

[21] Hunt, *The Retrieval of Liberalism in Policing*, 197.

[22] Note that "acute" often means "imminent," but not always. In the context of deception and dishonesty on par with fraud, acute is the appropriate term given the difficulty of establishing the imminence of a threat outside of real-time deadly force situations. For example, the FBI deadly force policy with which I opened this chapter is based on imminence, which makes sense because the policy is for situations in which it is reasonable to make imminence determinations (e.g., a situation in which a suspect is pointing a gun at a police officer).

[23] For a related legal doctrine ("public safety exception"), see New York v. Quarles, 467 U.S. 649 (1984) in which the U.S. Supreme Court held that police may deviate from Miranda rights in "a situation where concern for public safety must be paramount to adherence to the literal language of the prophylactic rules enunciated in Miranda."

Regarding the personhood constraint, one might think that when the police treat one with dishonesty it is inherently an affront to one's personhood and thus the personhood constraint would always be violated by a police DDD that is on par with fraud. However, as noted, there seems to be clear cases in which (deadly) force is justified, such that using force is not an affront to personhood in those cases (similar to justified cases of lethal self-defense, perhaps as well as the related idea of "death with dignity").

Killing one in self-defense suggests the value of personhood (protecting life), and that we may only kill others under very stringent conditions (which paradoxically respects their value as a person). One is only killed when they are responsible (moral agent) for breaking the social contract (reciprocator) by posing a serious threat to others; still, the killing must be done in a way that respects the criminal's dignity (instead of in, say, a tortuous or humiliating way).

Likewise, as noted, we can say that whenever force would be justified to make an arrest, dishonesty and deception on par with fraud would be as well. Of course, both justified force and a justified DDD would meet the other requirements of the prerogative power test, including the emergency constraint. What I have in mind for the personhood constraint is the prohibition of the use of a DDD that also involves degrading one's human dignity—treating one as if they have less worth or a lower status than others.

The broader point is that something along the lines of the prerogative power test provides a rough framework given our prior discussions regarding the connections between institutional bad faith, legitimacy, the rule of law, and fraud. The test is strict for good reason. No one seriously questions the need and justification for discretion in policing; to be sure, limited discretion is consistent with the rule of law. But the actual deviation from rule-of-law principles should have a high bar given that legitimacy through governance by law (free from bad faith that is on par with fraud) is foundational to viable societies. The police's pervasive use of proactive deception in non-emergency situations (to gather evidence against someone for using or selling illegal drugs, for instance) is a form of preemptive defection from good faith dealings. This is especially the case if one accepts Shelby's position discussed in Chapter 2, which is based on the idea that much criminal "deviance" is a (reasonable) response to bad faith policing that imposes an unfair distribution of security.[24]

---

[24] Tommie Shelby, "Justice, Deviance, and the Dark Ghetto," *Philosophy & Public Affairs* 35, no. 2 (2007).

Here is a brief application of the test. Recall the police's deceptive and dishonest threat in *Alexander v. DeAngelo* discussed in Chapter 2. The woman in that case was threatened by the police with a 40-year prison sentence when she was in fact facing only a 6-to-10-year sentence. Would such bad faith pass the prerogative power test? No. The police's threat was fraudulent, giving them an unjustified advantage in gathering evidence for the crime of soliciting a prostitute. Soliciting a prostitute involves no emergency or threat of serious injury that justified the police's bad faith; indeed, the fraudulent threat plausibly injured the rights and interests of the woman and was an affront to her personhood.

Consider one more preliminary application of this framework. Following the murder of George Floyd by police in 2020, there was a rise in homicides in major cities. Rightly or wrongly, legal scholars such as Paul G. Cassell argued that the spike in homicides was caused by the police scaling back proactive law enforcement tactics because they had to divert resources to patrolling antipolice demonstrations.[25] I take no position on this thesis aside from noting that we need compelling empirical evidence to make these sorts of causal connections.[26] But if we assume (for the sake of argument) that Cassell's thesis is correct, would the police be justified in renewing proactive policing (that entails dishonest, deceptive, and bad faith tactics that are on par with fraud) under the prerogative power test? Yes. If such proactive tactics are needed to prevent acute threats of gun violence and firearms crimes (and thus homicides), then they are justified under the prerogative power test. Again, though, it is vitally important to support any causal assumptions about homicide spikes with social scientific evidence. Accordingly, we can see a clear connection between the normative (moral) and descriptive (empirical).

Let me wrap up my description of the prerogative power test with this: If you were to press me, I would probably say that the ethical foundation for the prerogative power test is most similar to views in William David Ross's

---

[25] Paul G. Cassell, "Explaining the Recent Homicide Spikes in U.S. Cities: The "Minneapolis Effect" and the Decline in Proactive Policing," *The Federal Sentencing Reporter* (2020).

[26] Unfortunately, the empirical data regarding the narrow topic of this book is often lacking. However, there is a growing body of empirical work that is relevant to proactive policing generally, which often involves the use of deception and dishonesty. See, for example, National Academies of Sciences, Engineering, and Medicine, *Proactive Policing: Effects on Crime and Communities* (Consensus Study Report) (Washington, DC: National Academies Press, 2018); *Police Innovation: Contrasting Perspectives*, ed. David Weisburd and Anthony A. Braga (Cambridge: Cambridge University Press, 2019).

classic, *The Right and the Good*.[27] Although I approach the issues differently (via empirical generalizations and norms of political morality), I am sympathetic to the idea that there is a strong, or prima facie duty (in other words, "an actual duty on the condition that it doesn't conflict with another prima facie duty . . . of equal or greater importance"),[28] not to be deceptive and dishonest; and though such a duty may not be absolute, it often overrides utilitarian considerations. As the prerogative power test indicates, it is permissible to lie if doing so is necessary to save another person's life, but, otherwise, often wrong to lie when lying produces better consequences (achieving law enforcement goals, for example) than not lying.[29]

I am also sympathetic to the idea that there are implicit promises that create moral obligations and that lying is prima facie wrong because we typically promise (implicitly) to tell the truth when we speak. Recall Chapter 2's argument regarding how the relationship between the police and the community is contractual in nature (or at least quasi-contractual), creating obligations on the part of the police not to lie or deceive the people with whom they interact. Ross might not say that *deception* is prima facie wrong, but the upshot of my argument is that police deception and dishonesty are unjustified when they are on par with fraud. Of course, one might worry that any argument in this vein is ultimately based on mere intuitions (which vary wildly) about values. I have tried to mitigate such worries by stipulating certain empirical generalizations (Chapter 1) and norms of political morality (Chapter 2) regarding the societal role of mutual forbearance and trust. So while it is true that my arguments are conditional, the hope is the conditions on which I have relied are reasonably uncontroversial.[30]

---

[27] William David Ross, *The Right and the Good* (Oxford: Oxford University Press, 2007 [1930]). For insightful analysis of Ross's work on these points, see Thomas L. Carson, *Lying and Deception—Theory and Practice* (Oxford: Oxford University Press, 2010), 159–162.

[28] Thomas L. Carson, "The Range of Reasonable Views about the Morality of Lying," in *Lying: Language, Knowledge, Ethics, and Politics*, ed. Eliot Michaelson and Andreas Stokke (Oxford: Oxford University Press, 2018), 145–160.

[29] In other words, I wouldn't necessarily characterize the test in terms of, say, a "lesser evil" analysis (or proportionality analysis) regarding when deception and dishonesty is justified, but rather in terms of the principled priorities of societies that embrace the rule of law and permit narrow, principled deviations from the rule of law under specific circumstances (prerogative power). Compare with, for example: Helen Frowe, "Lesser-Evil Justifications for Harming: Why We're Required to Turn the Trolley," *Philosophical Quarterly* 68, no. 272 (2018): 460–480; Kerah Gordon-Solmon, "How (and How Not) to Defend Lesser-Evil Options," *Journal of Moral Philosophy* (2022).

[30] The point is that one may embrace the prerogative power test from a variety of theoretical perspectives. For example, a consequentialist might suggest that the test's constraints promote good consequences inasmuch as using deception and dishonesty when there is no emergency (or when it is not for the public good, and so on) will often lead to an erosion of trust of the police and therefore negative societal results. On the other hand, a deontologist might argue that the state lacks authority when it fails to respect the personhood constraint.

3. Other Approaches

The prerogative power test provides a normative framework that helps determine when the police are justified in departing from rule-of-law principles through deception and dishonesty that is on par with fraud. Although it is a rather broad normative framework, the next chapter narrows the framework through real-world application and concrete case studies.

First, though, I want to be clear that there are many other fruitful approaches to addressing police deception and dishonesty. Let's consider a few of them. In the book's Introduction, recall that we categorized police deceptive and dishonesty into two broad categories. *Investigative lies* involve deception and dishonesty to gather evidence and make arrests in investigations, while so-called *testilying* is the practice of lying in official documents and under oath in official proceedings (perjury) to get a conviction.[31]

Regarding testilying, legal scholar Christopher Slobogin has proposed a three-part *legal* remedy that focuses on changing institutional policies regarding constitutional constraints on the police: (1) stiff punishment for officers who commit perjury (conviction and dismissal), as well as significant rewards (promotion) for officers who act honestly—such as those who work to corroborate their testimony and those who expose perjury; (2) "flexify" the probable cause standard, which means that the requisite suspicion standards for the police to engage in a search would be treated in a more commonsensical and proportional way, such that the police have more discretion to engage in a (probable cause) search and thus less need to lie about meeting the standards of suspicion for those searches; and (3) abolish the exclusionary rule (the rule that prevents the government from using evidence gathered in violation of the United States Constitution); the idea here is not to address police behavior directly, but instead through judges and prosecutors: if improperly gathered evidence by the police is no longer subject to exclusion, then there is no reason for, say, prosecutors to "wink" (or look the other way) when the police lie about how they gathered the evidence—instead, they would have more motivation to expose and prosecute such lying.[32]

Regarding investigative lies, Slobogin starts with a broad claim about the justification of some investigative (and perjurious) lies: "lying that is

---

[31] See, e.g., Christopher Slobogin, "Deceit, Pretext, and Trickery: Investigative Lies by the Police," *Oregon Law Review* 76, no. 4 (Winter 1997): 776; Christopher Slobogin, "Testilying: Police Perjury and What to Do About It," *University of Colorado Law Review* 67 (1996): 1040.

[32] Slobogin, "Testilying," 1054–1059.

necessary to save a life may not only be acceptable but is generally applauded (even if it constitutes perjury)." As we will see, this is directly in line with the emergency constraint in my prerogative power test (and opposed to Kantian absolutism about lying).[33] But as Slobogin aptly notes: "Most types of police lies are of murkier morality."[34] For example, he is interested primarily in investigative lies that target suspects in the context of *undercover work* (which is inherently deceptive, involving fake identities and so on), *searches and seizures* (e.g., the police telling someone falsely that they have the authority to conduct a search, the police telling someone falsely that they have the authority to obtain a warrant to conduct a search, the police fabricating a traffic violation in order to stop and search a car), and *interrogation* (e.g., falsely leading a person to believe they have been implicated by another).[35] So these are lies with the goal of *catching* an (alleged) criminal (as in the case with which the next chapter opens), which the police tend to rationalize with a fairly broad *end justify the means* principle.

To address the murkiness of investigative lies, Slobogin draws upon philosopher Sissela Bok's classic book, *Lying: Moral Choice in Public and Private Life.*[36] Bok's work is in large part based on a "principle of veracity," standing for the idea (based on Aristotle's view) that "truthful statements are preferable to lies *in the absence of special considerations.*"[37] So we start with the initial assumption that truthfulness outweighs lying. And we then look for special reasons supporting exceptions to the priority of truthfulness. We have already covered—in the first part of the book—the value (and necessity) of truthfulness in society, so I want to focus on Bok's "special considerations" regarding when dishonesty might be justified.

---

[33] Sam Duncan argues that "in practically no real cases do [the police] have any reason to believe that failing to lie to a suspect will directly lead to the death of another person." Sam Duncan, "Why Police Shouldn't Be Allowed to Lie to Suspects," *Journal of the American Philosophical Association* 9, no. 2 (June 2023): 268–283. However, I can think of several cases (including some I experienced as an FBI Agent), in which the success or failure of an interrogation was quite relevant to serious future harm. Consider an active kidnapping case—or one involving an ongoing string of violent bank robberies—in which the police interrogate someone who might know the suspect's identity or location. Or consider a case involving the welfare of a child. Or one in which an officer needs to seize a person (which will necessarily involve some force, perhaps even deadly force); if such force is justified, then it's plausible to think lying to the suspect (to facilitate the arrest) would also be justified. These sorts of cases are essentially (common) "emergency" situations.

[34] Slobogin, "Deceit, Pretext, and Trickery," 776.

[35] Note that one of the central legal constraints on undercover operations is entrapment, which raises a number of issues beyond deception and dishonesty. I have discussed entrapment in detail in chapter 5 of my book, *The Retrieval of Liberalism in Policing*, and will return to the topic briefly in Chapter 3.

[36] Sissela Bok, *Lying—Moral Choice in Public and Private Life* (New York: Vintage, 1999 [1978]).

[37] Ibid., 30 (emphasis added).

For Bok, such considerations must be consistent with the concept of *publicity*. This means that moral considerations regarding the permissibility of dishonesty "must be capable of public statement and defense . . . directed to reasonable persons."[38] Bok's rationale for publicity will be particularly relevant in the next chapter when we explore *transparency*, as she notes the particular risk of justifying dishonesty based on "secret" moral principles relied upon by state institutions that occupy positions of trust.[39] So we will continue to see the deep connections between deception, dishonesty, trust, and transparency. Here, though, let's consider how Bok thinks reasonable persons should think about the public justification of dishonesty.

First, if there are no alternatives to deception and dishonesty, Bok suggests that we consider reasons that might excuse deception and dishonesty: (1) avoiding harm, (2) producing benefits, (3) fairness (as when one is said to deserve dishonesty because of some unjust act), and (4) veracity (as in paradoxical cases in which lying is said to *protect* the truth).[40] Although Bok thinks that reasonable persons would consider these excuses for dishonesty in good faith, she worries that the excuses would be abused by dishonest persons and entities—especially by powerful state actors:

> Reasonable persons might be especially eager to circumscribe the lies told by all those whose power renders their impact on human lives greater than usual. And they would wish to set up the clearest possible standards and safeguards in order to prevent these and other liars from drifting into more and more damaging practices—through misunderstanding, carelessness, or abuse.[41]

To be sure, this is a dire warning with respect to law enforcement tactics. Police have immense power and discretion to use deception and dishonesty in a way that manipulates one's liberty, as well as community trust.

Considering these worries, what sort of real-world scenarios does Bok have in mind? In the first two categories (avoiding harm and producing benefits), she considers "lies in crisis" cases such as when dishonesty may be necessary to address an imminent threat of death or serious bodily injury.[42]

---

[38] Ibid., 92 (drawing on John Rawls's *A Theory of Justice*).
[39] Ibid., 95.
[40] Ibid., 78–86.
[41] Ibid., 105.
[42] Ibid., chapter VIII.

Although such cases are justified (and, again, consistent with the emergency constraint of the prerogative power test), it is important to be wary of how such threats may be exaggerated by those in power.[43] We are all familiar with so-called ticking time bomb scenarios, in which a government agent must torture a suspect in order to find the location of a ticking time bomb that will kill many (millions!) of people. However, these scenarios are largely fictional and do not reflect the decisions of actual government agents.[44] Likewise, we must take care in our analysis of any "crisis" in which the state suggests that dishonesty and deception on par with fraud is necessary.

How about "fairness" scenarios in which we "lie to liars" because, presumably, that's what they deserve—or when we lie to our "enemies"?[45] This is surely relevant to the police, who deal with dishonest and deceptive criminal suspects routinely. Although Bok does not focus on the police specifically, she is generally wary of one justifying dishonesty based on another's dishonesty because "we are likely to invite vast increases in actual deception and to escalate the seriousness of lies told in retaliation . . . [which] would not stand up well under the test of publicity."[46] More to the present point, if the state is to characterize criminal suspects as "enemies," we must also consider how treating such persons with deception and dishonesty will affect the broader community (while keeping in mind the justification of dishonesty to prevent actual harm in an actual crisis). Bok writes: "Governments build up enormous, self-perpetuating machineries of deception in adversary contexts. And when a government is known to practice deception, the results are self-defeating and erosive."[47] It is difficult to find a better assessment of the current police institution given the pervasive (business as usual) use of deception and dishonesty—not to mention the erosion of community trust in the police.

Notwithstanding the above analysis, Bok suggests that it is more excusable to lie (if honesty is not a viable option) to persons who have been *publicly declared* to be enemies—such as *criminals*. Still, she is wary of such broad declarations given the potential for discrimination and the fact that "[w]ith

---

[43] Relatedly, consider cases in which the police escalate a situation such that it *becomes* an emergency in which lying (or force) is necessary. See Ben Jones, "Police-Generated Killings: The Gap between Ethics and Law," *Political Research Quarterly* 75, no. 2 (2022): 366–378.

[44] On this point, see generally Jeremy Waldron, *Torture, Terror, and Trade-Offs* (Oxford: Oxford University Press, 2010).

[45] Bok, *Lying*, Chapter IX and X.

[46] Ibid., 127.

[47] Ibid., 142.

the growing militarization of the world have come increased powers of brutal internal policing."[48] Here again, this is exactly the situation we find ourselves in today—which I have elsewhere described as a police "identity crisis" stemming in part from militarization steeped in a "warrior" ethos.[49] We will thus need to keep in mind the possibility that—based on concrete "warrior" training—the police might view the entire population of some communities (but not others) as an enemy with whom they are at war.

All in all, Bok makes the case that *most* dishonesty and deception is inexcusable because it harms the liar, the victim, and society. Applying this position to the police, legal scholars have found Bok's analysis convincing—with Slobogin writing that investigative lying by the police "harms the dupe, the liar, and society."[50] Specifically, he argues that police deception and dishonesty denigrate the dignity of the "dupe" (e.g., a criminal suspect subjected to an undercover or sting operation). Slobogin also thinks that police deception and dishonesty clearly harm society by undermining "trust in government" and leading to a "Big Brother" state.[51] Finally, he believes deception and dishonesty harm the police because "police lying feeds on itself" and "can lead to other [corrupting] effects."[52] But what about cases in which Bok is more sympathetic to deception and dishonesty—such as lying to avert a crisis or lying to an enemy?

As I have noted, the former is for the most part uncontroversial and consistent with the emergency constraint of my prerogative power test (police deception and dishonesty on par with fraud is justified when there is an acute threat of death or serious bodily injury). On the other hand, excusing lies to publicly declared "enemies" raises more questions. Slobogin concludes that such declarations would best be made with a "requirement of *ex ante* review by a judge, analogous to what occurs in the warrant process."[53] The idea is that a magistrate judge (the person who makes determinations of probable cause when the police seek a search warrant) would serve as a "proxy for the public" in determining who is an "enemy."[54] However, this sort of judicial authorization requirement would apply to only *active undercover operations* ("when the undercover operation takes on an active mode by going after a

---

[48] Ibid., 144–145.
[49] Luke William Hunt, *The Police Identity Crisis.*
[50] Slobogin, "Deceit, Pretext, and Trickery," 796.
[51] Ibid., 797–798.
[52] Ibid., 800.
[53] Ibid., 802.
[54] Ibid., 803.

specific target or targets thought to be criminal rather than seeking to lure criminals out of the general population"), not *passive undercover operations* (operations that "merely provide people with the opportunity to commit the crime, without importuning any particular person").[55]

Similarly, Slobogin argues that the same sort of judicial authorization should be required when the police want to engage in searches and seizures that entail dishonesty and deception (unless the dishonesty and deception are necessary to protect human life). This would include cases in which the police lie to a suspect about their authority to engage in a search, as well as pretextual searches and seizures such as stopping a "suspicious" vehicle under the pretext of a minor traffic infraction. Finally, Slobogin suggests that deceptive and dishonest *postarrest* interrogation tactics are permissible under Bok's framework. This is because the police are only tricking *declared* "enemies" (the criminal suspect who was arrested), which in turn puts the suspect on notice that they are in an adversarial setting. Accordingly, deception and dishonesty would only be restricted in *prearrest* interrogation.[56]

I am sympathetic to Bok's framework, as well as Slobogin's interpretation of the framework in the context of policing. They are both valuable contributions that enrich our understanding of the limits of police dishonesty and deception. And I think we are all in agreement on many of the important issues. As noted, there seems to be broad agreement that deception and dishonesty are justified (or at least excusable) when they would prevent death or serious bodily injury (or when the only alternative is the use of force), which is obviously a central issue in the context of policing.

In other respects, however, my framework departs significantly from the Bokian framework. First, I have alluded to how there are reasons to think that a public declaration of a person (i.e., a criminal suspect) as an "enemy" is an unjustified criterion for the state's use of deception and dishonesty. One of the central reasons is based on an assumption about societies (including liberal ones) that promote security through law enforcement, not "war" against law-breaker-enemies.[57] Law and philosophy scholar Seana Shiffin expresses the broader point this way: "we cannot do just anything to wrongdoers on the ground that they have strayed, even seriously strayed, from the moral

---

[55] Ibid., 805–808.

[56] Ibid., 808–815.

[57] See Hunt, *The Police Identity Crisis*, ch. 2. Of course, deceiving and lying to, say, criminal fugitives would likely be justified under the prerogative power framework, including because the emergency constraint would likely be satisfied (and recall that when force would be necessary, so would fraud).

path, and that we cannot entirely abandon them as members of our moral community."[58] This assumption is especially important in the context of political morality and the state's treatment of persons over whom it has power. The point has even more force if, again, we accept Shelby's position discussed in Chapter 2: much criminal "deviance" is a (reasonable) *response* to bad faith policing that imposes an unfair distribution of security.[59]

I also depart from Slobogin regarding the idea that police deception and dishonesty are excusable in the context of *passive undercover operations*. The pervasive use of these sorts operations would in many ways be the epitome of a police state that breeds community distrust: every person that one meets on the street becomes a potential undercover agent or informant, leading to distrust of both the police and one's friends, family, and neighbors. This point returns us to the arguments in the first part of the book regarding the societal necessity of good faith relations rather than preemptive defection.[60]

This last point leads to a broader distinction: The goal of this book is to identify a normative framework regarding the limits of police deception and dishonesty. As such, I am not focused on specific policy suggestions—such as creating a mechanism for magistrate judges to authorize police deception. I am focused on the moral, political, and legal limits of executive discretion and prerogative power within the police institution. It is for this reason that I think my approach to the issue of police deception and dishonesty might offer something missing from other approaches (keeping in mind the immense value of the other approaches we have considered).

The prerogative power test is uniquely suited in the police context because it recognizes an **institutional context** (including through the prudential

---

[58] Shiffrin, *Speech Matters*, 38. It is worth noting that Bernard Williams seems to be less sympathetic to this point when he writes, "it is a very natural thought, for instance, that it may be perfectly *fair* to deceive . . . [one who] has put himself out of line." Williams, *Truth and Truthfulness*, 120.

[59] Tommie Shelby, "Justice, Deviance, and the Dark Ghetto."

[60] The point is relevant even to (presumably) benign cases in which the police use deception to catch speeders with unmarked police cars (a potentially permissible tactic according to Bok and Slobogin). Happily, I myself have not received a speeding ticket in decades, but I still have reflexive anxiety when I enter areas that appear to be "speed traps" (areas in which the speed limit changes quickly and dramatically, and the police give high numbers of tickets to generate revenue). Coupled with further layers of deception—unmarked cars and so on—the police are likely eroding trust. The point is especially apt when considering that there are better ways to both generate revenue and encourage safe driving speeds. See, e.g., Chris W. Surprenant, "Policing and Punishment for Proft," *Journal of Business Ethics* 159 (2019): 119–131. Katherine Hawley has argued that, to be trustworthy, we must be careful about what commitments and promises we make. When we overcommit, we leave ourselves vulnerable to being untrustworthy even if we take on the commitments with the best of intentions. The police often operate under impossible expectations (enforce the law, generate revenue, and so on) given persistent background injustices in society. Katherine Hawley, *How to be Trustworthy* (Oxford: Oxford University Press, 2019).

constraint), a *substantive context* (including through the purpose and emergency constraints), and a *philosophical context* (including through the personhood constraint). The rule of law is foundational to most societies (certainly liberal, democratic societies), as well as the police institution specifically. The prerogative power test is tailored to assess state acts of dishonesty and deception and determine whether they promote legitimacy through governance by law (free from bad faith that is on par with fraud).

4. Trust

A necessary condition of co-operative activity is trust, where this involves the willingness of one party to rely on another to act in certain ways.

—Bernard Williams[61]

[T]rust is a social good to be protected just as much as the air we breathe or the water we drink. When it is damaged, the community as a whole suffers; and when it is destroyed, societies falter and collapse.

—Sissela Bok[62]

One of the practical takeaways from this Interlude is the value of *trust* in interpersonal and institutional relations. Indeed, one of the book's central themes has been the correlative relationship between force and fraud ("war") on one hand, and, on the other hand, cooperation and good faith. If our philosophical theories about the police are to have any traction in the actual world, then they must generate trust in their application.

In Chapters 1 and 2, we considered how social interaction is contingent upon trust, especially the expectation that others will not defect preemptively and rely on force and violence.[63] When people have recurring interactions over the long term, social cooperation is not possible without the disposition of trustworthiness—in other words, trust has *intrinsic value* considering that it is necessary for basic human purposes and needs.[64]

---

[61] Bernard Williams, *Truth and Truthfulness*, 88.
[62] Bok, *Lying*, 26–27.
[63] See also Williams, *Truth and Truthfulness*, 88.
[64] Ibid., 92.

Trustworthiness is a disposition that requires honesty. If one agrees to do X, then others must be able to rely on one to do X. We can't rely on those who act with dishonesty, deception, and bad faith. This is likewise true in the institutional (social contract) context: the state and its institutions will not be trusted if they deceive the public.[65] Interpersonal and institutional agreements are generally based on the norm that the agreement must be apparent from the objective terms rather than based upon the hidden, secret intentions of the parties. Otherwise, there would be no grounds for the parties to an agreement to trust each other.

Trust in this sense is deeply connected with good faith.[66] We rely on another's disposition of good faith when we enter contractual arrangements, and we accept the vulnerability of another's bad faith—though do not expect it given that good faith is a background norm (UPM) to contractual arrangements. If the police have been entrusted to provide security and reduce crime in a particular way (in a way that respects one's rights and personhood, for instance), then a lack of good faith in police tactics fosters distrust and the presumption of bad faith in the police institution because it is difficult to assess whether particular police strategies respect the rights and personhood of (all) members of a community.

Relatedly, within the domain of interactions regarding public goods such as security, the police are *incompetent* at providing security when they themselves are unable to evaluate and articulate their own security strategies (such as algorithmic policing, discussed in Chapter 4). This might be due to, say, the police's lack of transparency and their inability to communicate how and why a particular security strategy is used within a community.[67]

---

[65] But see Karen S. Cook, Russell Hardin, and Margaret Levi, *Cooperation Without Trust* (New York: Russell Sage Foundation, 2005), 104, suggesting that institutions consist of people "whom we could not trust in the sense of encapsulated interest because we cannot monitor them and do not have repeated interactions with them." For reasons discussed in Chapter 2, I think it makes perfectly good sense to say that an institution can be honest, transparent, and trustworthy (or not).

[66] Philosopher Annette Baier makes a related point, but in terms of good will: "When I trust another, I depend on her good will toward me . . . Trust then, on this first approximation, is accepted vulnerability to another's possible but not expected ill will (or lack of good will) toward one." Annette Baier, "Trust and Antitrust," *Ethics* 96, no. 2 (1986): 231, 235.

[67] This point is based on Karen Jones's illuminating framework for trustworthiness: "B is trustworthy with respect to A in domain of interaction D, if and only if she is competent with respect to that domain, and she would take the fact that A is counting on her, were A to do so in this domain, to be a compelling reason for acting as counted on." Karen Jones, "Trustworthiness," *Ethics* 123, no. 1 (2012): 61, 70–71. Jones adds that to be "richly trustworthy," you must *signal* to others depending on you that you are competent with respect to their needs. Although signaling is beyond the scope of this book, it is worth noting that some police practices (such as procedurally just community policing) may signal and communicate police competence. See also Russell Hardin, "Trusting Persons,

Ultimately, the point to emphasize continues to be the relationship between force and fraud ("war") and cooperation and good faith. Political philosopher Kevin Vallier puts it this way: We can head off political war if we "identify institutions that can create and sustain high levels of trust among persons with diverse values and commitments, specifically ones that sustain trust in society (social trust) and trust in political institutions (political trust)."[68] The challenge is to ground social trust in publicly available evidence—thus illustrating that people and institutions are trustworthy because they are committed to following moral rules for reasons that others can understand.[69]

The police cannot generate social and political trust if they deviate from UPM regarding force and fraud without the right reasons. If the police institution is to embrace a DDD (including a DDD that is on par with fraud), then it must do so for reasons that are intelligible to a diverse community. These reasons include institutional respect for the contours of personhood, legitimacy, and the rule of law, guided by principled frameworks such as the prerogative power test. Part II of the book illustrates how these considerations might look in practice.

Trusting Institutions," in *Strategy and Choice*, ed. Richard Zeckhauser (Cambridge, MA: MIT Press, 1991), 185–209; Russell Hardin, *Trust and Trustworthiness* (New York: Russell Sage Foundation, 2002), for a related account of trustworthiness. Note that the relation between transparency and competence works the other way, too: If the police become incompetent at providing security on which persons depend, then the police may cease to be counted on because they are not trustworthy.

[68] Kevin Vallier, *Trust in a Polarized Age* (New York: Oxford University Press), 20. Vallier aptly notes that for the police institution specifically, this means fair and professional police forces that do not operate in secret. Ibid., 62, 278.
[69] Consistent with many themes in this book, Vallier suggests that "liberal rights" facilitate trust for the right reasons. Ibid., 50.

PART II
THE STREET

Five Questions and Answers Explored in Chapter 3

1. **Q: Part I argued that good faith should be a normative foundation of policing, so will Part II's case studies show what good faith policing looks like?**

   A: Yes, but in a roundabout way (naturally). Despite good faith's foundational role, I am no absolutist about good faith policing (also: I would lie to a murderer at the door). There are cases in which a deliberate dishonest disposition (DDD) is justified. The problem is that a DDD involving bad faith and fraud has become the norm in policing, not the exception. Part II thus focuses on cases involving bad faith and then considers whether the police's departure from good faith was justified.

2. **Q: So the case studies will illustrate whether a DDD on par with fraud is justified considering the prerogative power test (PPT) introduced in the Interlude?**

   A: That's exactly right. It's worth noting that the PPT primarily helps evaluate deceptive, dishonest, and fraudulent actions, rather than a general law enforcement disposition. Legitimate policing is characterized by good faith, and the police may be said to have a good faith disposition in the cases in which dishonesty, deception, and fraud are justified under the PPT. But as a practical matter, it won't be important for us to focus on the difference between the actions and the disposition in our analysis of the case studies (especially considering that—as the case studies illustrate—a bad faith disposition isn't uncommon in policing).

3. **Q: The PPT seems strict, especially considering that a justified DDD on par with fraud requires satisfying an emergency constraint. Does this imply that vast changes are needed in police practice?**

   A: Yes, but recall that the use of police force is inherently an emergency because the use of force involves some risk of harm. And recall that whenever force would be justified to make an arrest, dishonesty and deception on par with fraud would be as well. On the other hand, the case studies imply the need for a revisionary theory—considering the police's vast use of dishonest, deceptive, and fraudulent tactics in nonemergency situations.

4. Q: Will we consider case studies involving "testilying" (the illegal practice of lying under oath in official proceedings)? I ask because that practice seems straightforwardly wrong, and I'm worried that testilying could be justified under your analytical framework.

A: Yes. About your worry: Testilying would clearly be unjustified under the PPT in most cases. But try to imagine being in a "murderer at the door" scenario while you're under oath. My analysis says it's still okay to lie in that rare situation.

5. Q: Can you give me one takeaway from Chapter 3's case studies?

A: Yes: A lot of police deception and dishonesty cannot be justified in liberal democracies.

3

Case Studies

Fraud and Deception as Law Enforcement Means

The whole business. . . . in many instances of being a Special Branch
Officer is based on lies. . . . And deception, otherwise you can't do
your job.

> —Officer Tony Robinson (United Kingdom's Special
> Metropolitan Police Special Demonstration Squad)[1]

Our Government is the potent, the omnipresent teacher. For good
or for ill, it teaches the whole people by its example. . . . To declare
that, in the administration of the criminal law, the end justifies the
means—to declare that the Government may commit crimes in
order to secure the conviction of a private criminal—would bring
terrible retribution.

> —Louis Brandeis[2]

Consider this ruse in which I participated as a law enforcement officer: Over
the course of an investigation, evidence of a crime is discovered leading to a
sealed indictment charging the subject of the investigation with violations
of federal criminal law. The subject needs to be arrested but is residing in a
distant land making arrest difficult for various administrative and political
reasons. Option 1: Contact the subject, explain the situation, and invite the
subject to return and submit to arrest. Option 2: Think of a ruse that deceit-
fully induces the subject to return to the United States, and then surprise the

---

[1] "True Spies: Subversive My Arse," *BBC*, broadcast on October 27, 2002; "Watching Subversives,"
BBC News, October 17, 2002, https://s3.documentcloud.org/documents/2642522/Transcript-True-
Spies-E1-Proofed-Transcript.pdf. In the aftermath of Vietnam War demonstrations, Scotland Yard's
Special Branch established the SDS due to concerns over a lack of intelligence regarding left-wing
groups in the United Kingdom. SDS officer went deep undercover over long periods of time, assuming new identities and infiltrating political groups.
[2] Olmstead v. United States, 277 U.S. 438, 485 (1928) (dissenting).

Police Deception and Dishonesty. Luke William Hunt, Oxford University Press. © Oxford University Press 2024.
DOI: 10.1093/oso/9780197672167.003.0005

subject with arrest upon arrival in the airport. If we assume these are the only practical options, it seems reasonable to think that option two is the most appropriate. There are at least two good reasons for this: first, the subject could simply refuse to return, and—having been informed of the investigation—could destroy evidence of the crime. Second, depending on the nature of the subject's alleged crimes, other people could be at risk while the subject is at large.

In practice, how do we square these intuitions with the claim in Chapter 2 that good faith is a normative foundation for the police as a political institution? So far, we have considered how a disposition of honesty is relevant to the police institution in terms of fulfilling law enforcement obligations in a way that protects reasonable expectations of those being policed. However, policing seems to inherently include tactics that fall completely outside the spectrum of honest thoughts, statements, and actions. Among other forms of deception and dishonesty, these tactics include the use of interrogation (intentionally misleading a suspect to get something from the suspect); informants (tasking a person to act as an agent of the state and acquire something under false pretenses); and ruse, sting, and undercover operations (constructing artificial scenarios to manipulate others). The international ruse is a good example.

Few would argue that the motivation to pursue these law enforcement ends *always* justifies deceptive and dishonest means (despite our intuitions about the ruse case). Consider the different questions raised by planting evidence to secure a conviction, lying about a colleague's abuse of a criminal suspect (or lying during testimony), and, on the other hand, engaging in a deceptive operation to rescue a victim of sex trafficking. The question, then, is how do we characterize the value of honesty in policing when lying and dishonesty seem morally justifiable in some policing contexts but not others?[3] In the Interlude, we introduced the prerogative power test (PPT) as a framework for examining the justification of a deliberate dishonest disposition (DDD) on par with fraud.

Over the course of this chapter, we will put our theories into practice—beginning with a preliminary objection to the way I have characterized good

---

[3] For a sample of the work on this question, see Don Fallis, "Lying and Deception," *Philosophers' Imprint* 10 (2010): 1–22; Thomas L. Carson, *Lying and Deception: Theory and Practice* (Oxford: Oxford University Press, 2010), Part I; Andreas Stokke, "Lying, Deceiving, and Misleading," *Philosophy Compass* 8 (2013): 348–59; Vladimir Krstić, "Can You Lie without Intending to Deceive?" *Pacific Philosophical Quarterly* 100 (2019): 642–60.

faith as a normative foundation of policing, followed by a preliminary response that addresses the above ruse case. The goal is to apply Part I's discussion of good faith, honesty, transparency, legitimacy, personhood—values that have a normative backdrop in universalistic positive morality (UPM)—to common scenarios in policing.

1. A Preliminary Objection and Case Study: International Ruse

The ruse scenario with which this chapter began raises a central objection to the argument we have been considering: Good faith cannot be a normative foundation for the police because the practical nature of the police role entails enforcing the law through dishonesty and deception, and that is inconsistent with good faith. To put it another way, good faith is not relevant (not a normative foundation, at least) because, obviously, *policing isn't like that*. Policing is instead a gritty job that requires getting one's hands dirty—including through dishonesty, deception, and the betrayal of trust—in order to promote security and safety in society.

1.1. Policing Isn't Like That

The issue is whether good faith is the rule—not the exception—in policing. This means we will need to decide whether a DDD is (and should be) so enmeshed in the police role that the police may engage in bad faith and trust betrayal whenever it serves a law enforcement end. As a practical matter, many law enforcement agencies require that certain thresholds be met before engaging in, say, a deceptive undercover operation. So even from a basic administrative perspective, law enforcement agencies often cannot engage in all forms of deception willy-nilly—and for good reason.

As we will see, police deception, dishonesty, and misrepresentation fall on a spectrum in terms of *legality* (analogous to how good faith falls on a spectrum between fraud and fiduciary). Bad faith must be so bad that it renders the interaction *involuntary* given the totality of the circumstances. But if we examine the issue from a broader normative perspective, we can ask whether the police should even be on this spectrum given commitments of political morality—and, if so, when? Consider an analogy to police brutality. Police have a range of legal options regarding their use of violence and force (including the intensity and duration of that violence and force) to fulfill their law enforcement obligations. But even if a department justifiably relies on use-of-force continuums, it would be odd to say that the police may act on a spectrum of *brutality* because that is a very different kind of spectrum. We simply say that all brutality is wrong and that police should not operate on that spectrum. I have not made that strong a claim with respect to bad faith, but the first part of the book came close given the fundamental role that good faith plays in political society.

Recall that, for many people, the police are the major connection between the community and the state. The police parole streets and highways; they question people who seem "suspicious" and they write tickets; they respond to automobile accidents, emergencies, and domestic disputes; they conduct surveillance on foot and in vehicles. In short, they touch many parts of everyday life. And yet they are officially sanctioned to lie, deceive, betray trust, and break what would otherwise be the law. This not only occurs in sophisticated undercover or ruse operations, but also informally while on patrol—as when a suspicious person is interrogated on the street (and perhaps then brought to the stationhouse for more formal interrogation).[4]

Law and philosophy scholar Seana Shiffrin's position about institutional duties of sincerity is apt here: "The police have institutionally grounded reasons not to lie, even effectively, to achieve their valid and admirable purposes. The practice of lying is in tension with the role the police play and should play in our scheme of epistemic moral cooperation."[5] Shiffrin is referring to the role police play in promoting moral agency in society through what I have described in terms of the norms of reciprocal relationships. In other words, recognizing our moral duties involves collective action, cooperation, and reciprocation that requires a "reliable epistemic environment."[6] Perhaps, then, the nature of the police institution is not so obvious.

If the police—as agents of the state—are sanctioned to engage in widespread acts of bad faith, deception, dishonesty, and (sanctioned) lawbreaking, then there is a sense in which the police as an institution erode

---

[4] I examined deceptive interrogation techniques from a rather esoteric, linguistic perspective in "Legal Speech and Implicit Content in the Law," *Ratio Juris* 29, no. 1 (2016): 3–22.

[5] Seana Valentine Shiffrin, *Speech Matters: On Lying, Morality, and the Law* (Princeton, NJ: Princeton University Press, 2014), 197.

[6] Ibid.

both the rule of law and trust within some communities—creating a culture of fear and suspicion in some (but not all) communities.[7] The upshot is that by acting in bad faith, the police subvert the foundation of a particular type of political community, namely: community based on respect for the moral agency of persons engaged in reciprocal political arrangements that require good faith interactions and a commitment to the rule of law.

1.2. Justifying a Deliberate Dishonest Disposition

There are a great many ways that the police could enhance their ability to enforce the law, reduce crime, and promote security. We can think of shocking tactics (such as torture and brutality) and less-shocking tactics (a DDD consisting of bad faith, deception, and trust betrayal). Assuming those tactics are unjustified in our interactions and agreements with others generally, then we have to answer why they are justified in the interactions and agreements between the police and those suspected of wrongdoing.

The answer we have been considering is the value of *security*. However, we do not want security at all costs (torture, brutality, and so on). For as we have seen, the concept of security is also about how safety is distributed within society (equitably between various societal groups), as well as the maintenance of particular ways of living (rather than simply safety and staying alive).[8] In the same way we don't want security that means living with torture and brutality, we have to ask whether we want security that means living with a police institution that relies on bad faith that is on par with fraud and deviations from the rule of law with respect to some groups but not others.

Is there a gray area—what Shiffrin would call a "justified suspended context"—in which the police may embrace a DDD? This is where we turned to the PPT introduced in the Interlude, illustrated below.

---

[7] See, e.g., Elizabeth Joh, "Breaking the Law to Enforce It," *Stanford Law Review* 62, no. 1 (2009): 191, stating: "Whether or not the action is justified as a matter of legal doctrine, the knowledge that the police are permitted to participate in crime, even for justifiable ends, erodes public trust in the police."

[8] Jeremy Waldron, *Torture, Terror, and Trade-Offs* (Oxford: Oxford University Press, 2010), 116–22.

Prerogative Power Test

When are the police justified in deviating from the rule of law through a deliberate dishonest disposition (DDD) on par with fraud?

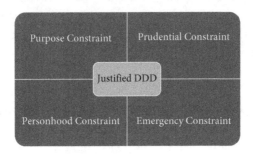

In short, the prerogative power test holds that the police are justified in engaging in a DDD on par with fraud when the DDD overlaps with the test's four constraints—in other words, when the underlying law enforcement action is consistent with the purpose, prudential, personhood, and emergency constraints.[9] We first applied this framework to the police's deceptive and dishonest threat in the *Alexander v. DeAngelo* case, in which a woman was threatened by the police with a 40-year prison sentence when she was in fact facing only a 6-to-10-year sentence.

Would the ruse scenario at the beginning of the chapter be justified under the above framework? If we assume the first three components were met (*purpose constraint*: the ruse supported a legitimate law enforcement purpose serving the public good; *prudential constraint*: there was no viable way to legislatively sanction any underlying bad faith and fraud in the ruse; and *personhood constraint*: the ruse was not an affront to the suspect's personhood), then it depends on the nature of the underlying crime. Was there an *emergency*—involving a threat of serious bodily injury—that could not be averted without bad faith and fraud? If so—if the case involved, say, crimes against children—then perhaps the ruse was justified. If not—if the case, say, involved the distribution of illegal drugs—then the ruse is unlikely to be justified.

---

[9] As the illustration suggests (and as discussed in the Interlude), a DDD on par with fraud is justified when all the prerogative power test's constraints are satisfied and overlap with the DDD. For example, the emergency constraint does not override the personhood constraint—in other words, the prerogative power test would not just justify, say, a DDD entailing an affront to personhood through brutality or torture in an emergency situation.

Of course, two people might reach different conclusions on these questions given that the analysis is based on a rough framework and we need more facts about the case. The larger point is to begin considering why there might be good reasons to radically rethink the extent to which the police should have open-ended authority to act with a DDD. Let's do that now.

2. Case Study: Covering Up

In January 2014, Larry Thompson, a Black man, lived in a Brooklyn apartment with his fiancée, their newborn baby, and Thompson's sister-in-law. The sister-in-law suffered from cognitive impairments and was cared for by the Thompsons. When the Thompson's baby was just one week old, Larry's sister-in-law secretly called 911 to report that Larry was sexually abusing the baby. When Emergency Medical Technicians (EMTs) arrived, Larry explained that they must have the wrong address because no one called 911. The EMTs left and then returned with four police officers. Larry asserted his rights by telling the police they could not enter his home without a warrant. In response, the police physically restrained Larry, handcuffed him to the floor, and conducted a warrantless search of Larry's home and child.

The EMTs took Larry's baby to the hospital, where medical professionals examined her and found no signs of abuse—only diaper rash. While all this was happening, Larry was arrested and charged with obstructing governmental administration and resisting arrest, as well as held in jail for two days. Subsequently, however, all charges against Larry were mysteriously dismissed with no explanation by the prosecutor or judge. It thus appeared that the police had charged Larry fraudulently to cover up the way they treated Larry, who had simply asserted his Fourth Amendment right against a warrantless search. Accordingly, Larry sued the officers for *malicious prosecution* in violation of his constitutional rights.

To be successful in his malicious prosecution suit, Larry had to demonstrate that he obtained a "favorable termination" in the criminal charges against him (obstruction, resisting arrest). Larry's suit against the police was dismissed because the court determined that "favorable termination" meant that Larry had to show that he was innocent (not merely that his prosecution ended without conviction). The problem was that Larry could not affirmatively show his innocence because he could not explain why his charges were dismissed (given that he received no explanation from the police, prosecutor, or judge). Larry's case went to the US Supreme Court on appeal.[10]

2.1. Legal and Philosophical Questions

Legal question: To demonstrate a "favorable termination" of a criminal prosecution in a malicious prosecution suit against the police, must Larry show that his criminal prosecution (for obstruction, resisting arrest) ended with some affirmative indication of innocence or simply that his prosecution ended without a conviction?[11]

Philosophical questions: If the police mischaracterized their authority to enter Larry's home without a warrant, was such dishonesty justified under the circumstances? If the police covered up their physical treatment of Larry by fraudulently charging him with obstruction and resisting arrest, was such dishonesty justified given the underlying case regarding the welfare of an infant? Or: Can an arrest or seizure be justified when it is the product of police lies?

2.2. Legal and Philosophical Analysis

Legal analysis: The Supreme Court explained that the malicious prosecution tort protects injuries to people relating to false imprisonment and harm to one's character or reputation. The elements of malicious prosecution (for obstruction and resisting arrest in Larry's case) are (1) the charge was brought without probable cause, (2) the motive for the charge was malicious (e.g., without probable cause and for a purpose other than bringing the charged person to justice), and (3) the charge was terminated with the acquittal or discharge of the person. The dispute in Larry's case was thus over the third element.

The Supreme Court held that—in a malicious prosecution suit against the police—Larry could show a "favorable termination" of his criminal prosecution (for obstruction, resisting arrest) by simply showing that his criminal prosecution ended without a conviction.

The Court's rationale was based in part on the underlying "values and purposes" of the Fourth Amendment. The Court also argued that it would

---

[10] Thompson v. Clark, 596 U.S. ___ (2022).
[11] Ibid.

be unreasonable for questions regarding whether one was wrongly charged (and whether one may seek redress for wrongful prosecution) to depend on "whether the prosecutor or court happened to explain why charges were dismissed."[12] The Court did not address issues relating to probable cause.

Philosophical analysis: Reconciling this case with the goal of *justice* is more difficult than it first appears. On one hand, it might seem like a straightforward case of dishonesty inasmuch as the police lied about their authority to enter Larry's home and then charged (and jailed) him to cover up their bad behavior. But on the other hand, we must contend with the value of *security*—especially considering that the alleged victim was an infant and could not speak for herself. We can thus frame the issue in terms of resolving the tension between security and safety and respecting Larry's rights.

When the police showed up at Larry's door, he was owed a duty of *good faith* by the police (so I have argued), which includes not purposefully distorting the facts as the police see them for good motivating reasons. We can also see how Larry might have been owed some degree of *transparency*, especially given that he received no explanation regarding why his charges were suddenly dropped.

Instead, one might construe the police's tactics as *fraudulent* inasmuch as the police dishonestly gained an unjust advantage over Larry and injured his rights and interests: they allegedly assaulted him after he invoked his right to be free from an unreasonable search and seizure—and then charged him with obstruction and resisting arrest to cover up their behavior (not to mention leaving him in jail for two days). There was thus a clear breakdown of cooperative dealings and a reliance on force and power. If the police's actions can be so characterized, then it seems clear that they were knowing and willful actions. And their actions were material because they harmed Larry, injuring his rights and interests.

If the police's dishonesty is on par with fraud, then such dishonesty raises questions about whether they are enforcing the law in a way that is consistent with the *rule of law*. Procedurally, the police may have circumvented the requirement that they only enter and search Larry's home (and seize Larry) with a warrant based on probable cause of criminal activity—or without a warrant, but with probable cause and exigent circumstances. This reflects a substantive commitment to the presumption of Larry's liberty, as well as a substantive commitment to judicial review of law enforcement action through the

----

[12] Ibid.

warrant process. Without a commitment to the rule of law in these ways, the police's actions would lack authority and thus legitimacy. And without a commitment to the rule of law, the police's action would not reflect a conception of Larry as moral agent with human dignity and the capacity for reciprocation.

But if we turn from Larry to his daughter and the allegation of abuse, how should we view Larry's rights considering his daughter's rights to security and safety? For police dishonesty to be a justified tactic for pursuing security, I assume that it should yield security equitably considering the commitments of liberal, democratic societies. This raises several questions given our assumptions about justice.

- Was the tactic used unfairly in Larry's case (e.g., was it used based on considerations regarding ethnicity or wealth)?
- Was this case an instance of a more general use of dishonest tactics that fall disproportionately on some groups of people (e.g., based on ethnicity or wealth)?
- Putting aside questions of equity, is the use of dishonesty even effective in these sorts of cases? For instance, is the police's use of dishonesty to enter a home (e.g., telling someone they have authority to enter when they do not) an effective way to stop crime?
- Is lying about a charge (e.g., mischaracterizing a person's actions as obstruction and resisting arrest) an effective police tactic—does it somehow deter crime?

Are there data or empirical methods available to help answer these questions? Regardless, even if we think the sort of dishonesty (dishonesty on par with fraud) in Larry's case involved effective tactics, are those tactics morally permissible given the prioritization of the rule of law, authority, legitimacy, and personhood in liberal societies?

There is no easy answer given the stakes (the welfare of an infant), but the prerogative power test may help us evaluate some of the various considerations. First, we should be clear that there are two potential areas of dishonesty in cases such as this: (1) the police mischaracterizing their authority to enter Larry's house without a warrant, and (2) the police mischaracterizing Larry's actions in order to cover their disrespect for his right to be free from an unreasonable search and seizure.

With respect to (1), the police seem to have acted within the *purpose* and *prudential* constraints of the prerogative power test given that the dishonesty was presumably used to promote an infant's safety and security in a timely manner. Likewise, under such circumstances, the *personhood* constraint was not violated because the police would have been justified in using force to protect an infant from harm (indeed, they did use force against Larry), as long as the force was not an affront to human dignity. The more pressing question is whether they complied with the *emergency* constraint of the test: Was dishonesty and fraud necessary to avoid death or a serious bodily injury?

The question boils down to the specific facts of the case.

- Did the police have good reason to force their way into Larry's home (and physically arrest him) *right then*?
- Were the police's reasons based merely on the phone call from Larry's sister-in-law, or were the police able to corroborate the sister-in-law's story independently? For example, did the police see or hear anything relevant when they arrived at Larry's door? Did they receive any indication that the infant was in danger?

We can put these issues in legal terms: Was there evidence suggesting a fair probability of crime, giving the police probable cause that the infant was in danger and that they needed to enter the home right away? If the police could not answer that question affirmatively, then mischaracterizing their authority to enter Larry's home was unjustified and they should have conducted further investigation to determine whether there was probable cause regarding the allegations against Larry. On the other hand, if the police could answer the question affirmatively, then they were justified in forcing their way into the home.[13]

The police's conduct is more problematic with respect to the second potential case of dishonesty: mischaracterizing Larry's conduct as obstruction and resisting arrest in order to cover up their own conduct and retaliate against Larry. Such dishonesty fails the *purpose* constraint of the prerogative power test because the conduct was self-serving, not for the public good. Moreover, questions about the infant's safety would have been irrelevant because any potential crisis had passed at the time the charges were filed; the conduct

---

[13] Note that if the police knew (or had reason to believe) that they in fact had probable cause, then there was of course no dishonesty involved in their entry of the home and the prerogative power test is not needed.

thus fails the emergency constraint of the test.[14] Of course, if the police in fact had evidence and reason to believe that Larry obstructed justice and resisted arrest, then their actions were not dishonest and the prerogative power test is not needed. However, the fact that they mysteriously dropped the charges against Larry without explanation suggest that the charging decision may not have been completely above board—not to mention how the police's conduct may have been an affront to Larry's human dignity. Greater transparency would be helpful here: the police could share their perspective on the case to promote epistemic goods (rather than relying on hidden, undisclosed intentions to misrepresent or alter their outward, objective words and actions).

2.3. Other Examples and Applications

Although every case is unique, the facts and analysis in Larry's case have broad application regarding police deception and dishonesty. Consider the well-known phenomenon of the police stopping and searching a vehicle or driver based on a "hunch" that drugs are in the vehicle. A hunch is not a valid evidential standard that would hold up in court. Accordingly, an officer might claim (falsely) in a police report that a stop was made based on some minor traffic infraction—and upon stopping the vehicle for the traffic infraction the officer saw drugs in the vehicle in plain view (making a search warrant unnecessary). Note that even if drugs are found in the vehicle, the dishonesty would not be permissible under the prerogative power test— including because there is no emergency regarding death or serious bodily harm that justifies the lie. It is not difficult to see how this sort of dishonesty in nonemergency situations (notwithstanding the potential discovery of criminality through the dishonest tactic) might have the effect of a more harmful erosion of trust within the community.

We can also consider the familiar scenario of the police stopping and frisking a person walking down a sidewalk based on a hunch that the person is a criminal with a weapon. Here again, such a stop would be illegal (if based merely on a hunch) and could only be justified through dishonesty. The police would need to report (falsely) that their suspicion of criminality

---

[14] Note that dishonesty would arguably pass the emergency constraint at this point if the police had reason to believe that potential abuse would be repeated; under such circumstances, the dishonesty would not be self-serving and would thus pass the purpose constraint.

was reasonable, including because they observed, say, a bulging object in the person's hoodie that required a pat-down search for officer safety (but with the goal of simply finding drugs on the person). These scenarios regarding dishonest and deceptive searches for drugs and guns often overlap with the facts in situations such as Larry's case, in which the police want to enter a person's home to look for contraband. It is of course unconstitutional to search a person's home for contraband without meeting requisite legal standards. The police thus need to claim (falsely) that, say, they saw drugs in plain view when they knocked on the door and the person answered the door.

Here is the broader takeaway: When the police intentionally devise schemes to obtain evidence in nonemergency situations and cover their tracks by means of false or fraudulent pretenses, they deviate from basic political, legal, and moral norms in ways that cannot be justified in liberal democracies and in ways that are likely to erode community trust.

3. Case Study: Controlling Citizens

Daniel Holtzclaw excelled as a high school and college athlete, including playing football at Eastern Michigan University. He became a police officer in Oklahoma City after graduating from college. Then he began deceptively using his police power to control women for his personal enjoyment. Holtzclaw followed a very specific modus operandi. Using police resources, he would identify mostly poor, Black women who he believed would be easy to deceive and control. Many of his victims were elderly. Many also had criminal records or outstanding warrants, which provided Holtzclaw with a legal basis to arrest them. Given their history, the victims were less likely to report Holtzclaw's crimes, including because they feared their stories would not be believed.[15]

A 48-year-old woman (identified as "S.B.") was walking along a street when Holtzclaw stopped his patrol car beside her. He asked S.B. where she was coming from and where she was going, as well as whether she had any drugs or weapons on her. Although S.B. had no outstanding warrants, she had been drinking alcohol earlier and Holtzclaw said (falsely) she had only two options: jail or detox. After responding that she wanted to go home,

---

[15] Dave Philipps, "Former Oklahoma City Police Officer Found Guilty of Rapes," *New York Times*, December 10, 2015.

Holtzclaw said (falsely) he would drive her home. Instead, he drove S.B. to a secluded area and gave her (falsely) a new set of options: oral sex and sex (rape) or jail. Given these options, she said "okay" and was forced into the sex acts. Holtzclaw then allowed S.B. to exit his car and she walked home.[16]

Several other victims provided similar accounts in the context of vehicle stops: Holtzclaw pulled over the woman's vehicle and ask whether she was intoxicated or had any contraband; he would then run the woman's information in a police database. With any relevant criminal history on hand, Holtzclaw would then order the woman out of the vehicle for a pat-down search. At this point, Holtzclaw would command the woman to lift up her clothes and kneel, forcing the woman to perform oral sodomy on him. Holtzclaw would then rely on a variety of lies after the assault, such as telling the woman that the police would not help her (in other words, *he* was the police) and that no one would believe her story.[17]

3.1. Legal and Philosophical Questions

Legal question: If Holtzclaw used his police power to control citizens by forcing them to engage in sexual acts, did those actions satisfy the elements of assault and rape?

Philosophical questions: If we assume that the central reason Holtzclaw's actions were wrong is because violating one's bodily integrity through assault and rape is wrong, how are his actions related to broader issues of bad faith, deception, and dishonesty?

3.2. Legal and Philosophical Analysis

Legal analysis: Holtzclaw was convicted on 18 of 36 counts of sexual assault in attacks on thirteen women. The evidence at trial included the testimony of thirteen women who described sexual assaults that began with groping and progressed to forced oral sex and rape. Several of the victims stated that Holtzclaw found them with drugs, then used his police powers

[16] Jessica Testa, "The 13 Women Who Accused a Cop of Sexual Assault, in Their Own Words," *BuzzFeed News*, December 8, 2015.
[17] Ibid.

to get the victims to do as he said. Physical evidence included DNA found near Holtzclaw's pants zipper that matched the DNA of a 17-year-old girl who testified that she was raped by Holtzclaw. Holtzclaw declined to testify at trial, though his ex-girlfriend testified that Holtzclaw never did anything to make her feel uncomfortable.[18]

Philosophical analysis: Unlike the prior case study, it may appear that there is no (difficult) philosophical problem to address in the Holtzclaw case. If the facts are as described, then we do not need much philosophy to understand why Holtzclaw's actions were wrong. Rape is one of the most heinous crimes imaginable. It is an intimate violation of one's bodily integrity—the forceful, nonconsensual use of another's body for sexual gratification.

As bad as any rape is, Holtzclaw's case includes aggravating factors that make his actions particularly despicable: He was an agent of the state who used his power to control and harm the citizens he was entrusted to protect. As we discussed in the last chapter, society has entrusted policing to agents of the state to permit a mutually beneficial division of labor. And it is through this *entrustment* that persons can be thought of as having a right to be secured in good faith. Accordingly, good faith is a fundamental component of modes of political deliberation and agreement through which persons (the victims in this case) entrust the state with (legitimate) authority.

It is through this entrustment that Holtzclaw could be thought of as having an obligation to promote security (and that his victims could be thought of as having a correlative right to be secured by him) in good faith. However, he merely acted under *color of law* (or the pretense of law) given that assault and rape are obviously not part of the police role: he illegitimately used the power of his role to control his victims. This bad faith manipulation of an entrusted role connects his actions to broader issues of deception and dishonesty.[19]

When Holtzclaw drove his police vehicle alongside a woman walking down the street—or pulled over a woman for a minor traffic violation—the women were owed a duty of *good faith* that included him not purposefully distorting the facts of their situation. This is especially the case given that it is unlikely that his victims (who were often elderly and impoverished) knew

[18] Philipps, "Former Oklahoma City Police Officer."
[19] Of course, it might be true that some of Holtzclaw's victims were engaging in criminality (e.g., drug use) and subject to sanction. It is thus possible that one's account of justice would entail a law enforcement response such as arrest, but obviously not assault and rape. The idea would be that investigating and sanctioning drug users promotes an (equitable) distribution of societal security (though I myself disagree with such claims for reasons discussed in Part I).

their options and rights—for example, whether Holtzclaw had the power to arrest them, take them to jail, take them to detox, or simply release them. Accordingly, they did not choose to engage in the sexual acts; they had no real choice. He had complete control over them and forced them to submit based upon his *fraudulent* use of the police role. He dishonestly leveraged his power to gain an unjust advantage over the women in a way that injured their rights and interests in a most intimate and horrifying way.

In this case, then, it is quite clear how dishonesty and fraud were contrary to the *rule of law*. Holtzclaw substituted governance by law with governance according to his personal sexual gratification. Under the *prerogative power test*, such dishonesty and fraud are clearly contrary to the *purpose* constraint given that the dishonesty was used for personal reasons (notwithstanding that he deceptively detained his victims for ostensibly justified reasons such as drug use or traffic infractions). And it should go without saying that his actions were contrary to the *emergency* constraint. But I want to focus on how his actions are an affront to the *personhood* constraint of the prerogative power test. The personhood constraint connects the Holtzclaw case to a broader range of more common police tactics involving bad faith.

We should be clear about the nature of Holtzclaw's dishonesty: At a minimum, he mischaracterized his authority to arrest the women and his authority to have them incarcerated and/or entered into "detox." He surely had the power to take some law enforcement action in some cases, but there is no question that he mischaracterized his actual authority as well as the actual rights and options the women had. Dishonestly acting under the pretense of authority, he treated his victims as *objects* that could be used for his sexual gratification. In other words, he did not respect the intrinsic value his victims had as persons—the high-ranking status they share with all persons, regardless of their specific backgrounds or specific socioeconomic positions. This is another way of saying that Holtzclaw denigrated what liberal (and other) societies call the *human dignity* of his victims.[20]

---

[20] Unfortunately, Holtzclaw's actions were not the only afront to the victim's human dignity. Some commentators observed that the media—along with many feminist and racial justice advocates—gave Holtzclaw's case little attention (compared to other cases) because of the victims' ethnicity and socioeconomic status. See, e.g., Ken Ford, "A Guilty Verdict for Daniel Holtzclaw," *The Atlantic*, December 11, 2015; Molly Redden, "Daniel Holtzclaw: Former Oklahoma City Police Officer Guilty of Rape," *The Guardian*, December 10, 2015; Jessica Lussenhop, "Daniel Holtzclaw Trial: Standing with 'Imperfect' Accusers," *BBC News*, November 13, 2015; Treva Lindsey, "The Media Failed Black Women By Not Covering This Rape Trial," *Cosmopolitan*, December 15, 2015. This suggests a view

3.3. Other Examples and Applications

One might think that this is a one-off case that has little relevance to policing broadly; in other words, Holtzclaw was simply a bad apple and we need not worry about police affronts to human dignity generally. This is where empirical data can be helpful. Following Holtzclaw's case, the *Associated Press* conduced a yearlong examination of sexual misconduct by police officers, determining that approximately 1,000 officers in the United States lost their licenses for sex crimes or other sexual misconduct over a six-year period. However, the investigation indicated that those numbers do not reflect the gravity of the problem because some states do not have a process that bans officers who engage in sexual misconduct. Moreover, the states that do revoke officer licensure have varying reporting requirements—thus raising problems of transparency.[21] In short, there is empirical evidence that the dishonest policing in the Holtzclaw case does not represent an isolated problem; such evidence can help inform the way we think about and reform police power.

The worry about disrespecting one's personhood with affronts to human dignity is broad in scope. Recall the facts of the *Alexander v. DeAngelo* case discussed in Chapter 2: The police told a woman she was facing a forty-year prison sentence for a drug charge unless she served as a police informant. The police wanted the woman to have oral sex for money with the target of an investigation so the police could charge the target with soliciting a prostitute. They wired the woman to record the encounter and they gave her a napkin, instructing her to spit the target's semen into it to provide physical evidence of the sex act. The woman completed the act. But in fact, she was only facing a six-to-ten-year prison sentence for the drug charge.

Although the court did not find the police liable for this conduct (in part based on their qualified immunity), it did consider how the police's conduct could be construed as facilitating *rape by fraud*.[22] In other words, there was at least a plausible legal question regarding whether the police obtained the

that some persons are worth less than others, pointing toward an unfair societal distribution of security.

[21] Sean Murphy, "Ex-Oklahoma Officer Gets 263 Years for Rapes, Sex Assaults," *Associated Press*, January 21, 2016.

[22] It is worth noting the distinction between rape by fraud or deceit and rape by coercion or threat, which each raise different issues. For a comprehensive discussion, see Stuart P. Green, *Criminalizing Sex: A Unified Liberal Theory* (New York: Oxford University Press, 2020), chapters 6–7.

woman's consent to sex by fraud, which would be grounds for a battery because a "false threat of lengthy imprisonment is a form of coercion that can vitiate consent to sex and turn the sex into battery."[23] Recall that the court ultimately found that the woman was not raped by the police in the "ordinary sense of the term "rape.'" Now, that *may* be the correct *legal* analysis (I am doubtful), but, here, we are focused on philosophical analysis and what the police *should* do. Even if it is legal for the police to dishonestly trick people into engaging in sex acts to support a police investigation, should they do that? We have already discussed how the tactic in the *Alexander* case fails the *emergency* constraint of the prerogative power test. But I hope it is now more apparent how the case fails the *personhood* constraint of the test in a way that is similar to the Holtzclaw case—even if the facts are less shocking than the Holtzclaw case at first glance.

Moving beyond sexual crime, how else may the police use deception and dishonesty to control citizens? The possibilities are almost endless, so let us consider just two common scenarios that are similar to many real-world cases. First, consider a scenario in which a young college student is stopped by campus police for a minor traffic infraction. The police find almost an ounce of marijuana in the student's vehicle and she is ordered to follow the police officer to her apartment. The officer states (falsely): "You don't have to let me in, but if you refuse then I can go get a search warrant." The student "consents" to the officer searching her apartment, and the officer finds and seizes five more ounces of marijuana along with some Ecstasy and Valium pills.

The officer tells the student (falsely) that the seized items make her liable for a twenty-year felony prison sentence and that her life will be ruined if she doesn't agree to work for the police as an informant. The student thus "consents" because she feels like she has no other choice. The police subsequently task the student to participate in an undercover sting operation requiring her to meet a convicted felon in an isolated location to buy heroin and a handgun (even though the student had never owned or shot a gun). On the day of the operation, things unfortunately do not go as planned and the police lose track of the student. She is found unconscious the next day in a ravine, having been severely beaten and sexually assaulted by the man she was sent to meet.[24]

---

[23] Alexander v. Deangelo, 329 F.3d 912 (7th Cir. 2003).

[24] This hypothetical scenario is based loosely on the real-world case of Rachel Hoffman, which has been covered extensively. See Sarah Stillman, "The Throwaways," *The New Yorker*, September 3, 2012, as well as chapter 4 of my *The Retrieval of Liberalism in Policing* (2019). Unlike the hypothetical

Now consider a second, common scenario.[25] As the result of a traumatic accident in high school, a young man in the rural south struggled with addiction to prescription pain pills for years. In and out of rehab, he finally achieved one year of sobriety and seemed to be getting his life together. However, he succumbed to temptation and relapsed after meeting up with his old high school friends who were using drugs at a house party. The young man was found by police the next morning in a gas station parking lot, passed out behind the steering wheel of his truck with a significant number of pills in his backpack.

The police took the man to the emergency room. Upon waking, the first person the man saw was a drug detective. Because the man was already on probation for drug charges, the detective stated (falsely) that he could either (1) *go to jail immediately and probably not see the light of day for a couple of decades*, or (2) *work for me as an undercover drug informant so I can get your legal problems all cleared up*. As in the other cases we have considered, the man felt that he had no other choice but to "consent" to work for the police as a drug informant.

Over the next few weeks, the man began making controlled buys of heroin for the police. Having struggled with substance abuse since high school, the man's relapse progressed, and he began using the drugs he was sent to buy for the police. The man's drug addiction was of course well-known to the police, given the circumstances under which their agreement was reached. Indeed, while working as a drug informant, the man sent a desperate text message to his police handler, stating, *I know I messed up and failed the drug test, but please don't send me to jail. It won't happen again, and I will find more drug users to inform on.* Within a week of sending that message, the man overdosed on the same drugs he was supposed to buy for the police. He had planned to begin a new job on the day he died. The day after he died, a text message from the police arrived on the man's phone: *Keep making buys and I'll keep doing my best to get your legal problems cleared up with the prosecutor.*

In both scenarios, the police's use of deception and dishonesty to mischaracterize facts and control citizens fails the prerogative power test—not least because the underlying facts do not satisfy the test's *emergency*

---

scenario I have described, Hoffman was found dead in a ravine, having been shot multiple times in the head and chest with the same gun that the police had arranged for her to purchase.

[25] This hypothetical scenario is based on the real-world case of Troy Howlett, as reported in Jason Biba, "Her Son Needed Help. First, He Had to Help the Police," *The New Republic*, January 4, 2022.

constraint. But as with the Holtzclaw case and the *Alexander v. Deangelo* case, there is a clear sense in which these cases do not pass the *personhood* constraint of the test. In both scenarios, the police use deception and dishonesty to control citizens, coercing them to participate in dangerous undercover operations that may result in death or serious bodily injury (no matter how many precautions the police might try to make).[26]

There is thus a straightforward sense in which the police's use of deception and dishonesty in these scenarios underscore the view that some citizens may be treated simply as a means to a law enforcement end. By mischaracterizing and exaggerating the person's rights, options, and potential criminal liability, the police make it impossible for the person to make a real, informed choice about whether to work for the police. Deception and dishonesty are thus tools for manipulating the person's autonomy and moral agency, as well as human dignity—especially considering that the police are willing to put the person in a situation in which there is a not insignificant risk of being assaulted or relapsing.

4. Case Study: Catching Criminals

Shahed Hussain agreed to work as an undercover informant for the FBI during the 2007–2009 timeframe. A Pakistani national, Hussain agreed to this role to avoid being deported due to a fraud conviction. The FBI tasked Hussain with identifying "disaffected Muslims who might be harboring terrorist designs on the United States." Hussain began presenting himself as a wealthy businessman with knowledge of Islam. With this cover story, Hussain befriended James Cromitie.[27]

Cromitie had very limited financial means and tried to sustain himself by committing petty drug offenses and working a night shift at Walmart; he earned less than $14,000 per year. In 2008, Cromitie approached Hussain in a mosque parking lot, mentioning that he had family in Afghanistan. Hussain asked Cromitie if he would like to travel to Afghanistan, and Cromitie responded that he would and that he wanted to die as a martyr and go to

---

[26] To be sure, subjecting informants to dangerous operations may be wrong for considerations apart from deception and dishonesty—as discussed in Chapter 4 of my *The Retrieval of Liberalism in Policing*.

[27] See United States v. Cromitie, 727 F.3d 194 (2d Cir. 2013), from which the facts in this section are drawn.

paradise; he wanted to "to do something to America." Hussain informed Cromitie that military planes flew arms and ammunition to Afghanistan and Iraq from an Air National Guard base at Stewart Airport (New York).

Hussain continued to meet with (and covertly record) Cromitie, documenting statements regarding Cromitie's hatred of America and his desire to harm Americans. In response, the FBI instructed Hussain to tell Cromitie that he, Hussain, was a representative of a Pakistani terrorist group and had the ability to obtain guns and rockets. Cromitie indicated that he would like to join and help the group, boasting that he had stolen guns from Walmart and that he could put a "team" and "plan" together. He also said he was interested in buying "stuff" from Hussain, given Hussain's stated access to guns and rockets. He told Hussain he wanted to "hit" the George Washington Bridge, but Hussain advised that bridges are difficult targets. When Hussain said they should pick a different target, Cromitie suggested Stewart Airport (the location previously referred to by Hussain). Approximately two months later, Hussain purchased a camera for Cromitie and drove him to Stewart Airport to conduct surveillance.

Thereafter, Hussain and Cromitie had no contact for over a month, at which point Cromitie told Hussain he was having financial problems and needed to make money. Hussain replied, "I told you, I can make you 250,000 dollars, but you don't want it brother. What can I tell you?" Cromitie responded, "Okay, come see me brother."

Hussain told Cromitie that his terrorist group had taken significant steps to support the operation and that "[t]he missile was ready." Cromitie subsequently introduced "lookouts" to help with the operation (who became the other defendants in the case), and the men began taking photographs of their targets—Stewart Airport as well as a synagogue and Jewish Center. Hussain advised that he would teach Cromitie how to use a rocket launcher; the group continued to discuss and plan a terrorist attack.

Eventually, Hussain drove Cromitie and the other members of the group to a warehouse in which the FBI had stored fake bombs and Stinger missiles; Hussain taught the other men how to wire the bombs and launch the missiles. Hussain then drove the fake bombs and missiles to New York, where he had rented a storage room. The group unloaded the fake weapons into the storage room and settled on a date for the attack. On the planned day of the attack, the group drove to the storage room and picked up the fake weapons, placing them in two vehicles (that were parked by the FBI for the operation) in front of the synagogue and Jewish Center. FBI agents then arrested all the men.

4.1. Legal and Philosophical Questions

Legal questions: Did the FBI entrap Cromitie through their use of Hussain as an informant, and were the tactics used by the FBI to persuade Cromitie to participate in the plan "outrageous" conduct in violation of the Due Process Clause (for example, outrageous as described in Chapter 1's discussion of the *Rochin v. California* case)?

Philosophical question: Was the FBI justified in the extensive use of deception and dishonesty in the undercover operation considering that the under-cover scenario was constructed to catch terrorists?

4.2. Legal and Philosophical Analysis

Legal analysis: The doctrine of entrapment includes two tests in the United States: Under the *subjective test*—the predominant test based upon federal precedent (and thus the test under which this case was evaluated)—a person is entrapped when the government induces the person to commit a crime that the person is *not predisposed* to commit.[28] In other words, the government must show that the defendant would have committed the crime even if (in some possible world) the defendant had not been induced by the government. Under the *objective test*—embraced by the Model Penal Code and adopted in a minority of jurisdictions—a person is entrapped when the police use unreasonable tactics: "Methods of persuasion or inducement . . . [that] create a substantial risk that . . . an offense will be committed by persons other than those who are ready to commit it."[29] Accordingly, the subjective test is about what is in the mind of the defendant (a question of criminal law), and the objective test is about the reasonableness of the police's conduct (a question of criminal procedure).[30]

The court concluded that a reasonable jury could find—based on the facts presented—that Cromitie had a predisposition to inflict serious harm on the United States, even though the FBI provided him with the

---

[28] See Jacobson v. United States, 503 U.S. 540 (1992).

[29] American Law Institute, Model penal code: official draft and explanatory notes: complete text of model penal code as adopted at the 1962 annual meeting of the American Law Institute at Washington, D.C., May 24, 1962, § 2.13.

[30] In chapter 5 of *The Retrieval of Liberalism in Policing*, I argue that there are four problems with the subjective test (the metaphysical problem, the epistemological problems, the ethical problem, and the political problem), and that any theory of entrapment and sting operations must exist within

opportunity and the "pseudo" (fake) weapons to inflict the harm on specific targets. With respect to the claim that the FBI engaged in "outrageous" conduct, the court determined that—despite the vast number of different tactics used by the FBI against Cromitie—the FBI's persistence was justified considering that Cromitie seemed to be ready and willing to commit terrorist acts. Moreover, the court did not find any coercion, duress, or physical deprivation used on Cromitie by the FBI. The court thus concluded that the techniques Hussain used to persuade Cromitie to participate in the FBI-devised plan were not "outrageous" and did not violate the Due Process Clause.

Cromitie (and the other defendants) were sentenced to twenty-five years in federal prison. It is worth noting that HBO subsequently produced a documentary about the case, *The Newburgh Sting*, which made extensive use of the FBI's surveillance video. The film suggests that the FBI's conduct constitutes a clear case of entrapment because the terrorist attack plans and (fake) materials were all supplied by the FBI's informant (Hussain), who coaxed the defendants into participating (including by offering Cromitie $250,000). A prominent review of the film in *The New York Times* concluded with this:

> [P]erhaps perversely, it's hard not to come away without some degree of admiration for Mr. Hussain, seen and heard only in the grainy videos shot in his car and living room. He puts on a superior performance over a long period of time and lies with breathtaking ease and quickness. If there were Oscars for informants, he'd be on the red carpet every year.[31]

If this assessment is even modestly accurate, it is difficult to see how men such as Cromitie stood much of a chance against a government willing to spare no expense in making its lies believable and providing Cromitie with unlimited opportunity to make bad choices. So much for the law; let's turn to philosophy.

Philosophical analysis: As with the *Thompsons v. Clark* case, reconciling the *Cromitie* case with the goal of justice is more difficult than it first appears.

---

the broader constraints upon the police's power to break the law (which would be more consistent with an objective-style test).

[31] Mike Hale, "Revisiting the Facts, after the Convictions," *The New York Times*, July 20, 2014.

On one hand, it is clear that the FBI was willing to move heaven and earth to construct deceptive, artificial scenarios that induce and ensnare persons in criminality. On the other hand, it is also clear that—once the FBI trap was set—Cromitie expressed a willingness to follow through with plans to harm the United States in deadly terrorist attacks (had the weapons been real). We must contend with the value of *security* as it relates to potential victims of terrorist attacks—*and* as it relates to persons who may be targeted by the government in deceptive undercover operations.

Considering that this section is focused on philosophical analysis, let's try not to get bogged down in doctrinal questions regarding the law of entrapment—which I have written about elsewhere.[32] Instead, let's begin with a very basic conception of liberty, specifically, negative liberty: the idea (especially prominent in liberal societies) of being free from interference by other people and entities, including the state and agents of the state.[33] This conception of liberty connects with our discussion of good faith policing in the first part of the book—the commitment to cooperative relations, which entail an honest disposition that precludes fraudulent interactions that injure rights and interests. Given such commitments, it is plausible to think one has a right to be free from dishonest, deceptive, fraudulent interference from the police (and the police have a correlative duty to respect that right).

There was a clear departure from (and breakdown of) these normative commitments in the *Cromitie* case. Recall that the FBI took *preemptive* deceptive action by tasking an informant (Hussain) with identifying "disaffected Muslims who might be harboring terrorist designs on the United States." Hussain thus began presenting himself (falsely) as a wealthy businessman with knowledge of Islam, befriending Cromitie through this cover story. We should thus ask whether the FBI was justified—at this stage in the case—in defecting from cooperative relations and taking preemptive action to deceive Cromitie and others. Under the prerogative power test, the FBI's actions likely satisfy the *purpose* and *prudential* constraints, given the goal of stopping terrorist attacks on the United States in a timely manner. However,

---

[32] Hunt, *The Retrieval of Liberalism in Policing*, chapter 5. See also the illuminating account of entrapment by Daniel J. Hill, Stephen K. McLeod, and Attila Tanyi, "The Concept of Entrapment," *Criminal Law and Philosophy* 12 (2018): 539–554.

[33] See, e.g., Isaiah Berlin, *Liberty* (Oxford: Oxford University Press, 2002).

there is deep tension between the FBI's actions and the *personhood* and *emergency* constraints of the test.

With respect to the personhood constraint, it is plausible to think that the FBI's relentless targeting of Cromitie undermined his agency and failed to treat him as a moral agent. We might describe the FBI's actions in terms of a deviation from what John Rawls called the "principle of responsibility," a principle that is inextricably intertwined with liberty.[34] Roughly, the principle of responsibility is based upon the idea that a just political system should give one a fair opportunity to account for penal sanctions, address one as a rational person, and give appropriate weight to one's liberty. The principle thus has natural overlap with liberal conceptions of personhood. However, the FBI's extensive use of dishonesty and deception against Cromitie would seem to treat him as incapable of responsible action: It justifies the use of tactics to induce him to commit a crime because there is a presumption that he would commit the crime anyway (because he was "predisposed").[35] Arguably, then, one might say the FBI's actions do not reflect a conception of Cromitie as a moral agent with human dignity and the capacity for reciprocation.

With respect to the *emergency* constraint of the test, there is good reason to think that the FBI's actions did not meet the requirement because there was no evidence of an acute threat to life that could be averted only through the use of bad faith on par with fraud. Indeed, it took many months (and goading by the FBI's informant) to *construct* a scenario (with material resources provided by the FBI) in which Cromitie was willing to harm the United States. The "emergency" in this case was thus artificially constructed and did not meet the requirement of the test. Accordingly, the investigation should have never moved forward.

But for the sake of argument, let's at least consider the serious terrorist threats that Cromitie made *after* being ensnared by the FBI. How should we view the FBI's actions considering the significant societal value of security (in this case, being shielded by the state from deadly terrorist attacks)? This is a fair question, but it must be considered in the context of a background norm of limited political power and authority. In other words, persons have a right to be kept secure legitimately within the bounds of authority. This suggests a moral foundation for enforcement grounded in limitations on the

---

[34] John Rawls, *A Theory of Justice* (rev. ed. 1999), 212.
[35] See Hunt, *The Retrieval of Liberalism in Policing*, chapter 5.

ways that security may be pursued by the state (security from enforcers, in other words).

The Cromitie case is the epitome of this idea. In the years following the 9/11 terrorist attacks, many people (e.g., those who seemed "normal" or "unsuspicious") benefited from an enhanced sense of improved security (due to strict, new security measures and proactive investigation imposed by the state) at the expense of other people (e.g., those who dressed, looked, and worshipped differently from the "normals," and were thus disproportionality affected by the new security measures). This suggests a deep connection between security and legitimacy, namely, states act illegitimately when they recklessly impose measures that affect the safety and security of some groups but not others.[36]

Again, for police dishonesty on par with fraud to be a justified tactic for pursuing security, I assume that it should yield security equitably considering the commitments of liberal, democratic societies. It is questionable whether the FBI's pursuit of security met this standard in the *Cromitie* case:

- Were deception, dishonesty, and fraudulent dealings used unfairly in Cromitie's case (for example, were such tactics used based on considerations regarding religion, ethnicity, or wealth)?
- Was this case an instance of a more general use of dishonest tactics that fall disproportionately on some groups of people (e.g., based on religion, ethnicity, or wealth)?
- Putting aside questions of equity, is the use of dishonesty even effective in these sorts of cases? For instance, did the FBI's use of dishonesty and deception stop a *real* terrorist who posed a *real* threat outside of government manipulation?
- Do these types of deceptive law enforcement "fishing expeditions" in fact deter crime?

Perhaps there are social-scientific data or empirical methods that can help answer these questions.[37] Regardless, we will have to contend with questions

---

[36] Waldron, *Torture, Terror, and Trade-Offs*, 148; Luke William Hunt, "The Limits of Reallocative and Algorithmic Policing," *Criminal Justice Ethics* 41, no. 1 (2022).

[37] Again, the empirical data regarding the narrow topic of this book is often lacking, though we can at least look to the growing body of empirical work on proactive policing generally (which is often tied to tactics involving deception and dishonesty). See, for example, National Academies of Sciences, Engineering, and Medicine, *Proactive Policing: Effects on Crime and Communities* (Consensus Study Report) (Washington, DC: National Academies Press, 2018); *Police Innovation: Contrasting*

about the moral permissibility of such deception given competing priorities of liberty, the rule of law, authority, legitimacy, and personhood in liberal societies.

4.3. Other Examples and Applications

There are a great many examples of the police's use of deceptive sting and uncover operations to catch criminals. However, we can conclude this section by briefly returning to the ruse scenario with which this chapter opened. Would the ruse scenario at the beginning of the chapter be justified under the prerogative power test? As discussed, it very well may have been justified—if, say, the case involved an emergency that could not be averted without bad faith and fraud. So the important takeaway is that deceptive and dishonest sting and undercover operations are most certainly justified under the test when there is no other way to prevent death or serious bodily injuries. On the other hand, the pervasive, default use of such tactics by law enforcement in non-emergency situations conflicts with some of the most basic principles of political morality.

5. Case Study: Coercing Confessions

Over the course of a murder investigation, the Boston homicide unit (including detectives Harris and Murray) received information that several people (Selby, Edwards, Gunter, and McConnico) were at the victim's residence on the day the victim was shot and killed. Upon being arrested, Selby was read his Miranda rights and interrogated.

Selby stated that—on the day of the murder—Edwards called Selby and told him that he had been robbed. Edwards asked Selby to go with him to the victim's residence; both Selby and Edwards brought a gun. But Selby told the detectives that he and McConnico stayed on the victim's front porch while Edwards went inside the victim's residence. After hearing noise inside, Selby and McConnico ran to the car; Edwards exited the victim's residence and the group drove away.

After giving this statement, Detective Murray removed a photocopy of a handprint from a file. He then asked Selby: How could the police have your

Perspectives, ed. David Weisburd and Anthony A. Braga (Cambridge: Cambridge University Press, 2019).

print in the victim's house if you never entered the house? Unbeknownst to Selby, the handprint was not his. In fact, the handprint had nothing to do with the murder; it was simply a deceptive prop used by Detective Murray to facilitate his interrogation of Selby.

Murray's ploy worked, and Selby changed his story—stating that he had been in the "hallway" of the victim's house along with Edwards and McConnico. Selby now said that he, Edwards, and McConnico entered the house with guns drawn, an argument ensued, and, upon hearing shots fired, Selby and McConnico fled the house. When Detective Murray asked Selby to go over the facts again, he also asked whether there were "any reasons why we found your fingerprints on the shell casings inside the house?" Here again, the police had not found any such fingerprints. Selby stated that he had been playing with a nine-millimeter gun earlier but had not been armed with that particular gun when the shooting occurred.

Following a short break in the interrogation, Selby told the detective he wanted to clear up a mistake he made in his story. Selby then told the detective that he went to the victim's house armed with a nine-millimeter handgun to retrieve money and drugs; Edwards was also there with a nine-millimeter. The occupants of the house (including the victim) were in the kitchen, and the victim grabbed Selby's hand and his gun went off, firing two or three shots. Selby said he later learned that the victim had died.

5.1. Legal and Philosophical Questions

Legal question: Did the detectives' intentional use of false information (palm print and fingerprints) during the interrogation elicit incriminating responses from Selby in a way that made Selby's confession involuntary?

Philosophical question: Were the police justified in using fake evidence in a murder investigation to trick Selby into confessing?

5.2. Legal and Philosophical Analysis

Legal analysis: The key legal issue is whether Selby's incriminating statements were "voluntary" based on the totality of the circumstances. This is a difficult question because Selby changed his story and made incriminating statements shortly *after* the police lied to him about the evidence they had against him. The court interpreted "voluntary" to mean a product of a "rational intellect" and a "free will," which perhaps raises more questions than answers. In any case, the state has the burden of proving—beyond a reasonable doubt—that Selby's statements were made voluntarily. On what evidence did they rely?

Regarding Selby's claim that the deceptive use of "nonexistent incriminatory information" to elicit incriminating statements amounted to psychological coercion, the court simply reasoned that *misinformation alone* is not sufficient to show involuntariness. Beyond the use of lies and phony props (photocopy of prints) by police officers in an interrogation room, what more is needed? Selby was read his Miranda rights, and the court indicated that there was no evidence that Selby was incapacitated or incompetent during the interrogation. Presumably, then, the police may have a legal right to lie and use fake evidence as long as the suspect has been properly Mirandized, is not incompetent, and is not, say, high or drunk. This strikes me as a rather low bar.

Philosophical analysis: We will consider a few more examples in the next section, but I think we can safely say that it is relatively routine for the police to intentionally prompt confessions by fabricating evidence (as in the Selby case) or by misrepresenting the seriousness of a suspect's crime.[38] As noted above, for this sort of misrepresentation to violate a *legal* right, it must result in an *involuntary* confession.[39] But general bad faith by the police regarding evidence in the police's possession does not typically render a defendant's confession involuntary.[40] Even if these practices are legal, are they justified considering the assumptions about political morality we have been discussing?

It is instructive to compare these sorts of deceptive police tactics to the doctrine of "puffery" in commercial sales.[41] Although a business may not engage in fraudulent advertising (misrepresenting specific facts), businesses are free from liability when using advertising tactics that invoke (exaggerated)

---

[38] See, e.g., State v. Walker, 493 N.W.2d 329, 334 (Neb. 1992), holding that a defendant's confession was not invalidated because of the police's misrepresentation that consensual sex with a minor is not a crime; Conner v. McBride, 375 F.3d 643, 653 (7th Cir. 2004), denying relief to a defendant that confessed after police indicated that defendant's conduct amounted to manslaughter, not murder (discussed in the next section).

[39] See, e.g., Moran v. Burbine, 475 U.S. 412, 421 (1986).

[40] See, e.g., Fraizer v. Cupp, 394 U.S. 731, 739 (1969).

[41] See Shiffrin, *Speech Matters*, 188–191, for an illuminating discussion of this doctrine as it relates to institutions generally.

opinions about the quality of their product.[42] Accordingly, one might argue that if it is okay to advertise the "best vacuum cleaner in the universe" on television, then surely it is okay for the police to engage in a bit of puffery to achieve a justified law enforcement end. But the examples that have been discussed are less like puffery (telling a suspect, insincerely, "I don't think what you did is a big deal") and more like *fraud*—as when the police tell a suspect (falsely):

- "You should agree to be an informant because you're facing forty years," when the person is facing six years.
- "We have your DNA at the crime scene," when no such evidence exists.
- "What happened qualifies as manslaughter, not murder," when the homicide in question qualifies as murder as a matter of law.

For the sake of argument, suppose you still think these sorts of examples are closer to puffery. Even if that's the case, it is at least reasonable to think the police should generally refrain from such a disposition. To put it a bit glibly, state officials in liberal democracies should be more trustworthy than vacuum cleaner advertisements.

To be sure, there will always be exceptions such that a fraudulent DDD is justified—as we have discussed in the prior case studies and their relation to the prerogative power test. In the present case, I will just note briefly that—again—the deception and dishonesty used against Selby does not comply with the emergency constraint. Although it is no doubt a serious case (and there was no doubt strong evidence against Selby, independent of his confession), there is no emergency in which a DDD is necessary to prevent serious harm.

I do not want to sound alarmist, but the use of phony, fabricated evidence in an interrogation room is on the spectrum of tactics used by countries that rely on show trials in which authorities have already determined the guilt or innocence of the defendant. To be fair—in the case we have considered—the police likely have good intentions (seeking justice by obtaining a confession from the person they "know" to be the murderer), not merely publicity or self-interested professional advancement. But there is good evidence that the practice of manipulating people with false evidence can have disastrous results.

[42] *Restatement (Second) of Contracts*, § 168, § 168 cmts. B& c, § 169 (1981).

The "Central Park Five" case—discussed in the book's Introduction—is an infamous example. One of the teenagers was interrogated by the police about his involvement in the rape of a woman in a park. The teen says he didn't do it. The police say they know the teen is lying because they have fingerprints from the victim's pants—though no fingerprints exist. The teen confesses and is incarcerated for several years, but it is later discovered that the teen was not the rapist. There are indeed compelling reasons why states should not deviate from foundational commitments of political morality steeped in UPM.

5.3. Other Examples and Applications

We have focused mostly on fraudulent misrepresentations of fact (fake evidence, for example) by the police, but let us consider misrepresentation of law briefly. First, consider a scenario in which a man is arrested for killing three people after an argument occurred while drinking alcohol.[43] The man is subsequently arrested and interrogated by the police. During the interrogation, the police produce the state criminal codebook, which defines the elements of each type of homicide in the state (murder, manslaughter, and so on). The police show the suspect the codebook, and intentionally misrepresent the suspect's alleged conduct as meeting the elements of manslaughter only—not the more serious charge of murder. The suspect subsequently confesses to the crime and is charged and convicted of murder. On appeal, the court upholds the finding that such a confession is not unreasonable.

Now consider a scenario in which a fifteen-year-old girl tells her stepmother that she submitted to sexual contact with a thirty-two-year-old man.[44] The girl stated that the man had phoned her, picked her up in his car, and asked her to perform oral sex—which she did. The two then drove to a wooded area and had sexual intercourse; afterward, the man dropped off the girl near her father's house.

During an interview and interrogation with the police, the man initially denies any sexual contact with the girl. One of the officers then tells the man that if the sex was mutually agreed upon, it did not constitute sexual assault. The officer continues the interrogation, adding that it is not uncommon for such sexual contact to be agreed upon. The man eventually admits to having

---

[43] This scenario is based on Connor v. McBride 375 F.3d 643, 653 (7th Cir. 2004).
[44] This scenario is based on State v. Walker, 493 N.W.2d 329 (1992).

intercourse with the victim. However, in fact, the law in the relevant jurisdiction states that "any person who subjects another person to sexual pen-
etration and . . . the actor is nineteen years of age or older and the victim is
less than sixteen years of age is guilty of sexual assault in the first degree." The
man is thus convicted of first-degree sexual assault on a child.

In both these cases, one might think it is just to uphold these
misrepresentations of law based on the well-established principle of legal ignorance, which stands for the idea that ignorance or mistake of the law is no
excuse. The principle is based on the idea that we are responsible for knowing
our legal duties. One argument in favor of this principle is that there would
be lawlessness without the principle because people would claim ignorance
of the law all the time. Whatever you think about that argument, note the important distinction in the cases we have been discussing: The defendant (reasonably) relied on the police—whose job it is to enforce the law—to explain
the nature of the offenses in question.

Indeed, there is a reasonable reliance legal doctrine standing for the idea
that a person will be excused because of a mistake of law if the person reasonably relies on an official (but erroneous) statement of the law obtained from
a public official with responsibility for the interpretation, administration, or
enforcement of the law. Although the legal doctrine may not be perfectly apt
in the scenarios we have been considering (because, say, the police are relatively low-ranking state officials), the underlying principle is clearly relevant.
If you cannot trust the police to tell you what conduct is and is not a violation of a particular law, who can you trust? Given that police are tasked with
enforcing the law, it stands to reason that people are entitled to a good faith
account of the truth in these matters.[45] And given that the police are not held
to this standard—because, say, the confession is interpreted as "voluntary"
or a product of "free will"—it is not difficult to see why the police institution
suffers from a lack of trust.

6. Case Study: Convicting Citizens

We close this chapter with a brief case study illustrating the underlying motivation and rationale for police deception and dishonesty in almost all the

---

[45] Of course, there may be rare cases in which lying to one about the content of the law can be justified under the prerogative power test—such as an emergency situation in which there is an acute
threat to life.

cases we have examined: a means justified by the end, namely, securing a conviction.

Three men carjack Orhan Polat, a cabdriver in New York City, in 2015. The men forced Polat out of his vehicle at gunpoint and then stole his vehicle. The police show Polat photographs of men who fit the description of the carjackers, but he initially recognizes only one of the carjackers. Detective Michael Fodor, New York Police Department, later testifies in court about what happened next in the investigation. Fodor testifies that he prepared two photo lineups that included the additional two suspects, and that Polat identified the two suspects from the lineup. The two additional suspects were charged with the carjacking based primarily on these lineups.

Foder dated each photo lineup that was administered to Polat, noting the suspect's photo that was selected by Polat. However, lawyers discovered that some of the photos in the lineups did not even exist at the time Fodor testified that he administered the lineups; they were taken a month after Polat supposedly viewed the lineups. The lineups were fabrications.[46]

6.1. Legal and Philosophical Questions

Legal question: Did Detective Fodor engage in perjury and obstruction of an official proceeding, falsifying documentation relating to the purported identifications made by Polat in the carjacking case?

Philosophical question: Was Detective Fodor justified in lying and tampering with witness identifications to secure convictions against carjackers?

6.2. Legal and Philosophical Analysis

Legal analysis: Detective Fodor eventually pleaded guilty to perjury in connection with the false statements he made under oath during the criminal proceeding. He was sentenced in federal court to three months imprisonment. In announcing his sentence, the prosecutors and investigators

---

[46] Joseph Goldstein, "New York Detective Charged with Faking Lineup Results," *The New York Times*, February 27, 2018.

stated: "In choosing to lie, this defendant undermined fellow officers and rendered himself unfit to serve as a law enforcement officer."[47]

After they pleaded guilty to an unrelated crime, the carjacking charges were dropped against the two suspects who had been arrested based on the fabricated photo lineups.

Philosophical analysis: This case seems straightforward. After all, most people think that tampering with evidence—witness identification evidence, no less—and then lying about it under oath is pretty bad. And this behavior seems especially bad when it comes from within the police institution—an institution that is supposed to engender public trust. Briefly, I want to add two wrinkles to these intuitions.

First, it seems to me that there *are* cases in which police perjury would be justified—including for reasons that make such dishonesty justified under the prerogative power test. Imagine a case in which the boss of a mafia crime family is on trial for extortion and murder. An FBI agent is scheduled to give crucial testimony at 9:00 a.m. on the last day of the trial; the entire case hinges on the agent's testimony. The agent leaves his hotel at 8:00 a.m. to walk to the courthouse. On the way he is grabbed and pulled into a small, dark alley, restrained by three men. One of the men shows the agent a live video call on the man's phone. It is the agent's wife on the call, who says that she has been kidnapped and that she will be raped and killed if the agent does not give false testimony (to aid the crime boss on trial) on the witness stand at 9:00 a.m.

This scenario is probably not as farfetched as it might seem given what we know about the ruthless tactics of crime families. In any event, if the agent decides to perjure himself on the witness stand, such dishonesty seems clearly consistent with the public and prudential constraints of the prerogative power test inasmuch as the dishonesty is motivated by the timely prevention of a rape and murder (he has a personal connection in this instance, but all rapes and murders are crimes against the public), and his lie would not raise any issues regarding affronts to personhood. Moreover, given the compelling, real-time evidence, this scenario represents the rare case in which the agent's "testilying" would be consistent with the emergency constraint of the prerogative power rest. So the justification for the dishonesty in this

---

[47] "Former NYPD Detective Sentenced to Three Months' Imprisonment for Committing Perjury in a Federal Prosecution," Department of Justice, U.S. Attorney's Office, Eastern District of New York (Feb. 25, 2019), https://www.justice.gov/usao-edny/pr/former-nypd-detective-sentenced-three-months-imprisonment-committing-perjury-federal

case is not to get a conviction, but rather to address a dangerous emergency situation.

The broader point is that—as radical as it may seem to argue that good faith is a normative foundation for policing—our overall framework is flexible enough to justify dishonesty when it counts. There is no Kantian "murderer at the door" rigidity here.

There is one more wrinkle to consider that points in the other direction. In contrast to the mafia scenario, Detective Fodor's dishonesty is clearly inconsistent with the prerogative power test. His lies were not based on averting an emergency; they rather seemed to be a lazy, self-serving way to secure a conviction. But if that's the case, why are we (or the courts) okay with securing confessions with phony, fabricated evidence in other contexts? Recall the Selby case in the last section: In his interrogation of Selby for homicide, the detective shows Selby a handprint and asks: *How could the police have your print in the victim's house if you never entered the house?* The handprint was not Selby's and had nothing to do with the murder; it was a fake used by the detective to enhance his interrogation of Selby and secure a confession. Although there is a legal distinction, it is far from clear what the moral distinction is between the dishonesty and fabrication in the Selby case and that in the Fodor case.

6.3. Other Examples and Applications

Just a month before Fodor was charged, another NYPD detective was convicted of lying under oath in order to secure a conviction. A jury found that NYPD Detective Kevin Desormeau lied in court about observing a suspect deal drugs to two women on a street corner. Desormeau swore that he stopped and arrested the suspect on the sidewalk after observing the drug deal. However, security cameras told a different story. The videos showed that the suspect had been playing pool inside a restaurant at the time Desormeau said he observed the suspect selling drugs outside. It thus seemed impossible for Desormeau to witness the suspect selling drugs; instead, it appears that he simply decided to search the suspect based on a hunch, covering up the illegal search with a phony cover story so he could secure a conviction.[48]

---

[48] Joseph Goldstein and John Surico, "New York Detective Guilty of Lying About Drug Arrest," *The New York Times*, January 24, 2018. The detective's hunch turned out to be correct because the man was found with drugs on him.

I want to close this chapter with a few reactions to the Desormeau and Fodor cases: First, it was reported that officers from his old unit (the Queens gang squad) patted Desormeau on the back in support as Desormeau left the courtroom after his conviction; one of the officers supporting Desormeau called the case a "witch hunt."[49] Second, Foder's lawyer was emphatic that Fodor investigated the carjacking "in good faith." Presumably, this was based on the view that Fodor's dishonesty was motivated by the goal of securing a conviction—a means to an end, as it were. Third, the police commissioner, James P. O'Neill, said the people of New York "expect the highest levels of integrity and truthfulness from our police officers."[50]

Ironically, these three reactions bolster the underlying themes we have been examining in this book: We need to revisit our understanding of good faith as it relates to the police institution, as well as how that understanding affects our trust in the police and expectations regarding their truthfulness.

[49] Ibid.
[50] Goldstein, "New York Detective Charged with Faking Lineup Results."

Five Questions and Answers Explored in Chapter 4

1. **Q: Why do chapter 4's case studies focus on transparency when it doesn't seem that good faith even requires transparency? I mean, can I not negotiate the purchase of a car in good faith without being transparent about the highest price I'll pay?**

   A: In the same way good faith falls on a spectrum (good faith requires more than merely refraining from fraud, but it requires less than fiduciary loyalty), the justification of opacity falls on a spectrum: there will be some cases in which a person's opacity is closer to the fraudulent end of a transparency spectrum. Likewise, pursuing security through opaque policing can be closer to the fraudulent end of the transparency spectrum. (For what it's worth, I hope you get a great deal on your car.)

2. **Q: Fair enough, but how is all this related to democratic values?**

   A: It's implausible to think the public can reasonably trust that rights will be respected honestly if the state's pursuit of security is opaque (recall Chapter 2's discussion of Hobbes, Locke, and Shelby). On the other hand, it's also implausible to think the state can provide security (especially "national security") without opacity. Our analysis will thus seek a pragmatic compromise: transparency regarding things such as investigatory evidence (*substantive transparency*) is not always justified, but transparency regarding procedures and processes by which state institutions wield their power (*procedural transparency*) is much more likely to be justified given democratic goals of accountability, authority, and legitimacy.

3. **Q: Can you say a bit more? For example, what about the prerogative power test (PPT)?**

   A: Yes. Failures of transparency make it difficult for the public to evaluate institutional authority (and thus legitimacy). The PPT is well-suited to assess failures of procedural transparency, helping us determine whether instances of law enforcement opacity are consistent with governance by law that is free from bad faith that is on par with fraud.

4. Q: Chapter 4's case studies cover a wide range of topics—from the 2016 election and the COVID-19 pandemic to the overturning of *Roe v. Wade* and predictive policing. Why these particular case studies?

A: These cases illustrate how some of the most significant issues (historic and ongoing) of public concern are deeply connected to questions about honesty, transparency, and democracy.

5. Q: Honestly—and just between you and me—are you using your immense power as a university professor to spread radical propaganda and corrupt the minds of the next generation?

A: Is that a trick question?

4

Case Studies

Honesty, Transparency, and Democracy

In concrete problems of any gravity . . . publicity requires us to go beyond merely turning to our conscience or to imagined others for the
justification of our lies. This is especially true for deceptive *practices*,
as in government, where those who deceive occupy positions
of trust.

—Sissela Bok[1]

Publicity is justly commended as a remedy for social and industrial
diseases. Sunlight is said to be the best of disinfectants; electric light
the most efficient policeman.

—Louis D. Brandeis[2]

We must remember the fact which we have encountered several
times . . . that "democracy" as such is opposed to the "rule" of bureaucracy, in spite and perhaps because of its unavoidable yet unin-
tended promotion of bureaucratization. . . . For this reason, it must
also remain an open question whether the *power* of bureaucracy is
increasing in the modern states in which it is spreading.

—Max Weber[3]

Suppose a person has two career options: (1) accept a job offer and move to a
new state, or (2) stay put in their current job. Prior to receiving the job offer,
the person was quite excited about the prospect of moving and was almost
certain they would accept any offer received (including for reasons relating

---

[1] See Sissela Bok, *Lying: Moral Choice in Public and Private Life* (New York: Vintage, 1999) (1978).
[2] Louis D. Brandeis, *Other People's Money and How the Bankers Use It* (New York: Frederick
A. Stokes, 1914), 92.
[3] Max Weber, "The Power Position of the Bureaucracy," in *Economy and Society: An Outline of
Interpretative Sociology* (New York: Bedminster Press, 1968), 990–994.

Police Deception and Dishonesty. Luke William Hunt, Oxford University Press. © Oxford University Press 2024.
DOI: 10.1093/oso/9780197672167.003.0006

to proximity to family). However, when the person does receive the offer, they learn some peculiar (undesirable) things about the new job that gives them pause. These were idiosyncratic issues about the job that were impossible to know during the interviewing phase. Although torn, the person is *almost* certain that the new information means that they will turn down the job offer.

In many lines of work—including academia—it is at this point in which you notify your current employer of the new job offer. This gives your current employer an opportunity to make what is known as a retention offer: your current employer can try to entice you not to leave (by offering a raise or other benefits, for example). Following this standard practice, suppose the person in our example presents the new job offer to their current employer, with the understanding that their current employer has the opportunity to retain them by matching the offer the person received. As you might guess, the person does not inform their employer that they are having doubts about the new job.

My sense is that such a person is within their rights to negotiate in this way—in other words, in a way that is less than completely transparent about their intentions. I tend to think that such a lack of transparency is justified given the situation (though I am not certain about that). There is no question that the person was legally justified, and my sense is that—all things considered—it was not morally wrong to leverage the new job offer into a retention offer from the person's employer. Even if there had been some sense in which the person's lack of transparency was deceptive (had the person exaggerated their interest in the new job offer, for instance), then it would have arguably fallen on the justified end of a transparency spectrum (assuming that one has a right to negotiate strongly). Again, though, I'm not certain about that. What does seem plausible is that questions about the justification (or lack thereof) of opacity fall on this sort of a spectrum.

There are certainly cases in which a person's opacity is closer to the fraudulent end of a transparency spectrum. Consider a different case in which a potential job offer comes with the "understanding and expectation that the successful job applicant will remain in the job for at least one year," though the understanding and expectation are not legally binding. The hiring company's rationale is based on the significant relocation expenses (paid by the hiring company) associated with moving new employees across the country. Suppose a successful job candidate is opaque about their commitment to the company and quits after working at the company for three months (after the company spends $25,000 on the person's relocation). All along, the person had planned to merely use the company as a cost-effective way to move from one side of the country to another; the person's opacity was based on deception or dishonesty to gain an unjust advantage, injuring the company's material interests. If you don't like that example, we can flip it: The job offer comes with the understanding and expectation that employment will continue for at least one year, but the employee is fired (without cause) after three months (and after uprooting and moving across the country).

Pursuing *security* through *opaque policing* can also be closer to the *fraudulent* end of the transparency spectrum. Security is often conceived in terms of social utility. Under this conception, problems of security may be addressed by maximizing the satisfaction of the underlying social interests. For example, President Biden's Administration issued a 2021 intelligence report about the rising threat of far-right militias and white supremacists and the need to better fight homegrown extremism.[4] Shortly thereafter, Biden's Administration issued the *National Strategy for Countering Domestic Terrorism*.[5] These are serious documents regarding organizations with centralized structures that pose real security threats. At the same time, the report highlights the well-known, inherent tension between security and liberty.

The idea is to enhance security in part by gathering and disseminating more information, including "open-source information" such as domestic terrorism threat intelligence provided by non-government third parties. Importantly, the report adds that securing the nation from domestic terrorism must be done in a way that is "consistent with civil liberties and privacy protections."[6] In other words, individual rights must be respected in the pursuit of societal security. But there is another—often overlooked—issue on which we will focus: the relationship and balance between security on the one hand, and transparency and honesty on the other. We can frame the issue with two questions.

First, how can the public reasonably trust that individual rights will be respected honestly if the state's pursuit of security is not transparent? For example, if the state generally (and the police specifically) has vast discretion

---

[4] Office of the Director of National Intelligence, *Domestic Violent Extremism Poses Heightened Threat in 2021* (March 2021).

[5] United States National Security Council, *National Strategy for Countering Domestic Terrorism* (June 2021).

[6] Ibid.

to opaquely collect extremely large ("public" and "open-source") data sets regarding one's life and identity, then is such surveillance power consistent with the legal, political, and moral principles underpinning the rule of law?[7] Second, how is security (especially "national security") to be achieved *without* opacity?

To address these questions, we turn to case studies that are in tension with the prerogative power test (PPT). We will see that not all opacity is unjustified. It would certainly be odd to think that transparency regarding things such as investigatory evidence (what I call *substantive transparency*) is always justified. On the other hand, transparency regarding procedures and processes by which state institutions wield their power (what I call *procedural transparency*) is much more likely to be justified given democratic goals of accountability, authority, and legitimacy.

Ultimately, we will see that transparency is deeply connected to governance by rule of law principles. When law enforcement institutions act outside of their power they act fraudulently and without authority—and thus without legitimacy. Failing to take procedural transparency seriously makes it difficult for the public to hold law enforcement institutions accountable to a good faith commitment to the rule of law—and that is anathema to the democratic process itself.

1. A Preliminary Objection and Case Study: FISA Fiasco

It is difficult to overstate the strangeness of the 2016 US presidential election and its immediate aftermath. For starters, many powerful Republicans strongly opposed Donald Trump—a reality television star and businessperson with multiple corporate bankruptcies—becoming the Republican nominee for president. Indeed, wealthy Republicans funded a Washington research

---

[7] Of course, one might argue that state opacity regarding surveillance and related security objectives is not lying or deception on the part of state officials, but rather invasions of privacy about which the state fails to inform people. Thomas Carson's distinction between "negative" and "positive" honesty is instructive on this point: honesty in a negative sense ("having a strong principled disinclination to tell lies or deceive others") and honesty in the positive sense ("being candid, open, and willing to reveal information"). Carson argues that honesty in the former sense is a cardinal virtue in ordinary circumstances, but honesty in the latter sense is often not a virtue. Thomas L. Carson, *Lying and Deception—Theory and Practice* (Oxford: Oxford University Press, 2010), 257. I have no issue with Caron's position, which strikes me as quite plausible; instead, my goal is to carve out and focus on a narrower issue: cases in which a person's opacity is closer to the fraudulent (and hence dishonest) end of a transparency spectrum.

firm (Fusion GPS) to create a dossier documenting why Trump's personal and professional history would make him a poor nominee. In other words, Fusion GPS was hired by Republicans for "opposition research" on Trump.[8] As a private firm, Fusion GPS relied on information (or "intelligence") derived from public sources such as reporting by journalists, court documents, and so on—which is often referred to as "open source intelligence."

However, Republican interest in funding the dossier ended when it became clear that the Trump Train, as it were, could not be stopped. Trump would be selected as the Republican nominee for President of the United States. With respect to Fusion GPS, Trump's nomination simply meant that there was a new market for opposition research against Trump: the Democratic party and supporters of their nominee, Hilary Clinton. Fusion GPS thus continued its research against Trump, but now on behalf of Democrats.[9] This is when things get really weird.

As Clinton ramped up her campaign efforts, the Democratic National Committee (DNC) was hacked by Russian agents, who began posting stolen DNC documents online. Fusion GPS thus hired Christopher Steele—a former British spy with extensive experience in Russia—to assist with opposition research against Trump. Steele documented his work for GPS Fusion through December 2016—by which point Trump had won the election and GPS Fusion was no longer being paid for their work. These documents became known as the "Steele Dossier," and supposedly documented Russia's efforts to influence Trump—as well as contacts between Trump's presidential campaign team and Russian officials regarding the DNC cyber hack.[10] Although much of the information in the dossier was difficult to confirm (or simply seemed mistaken), it was read and used by the FBI (which had prior relations with Steele) and British intelligence agencies who were interested in Trump's connections to Russia.

Parallel to these events, former FBI Director (and my former boss) Robert Mueller was tapped (in 2017) as Special Counsel to investigate Russian interference in the 2016 election, along with obstruction of justice and connections between Trump and his associates and Russian officials. Mueller's investigation resulted in the federal criminal indictment of 34 people (and three Russian organizations), including George Papadopoulos

---

[8] Scott Shane, Nicholas Confessore, and Matthew Rosenberg, "How a Sensational, Unverified Dossier Became a Crisis for Donald Trump, *The New York Times*, January 11, 2017.
[9] Ibid.
[10] Ibid.

(a Trump campaign foreign policy advisor), Paul Manafort (Trump's campaign chairman), Rick Gates (Trump's deputy campaign chairman), Michael Flynn (Trump's National Security Advisor), Michael Cohen (Trump's personal lawyer), and Roger Stone (Trump's political advisor), and numerous Russian nationals.

There is broad agreement that Mueller's investigation was immensely valuable, as it uncovered the extent to which Russia sought to manipulate the democratic processes of the United States. The investigation also uncovered vast criminality within Trump's inner circle. However, Mueller's report concluded that there was no evidence of a criminal conspiracy between Russian officials and Trump and his associates (including those noted in this chapter, who were charged with other crimes)—nor did the report reach a clear conclusion about the possibility that Trump obstructed justice.[11]

For our purposes, the pressing issue is how the FBI's investigation of Russian election interference went off the rails. To be clear, the goal of the investigation was justified inasmuch as we value *security*—specifically, security in our elections and democratic processes. On the other hand, some of the FBI's tactics raise serious questions about whether the end (security) justified the means. Indeed, government audits revealed numerous problems regarding the FBI's investigation of Trump's associates and their connections to Russian officials—as well as a pattern of abuses in national security investigations generally (beyond the Russia-Trump investigation).

These abuses largely related to the FBI's opaque use of the Foreign Intelligence Surveillance Act (FISA), which outlines the government's power to surveil persons and collect foreign intelligence between foreign powers (such as Russia) and agents of foreign powers (such as Russian officials who are in contact with US citizens) suspected of espionage or terrorism. To put it very simply, FBI agents document evidence from their investigation of persons affiliated with foreign powers, and specially assigned judges ("the FISA Court") decide whether the FBI may search and surveil (including wiretapping) the persons in question. This is of course all conducted outside of public view.

A notorious example was the FBI's request to conduct FISA surveillance on one of Trump's associates, Carter Page, who was known to have contacts in Russia. The FBI's FISA application relied in part on information provided

---

[11] Mark Mazzetti and Katie Benner, "Mueller Finds No Trump-Russia Conspiracy, but Stops Short of Exonerating President on Obstruction," *The New York Times*, March 24, 2019.

by Steele and the dossier he compiled on Trump, though the FBI failed to follow policy guidelines regarding the documentation of Steele's creditability and background. For example, the FBI failed to note that some of Steele's sources disagreed with how Steele characterized the information they provided to Steele.[12]

It thus seemed that FBI agents circumvented the rules by cherry-picking evidence regarding their investigation of Page. This included omitting important details about Page, such as the fact that he had been providing information to the Central Intelligence Agency (CIA) regarding his Russian contacts (not to mention that an FBI lawyer doctored an email regarding Page's CIA connection). However, the more significant revelation regarding the audit of the FBI was that the misconduct was not limited to the Page case. Ron Wyden, Democratic Senator for Oregon, put it this way: "The inspector general's findings of widespread abuses indicate that Carter Page was not singled out. Congress should write reforms into black-letter law to ensure that every American's rights are protected, not just friends of the president."[13] Here are the takeaways from this case study: (1) The Carter Page case was not a one-off incident for the FBI, and (2) the FBI's tactics were neither transparent nor honest. This is what happens when—as Brandeis put it in the epigraph—states lack the disinfectant of sunlight.

1.1. Objection: Law Enforcement Shouldn't be Transparent in Matters of National Security

Perhaps it seems obvious that law enforcement agencies should not be transparent in matters of national security (especially matters involving FISA investigations) because transparency would undermine sensitive investigations (and thus security).[14] This perspective returns us to the

---

[12] Charlie Savage, Adam Goldman, and Katie Benner, "Report on F.B.I. Russia Inquiry Finds Serious Errors but Debunks Anti-Trump Plot," *The New York Times*, December 9, 2019; Charlie Savage, "Problems in F.B.I. Wiretap Applications Go Beyond Trump Aide Surveillance, Review Finds," *The New York Times*, March 31, 2020.

[13] Ibid.

[14] Some scholars and practitioners argue, for example, that "the ethical principles applied to the work of intelligence agencies ought also to apply to law enforcement intelligence activities while accepting that the details of authorization procedures and oversight may differ." David Omand and Mark Phythian, *Principled Spying—The Ethics of Secret Intelligence* (Washington, DC: Georgetown University Press, 2018), 77. This raises an important and subtle point considering the discussion of social contract theory in Chapters 1 and 2, namely: It is plausible to think the moral principles governing intelligence agencies (such as the CIA) are different from those governing the police

question of balancing security with other values. But let's begin with a more basic question underlying the objection to transparency: Is transparency even a good thing in the first place? It might be surprising to hear that some people don't think so, including several prominent philosophers.

Philosopher (and crossbench member of the House of Lords) Onora O'Neill suggests that honesty and trust are often in direct opposition with transparency. This might sound odd, but she provides some good reasons to support the view. For instance, consider how transparency might encourage a person to increase their deception and dishonesty (and thus decrease their trustworthiness). If I am, say, a police chief, and I know that everything I say or write about policing will be available to the public, then I will be tempted to "massage" the truth. In private—among colleagues working to solve problems—I will likely feel pressured to cut to the chase. On the other hand, I may feel significant pressure to overstate (or understate) controversial points regarding data on the police's successes and failures when my statements are available for public consumption. Or I may simply be vague because I feel the information is sensitive and will not be received by the public with the appropriate context and nuance. In short, when I am required to be transparent, I may be more motivated to rely on "half-truths" and "political correctness" (or what may more accurately be described as deception and dishonesty).[15]

Philosopher C. Thi Nguyen builds upon O'Neill's work, arguing against *public transparency*, or "transparency to the public over expert domains."[16] Nguyen compellingly defends two positions: (1) transparency forces experts to explain their expert reasoning (which is often inaccessible to nonexperts)

---

institution inasmuch as the former operates internationally (and thus does not have the same sort of obligations derived from social contract theory) and the latter operates domestically. Agencies such as the FBI are hybrid in that they operate domestically in both criminal and national security cases, but their intelligence mission means that they also engage with foreign targets connected to the United States. The Carter Page FISA case is a good example because Page is a US citizen who was the subject of an international investigation involving foreign powers. There is no neat conclusion to these issues, though we will try to make headway by focusing on the distinction between justified substantive opacity and unjustified procedural opacity (keeping in mind cases in which procedural opacity may be justified under the prerogative power test). See Cécile Fabre, *Spying through a Glass Darkley: The Ethics of Espionage and Counter-Intelligence* (Oxford: Oxford University Press, 2022), for an illuminating study of morally permissive and morally obligatory uses of deception in national security settings.

[15] Onora O'Neill, *A Question of Trust: The BBC Reith Lectures 2002* (Cambridge: Cambridge University Press, 2002).
[16] C. Thi Nguyen, "Transparency is Surveillance," *Philosophy and Phenomenological Research* (2021): 1.

to nonexperts, which motivates experts to act only in ways that can be justified publicly, and (2) practical deliberation is often based on "intimate" reasons that are difficult to explain to those without the requisite background, and thus transparency pressures people to abandon important, intimate reasons derived from their unique backgrounds. This leads Nguyen to construe transparency as a type of *surveillance*. In other words, transparency might have benefits (such as bringing corruption to light, which is vital to achieve trust), but it also undermines "expert skill, sensitivity, and subtle shared understandings."[17] The upshot is an inherent tension between trust and transparency.

O'Neill's argument against transparency—and Nguyen's incisive development of the argument—are compelling. And a moment's reflection reveals (against our first, surprised reaction), that the arguments against transparency are quite intuitive. In my example about the police chief, the chief may not want to be dishonest with the public, but she is compelled to deception because it would be difficult (or impossible) to explain some components of policing to a non-expert public (a good example—discussed later in the chapter—might involve the complexities of algorithmic policing tactics such as "predictive policing"). Another law enforcement (and national security) example is the ridiculously complex FISA case mentioned in this chapter. Given the difficulty of transparency in such cases, law enforcement agencies may unnecessarily reduce or abandon (presumably good) policing tactics because it is impossible to justify their complexities to the public broadly.

But perhaps this is all beside the point. Indeed, there are many concrete political contexts in which we do not even seem to mind a lack of transparency. Consider voting. Most people seem comfortable with *secret voting* in democracies. Indeed, when a citizen votes in the United States, there are significant efforts to hide and conceal the person's vote: Election officials ask the voter to walk into an individual voting booth so that no one can see how the vote is cast.[18] We see very few objections to this sort of democratic opacity.

---

[17] Ibid.

[18] Defenders of secret voting include Jeremy Bentham, along with recent advocates such as Bernard Manin, "Why Open Voting in General Elections is Undesirable," in *Secrecy and Publicity in Votes and Debates*, edited by Jon Elster, 209–214 (Cambridge: Cambridge University Press, 2015); and James Johnson and Susan Orr, *Should Secret Voting Be Mandatory?* (Cambridge: Polity Press, 2020). Of course, some scholars have advocated for public voting in elections: John Stuart Mill defended open voting, and more recent defenders include Eric Beerbohm, *In Our Name: The Ethics of Democracy* (Princeton, NJ: Princeton University Press, 2012).

On the other hand, what about the votes cast by our *representatives*—should those votes be secret or transparent? I currently live in the state of Alabama, which is (somewhat embarrassingly) represented by a senator whose central qualification is coaching football. Fortunately, we have access to voting records. This is important because I (and other citizens) need to know how elected officials vote so that we can (try) to hold him account-able.[19] It is not adequate to focus (blindly) on the consequences of our representatives' votes; instead, many people want to know that their repre-sentatives' votes are improving their lives (or not) for the right reasons.

For example, suppose I live in a state in which my representative casts se-cret votes for legislation. And suppose my life improves under this opaque system: I make more money and my state has fewer threats to security. However, I may not want more money and more security at all costs. I may be willing to make less money if it means that social programs receive more state funding. I may be willing to be less secure if it means that peoples' rights are being protected by the police. Accordingly, I want to know how my rep-resentative voted with respect to legislation regarding taxes and security, not simply whether I am more secure and have more money.

The underlying idea is likewise relevant to state *executives* (and execu-tive institutions, such as the law enforcement institution). Recall President Obama's memorandum to the heads of executive departments and agencies on his first day in office, titled "Transparency and Open Government." The memorandum described the Administration's goal "to ensure the public trust and establish a system of transparency, participation, and collabora-tion," which "will strengthen our democracy."[20] In short, many people do not merely want to see good results from their government; they want to be in-volved and they want to know the means by which consequences (whether good or bad) were achieved. And we cannot know these things without transparency.

The broader point is that arguments against transparency are really only arguments against *too much* transparency—not that transparency itself is

---

[19] Philosophers such as Brian Kogelmann push back against this view, arguing that our legislative representatives should vote by secret ballot. Brian Kogelmann, *Secret Government—The Pathologies of Publicity* (Cambridge: Cambridge University Press, 2022), ch. 2. Kogelmann also argues that delib-eration among our legislative representatives should be done secretly—assuming that such delibera-tion is structured properly within our legislative institutions. Ibid., ch. 3.

[20] The White House, *Transparency and Open Government: Memorandum for the Heads of Executive Departments and Agencies* (January 21, 2009), https://obamawhitehouse.archives.gov/the-press-off ice/transparency-and-open-government.

inherently bad. Indeed, Nguyen states that "we also need transparency, pre-cisely because we often have good reason to distrust."[21] So even some of the most compelling critics of transparency readily acknowledge the underlying value and need for transparency.

With respect to policing specifically, many people think (reasonably) that the police institution cannot be trusted given its history of disrespecting rights, denigrating personhood and human dignity through brutality, widespread use of deception and dishonesty, and reflexive defense and cover up of bad (often illegal) police behavior. So it might just be the case that—considering what we have examined in this book so far—the police institution is in unique need of enhanced transparency. And this might mean that the burden of addressing O'Neill and Nguyen's worries (e.g., that requirements of transparency will sometimes increase deception) should be shifted to the police institution: *They have a duty to accept the burden of being both transparent and honest with the public.*

In a similar way, it is not clear that Nguyen's worry about transparency being a form of surveillance is problematic—at least in the context of the po-lice institution. The extent to which the police have the ability to surveil (liter-ally) the public is mindboggling, as we will discuss in the case studies relating to the third-party doctrine. It stands to reason, then, that the surveilling gaze should more equitably be flipped toward the police.[22] Nevertheless, Nguyen worries

that the demand for public transparency is a kind of institutional assholery, which fails to respect the incredibly rich ways in which dif-ferent communities and groups of experts can see the world in partic-ular and sensitive ways. It fails to respect the fact that other people might speak and think in justificatory language deeply distant from the general public's.[23]

---

[21] Ibid., 2.

[22] Although Nguyen's article does not focus on policing, he makes a similar point in the con-text of a similar domain: sentencing decisions by judges. For example, the COMPAS information system generates risk profiles for criminal defendants by combining a wide range of information about the defendant's social and criminal history. The risk profile can be used by judges to make sentencing determinations. As Nguyen notes, "transparency is extremely important in cases like this [because] . . . the cost of failure is so high, that we can justify the burdens of increased vigilance [and] . . . such projects have complex relationships to the public good." Ibid., 16. I have addressed COMPAS in "The Limits of Reallocative and Algorithmic Policing, *Criminal Justice Ethics* 41, no. 1 2022).

[23] Nguyen, "Transparency is Surveillance," 26.

No one wants to be guilty of assholery, so let's see if we can provide a fuller defense of transparency in the context of police deception and dishonesty.

1.2. Reconciling Security, Transparency, and Honesty

Recall the job offer examples at the beginning of the chapter: there are some cases in which a lack of transparency seems justified (assuming one has a right to negotiate strongly), while other cases (as when one misrepresents one's interest and commitment in a job for financial gain that injures the material interests of another party) fall closer on the fraud end of the transparency spectrum. The latter sort of opacity can likewise injure rights and interests in the domain of policing.

In the Carter Page case, the FBI agents applying to the FISA court for surveillance authority failed to follow policy guidelines regarding the evidence on which their application relied. Strictly speaking, then, they did not break the law, but rather failed to fulfill their administrative (policy) requirements. The failure took the form of an *omission*: They failed to disclose information that might cut against their surveillance application.[24] Of course, these sorts of investigations are highly complex and involve myriad pieces of information, which sometimes means that judgment calls must be made about what to include in applications to the court. However, in this case, it appears that the FBI's opacity and lack of transparency was *material*—they failed to disclose information that would have aided the FISA court's decision. This sort of opacity harms the interests of not only the subject of the investigation (Page), but also the democratic process itself: The FBI's opacity allowed it to circumvent regulations to (illegitimately) increase its investigatory power.

What is the philosophical foundation for this position? At the broadest level, reciprocal societies rely upon the sharing of perspectives to promote epistemic goods among its members. It is thus no mere platitude to say that transparency is a fundamental facet of democratic morality inasmuch as it facilitates the flow of rights and duties between citizenry and state. Transparency is required of state institutions if people are going to cooperate

---

[24] As Carson rightly notes, not all cases of omission (or withholding information) constitute deception. Thomas L. Carson, "Lying, Deception, and Related Concepts: A Conceptual Map for Ethics," in *From Lying to Perjury*, ed. Laurence R. Horn (Berlin: De Gruyter Mouton, 2022), 15–40. I will mostly avoid this distinction, arguing more broadly that police deception and dishonesty (including deception and dishonesty by omission) are unjustified when they are on par with fraud.

in the pursuit of epistemic goals and goods that cannot not be otherwise obtained.

As we saw in Chapter 1's discussion of universalistic positive morality (UPM)—and in Chapter 2's discussion of Hobbes and Locke—it is difficult (or impossible) for individuals to privately provide for their security in a way that respects the rights of others; on the other hand, state law enforcement agencies have the potential to accomplish such goals effectively and efficiently. Transparency is necessary to ensure that those goals are being achieved in a justified and legitimate way (beyond considerations of efficacy and efficiency). This means that transparency is not merely a way to *constrain* government power—for example, protecting rights of privacy and bodily integrity by limiting police surveillance.

Transparency is also a trait that *empowers* persons (who would otherwise be powerless) to secure their rights from the state: it *empowers* persons to hold the state accountable by ensuring that the state acts with *public authority* (for the whole society) and thus with *legitimacy*.[25] We thus return to the idea that rule of law, democratic societies are not merely about good results (security, wealth, and so on); they are also about ensuring that the good results are achieved legitimately and on behalf of the whole society (rather than select, privileged groups). Political societies interested in legitimate public deliberation must continually maintain the trait of transparency.

As I have alluded, complete transparency is not always required, especially when complete transparency would *fail* to promote public epistemic goods such as knowledge and true belief for the whole society. When the FBI keeps the *substance* of FISA investigations secret from the public, such secrecy ultimately *promotes* the public's epistemic goods. Consider how the public ultimately learned (as a result of secret investigations) that Russian agents tried to manipulate the democratic processes in the United States during the 2016 election. Accordingly, we can say that the FBI and other law enforcement agencies are justified in opacity regarding the substance of their investigations into national security threats such as espionage (which often includes FISA material).

The same is true for more traditional criminal investigations. It may be beneficial for the police to publicize information regarding a violent bank robbery or some other criminal investigation.[26] But sometimes it is best to

---

[25] Jeremy Waldron, *Political Political Theory* (Cambridge: Harvard University Press, 2016), ch. 2.

[26] Consider the Unabomber case, in which the FBI recommended that newspapers publicize what was known about the Unabomber—including a 35,000-word screed he wrote. The Unabomber's brother subsequently recognized the published facts and turned his brother in.

hold investigatory details close to the chest; likewise, there is an obvious need for secrecy in grand jury proceedings (as with FISA proceedings) given their function and the goal of protecting the privacy and reputations of targets and witnesses.[27] In short, *substantive transparency* (regarding things such as investigatory evidence) may not always be justified—at least in the case of law enforcement institutions.[28] On the other hand, it is plausible to think that *procedural transparency* (the procedures and processes by which state institutions wield their power) is almost always required given democratic goals of accountability.

There is no easy, bright-line rule that will neatly resolve all our questions regarding the balance between state opacity and procedural transparency. There will always be exceptions and counterexamples given the messiness of policing in the existing world. However, the PPT can provide a helpful framework as we try to make sense of the underlying tension between security and transparency. The basic idea is that the prerogative power test—with its emphasis on the purpose, prudential, personhood, and emergency constraints—can help us determine when state institutions such as the police may engage in opacity while also maintaining a commitment to the rule of law and public accountability.

We thus need to consider whether cases of police opacity are consistent with the timely pursuit of public goods in ways that respect personhood and prevent emergencies. We now turn to even trickier case studies, with the goal of assuaging the tension between state opacity and principles of democratic governance and public trust.

2. Case Study: Pandemic Privacy and Third-Party Opacity

The COVID-19 pandemic prompted an unprecedented push for scientific innovation. The pursuit of new treatments and vaccines was the most obvious area in which science and technology converged. There was also a worldwide

---

[27] See, e.g., Douglas Oil Co. of Cal. v. Petrol Stops Northwest, 441 US 211 (1979).

[28] Note that substantive transparency *is* justified in the case of, say, the voting record of legislative representatives; we want to know the substance of their votes, not just the procedures governing the voting process. This point reflects the differences between the legislative process (making law) and the executive process (enforcing law). Knowing how law is made (including the substance of a representative's vote) does not harm the legislative process in the same way knowing the substance of an investigation harms the executive (law enforcement) process. Moreover, it is plausible to think that greater transparency in the former (law) will result in great trust in the latter (law enforcement).

push to develop technological applications that identify and track people who come into contact with the coronavirus. *The MIT Technology Review* created a database documenting these tracking applications, noting that some contact tracing systems "are lightweight and temporary, while others are pervasive and invasive."[29] For example, "China's system . . . sucks up data including citizens' identity, location, and even online payment history so that local police can watch for those who break quarantine rules."[30] Despite the obvious privacy concerns, one might argue that a global health crisis justifies invasive carrier tracking. Besides, the tracking applications presumably are not used for criminal purposes (in most places, at least), but rather to protect the general health and welfare of the populace.

On the other hand, if we consider the underlying issues more broadly, there are a variety of questions that must be answered when evaluating the justification of a state's use of technology as it relates to transparency and law enforcement. For instance, how do corporations and governments obtain the vast troves of data allowing them to track millions of people? Relatedly, is it possible that similar data—derived through similar means—might sometimes be used by governments in criminal investigations? Is there adequate transparency in the relevant processes to ensure that people can hold the state accountable for how and when it uses such data?

A coronavirus tracking application is but one of many recent innovations illustrating the emerging connections between technology, transparency, and law enforcement. And as we will see, pandemics are not the only healthcare issues raised by such applications—especially considering the Supreme Court's decision overturning *Roe v. Wade* and ruling that the Constitution does confer a right to women to have an abortion.[31]

2.1. Legal and Philosophical Questions

Legal question: On what basis do law enforcement and intelligence agencies (such as the FBI) have the authority to opaquely obtain personal information about a person without a search warrant (or a FISA court order)?

---

[29] Patrick Howell O'Neill, Tate Ryan-Mosley, and Bobbie Johnson, "A Flood of Coronavirus Apps Are Tracking Us. Now It's Time to Keep Track of Them," *MIT Technology Review*, May 7, 2020.
[30] Ibid.
[31] Dobbs v. Jackson Women's Health Organization, No. 19–1392, 597 U.S. ___ (2022).

Philosophical questions: First, to what extent is the state—particularly the police institution—justified in the opaque use of algorithms to analyze the vast trove of online data created by our reliance on routine, everyday technology (such as smart phone "apps")? Second, if a person consents to turn over personal information (by using a smart phone app, for example), then does the person's consent nullify any rights to transparency regarding how their information is used?

2.2. Legal Analysis

Martin Scorsese's film, *The Irishman*, is a fictionalized true crime story about the disappearance of labor union leader Jimmy Hoffa. Hoffa—who was involved with organized crime—went to prison for jury tampering in 1967. Some of the relevant evidence against him was secretly obtained by a government informant, who revealed several conversations with Hoffa about Hoffa's attempt to tamper with a jury. Hoffa had invited the informant to participate in the conversations, but later argued that the government's deceptive use of the informant violated his privacy rights.

The US Supreme Court disagreed, holding that the Fourth Amendment does not protect "a wrongdoer's misplaced belief that a person to whom he voluntarily confides his wrongdoing will not reveal it."[32] The Court's ruling helped establish what came to be known as the third-party doctrine: "a person has no legitimate expectation of privacy in information that he voluntarily turns over to third parties."[33]

The year after *Hoffa* was decided, the Court set forth—in the landmark case, *Katz v. United States* (1967)—a new framework for evaluating the Fourth Amendment. The Fourth Amendment contains two central parts: the "reasonableness clause" ("right . . . to be secure . . . against unreasonable searches and seizures") and the "warrant clause," which lists specific requirements for the issuance of a valid warrant.[34] Generally speaking—notwithstanding the many exceptions—these two clauses conjoin to mean that a government search is reasonable when it is conducted pursuant to a valid warrant.

---

[32] Hoffa v. United States, 385 U.S. 293 (1966).
[33] Smith v. Maryland, 442 U.S. 735 (1979).
[34] U.S. Const. amend. IV.

The *Katz* case thus combined the two clauses to establish a *reasonable expectation of privacy* test. The test has been understood to include both a subjective and an objective component: an actual expectation of privacy by the subject (subjective component) that society recognizes as reasonable (objective component). Accordingly, if the two components are established, the police are required to obtain a warrant before engaging in the "search." Otherwise, the search would be unreasonable. If the components are not established, the police do not need a warrant because their activity does not constitute a "search." This standard has guided the contours of the third-party doctrine, which allows the police to use vast troves of intimate data about persons without transparency and thus without accountability.

Following the *Hoffa* and *Katz* cases, the US Supreme Court ruled on two major third-party doctrine cases in the 1970s. In *Miller v. United States* (1976), the Court ruled that it was permissible for ATF agents to simply subpoena (rather that obtain a search warrant) banks for a customer's financial records.[35] In other words, if a person voluntarily conveys information to a bank (in the same way Hoffa voluntarily conveyed information to an undercover informant), that information may be shared by the third party (bank and informant, respectively) with the government without a search warrant. Three years after *Miller*, the Court significantly expanded the third-party doctrine in *Smith v. Maryland* (1979), holding that the police can request (without a warrant) that a telephone company install a "pen register" (which records the telephone numbers dialed from a person's home) on a person's phone. Again, if you give your information to a phone company, you have lost your right to control and protect that information.

The US Supreme Court has only recently constrained the way police rely upon new technology to exploit the third-party doctrine, and these limited constraints raise more questions than answers.[36] In *Carpenter v. United States*, the Court held that it was not permissible for the FBI to rely on a simple court order (rather than a search warrant requiring probable cause) to access detailed information from (third-party) cell service providers about

---

[35] Miller v. United States

[36] One of the first cases signaling a (potential) new direction for the third-party doctrine was *United States v. Jones*, 565 U.S. 400 (2012), which laid the groundwork for *Carpenter v. United States*, 585 U.S. ____ (2018). The concurring opinions in Jones worried about "the appropriateness of entrusting to the Executive, in the absence of any oversight from a coordinate branch, a tool [such as GPS monitoring] so amenable to misuse, especially in light of the Fourth Amendment's goal to curb arbitrary exercises of police power and prevent 'a too permeating police surveillance.'" *United States v. Jones* (2012).

a person's physical location (cell-site location information, or "CSLI"). The Court stated that the FBI should have obtained a search warrant because the target had a "legitimate expectation of privacy in the record of his physical movements." This is a significant crack in the third-party doctrine's foundation. However, given that *Carpenter* is limited to historical cell-site records, the interesting normative question is how the third-party doctrine should evolve moving forward considering concerns regarding transparency and accountability.

2.3. Philosophical Analysis

Despite the emphasis on privacy in this legal analysis, a parallel issue is the use of discretionary authority under cloak of darkness. This issue is important in part because limited discretionary authority is one of the foundations of political societies committed to the rule of law. If one assumes that there is a background norm in such states regarding a right to legitimate authority (or to be free from the illegitimate coercion of political and legal institutions), then a correlative is the state's general moral duty to transparently govern within the parameters of the rule of law so that people can hold the state accountable.

Around-the-clock electronic monitoring of "public" (third-party) information is a dramatic change from the police's routine ability to follow someone's vehicle in public places (or stake out their home or place of business) for a limited time period; the former is inconsistent with a societal commitment to limited discretionary authority.[37] Moreover, considering that one typically does not know when a third-party discloses information to the government (or what the government does with that information), the third-party doctrine bolsters state opacity and weakens a state's accountability for the use of its surveillance discretion.

---

[37] Given the surveillance state in which we now live, there are a variety of difficult questions that are beyond the scope of this book. Consider how there are CCTV cameras on every corner in Times Square in New York City. Is it deceptive for the police to review these videos of people who did not realize they were being watched? My sense is that such surveillance is generally unjustified inasmuch as it defrauds people of a right to move freely in public without being under the constant gaze of the state. On the other hand, in some cases, such surveillance could perhaps be justified under the prerogative power test's emergency constrain given, say, an imminent threat of harm to the public (e.g., heightened terrorist, security threats to a particular area). On these points, consider Foucault's work on disciplinary institutions and the analogy to big data and constant surveillance by the state. Michel Foucault, *Discipline and Punish: the Birth of the Prison* (1975).

This case study foreshadows the need for clarity (including through legislation) regarding the limits of the third-party doctrine given the value of transparent governance and democratic oversight of political authority. The pressing point is to establish a justified law enforcement need (or "predication," as discussed in the next case study), especially when law enforcement agencies depart from commitments to procedural transparency.

2.4. Objections: The Third-Party Doctrine and Consenting to Opacity

If one has a right to legitimate institutions, it is a corelative of a state's general moral requirement to govern within the parameters of the rule of law. If that's the case, why might the third-party doctrine's opacity be problematic if the doctrine is based upon *consent*?

Recall that the third-party doctrine means—as stated in *Smith v. Maryland* (1979)—that "a person has no legitimate expectation of privacy in information that he voluntarily turns over to third parties." In other words, if a person consents to turn over information to a third party, then the person's consent nullifies one's privacy and transparency interests in the information.

The *Carpenter* case limited the third-party doctrine's applicability in the narrow context of CSLI, with the Court reasoning: "when Smith was decided in 1979, few could have imagined a society in which a phone goes wherever its owner goes, conveying to the wireless carrier not just dialed digits, but a detailed and comprehensive record of the person's movements." The Court thus held "that an individual maintains a legitimate expectation of privacy in the record of his physical movements as captured through CSLI." Despite this rationale, the Court expressly stated that the holding is "a narrow one" and declined to limit the third-party doctrine beyond the context of CSLI. The holding in *Carpenter* (2018) does not disturb "the application of *Smith* and *Miller*," or "call into question conventional surveillance techniques and tools, such as security cameras," or "business records that might incidentally reveal location information."

This narrowness is in many ways bizarre. For example, when a person consents to the terms of a Gmail email account, does that mean that the government should be able to compel Google (without a warrant) to provide it with all the person's email conversations without the person's knowledge? Or consider direct-to-consumer genetic testing services in which customers provide a saliva sample that is analyzed in a laboratory. Should the government be able to obtain one's DNA from such companies without a warrant or probable cause, and without the person's knowledge? In principle (though not in practice), the third-party doctrine answers these questions in the affirmative.[38] This means the public has very little knowledge of how the police use personal third-party information and thus very few ways to hold the police accountable for that use.

On the other hand, perhaps we *consent* to such opacity. Legal principles regarding consent (*Volenti non fit injuria*) are well-established: "To one who has consented no wrong is done."[39] In support of the third-party doctrine, then, one could say a person is responsible for any third-party disclosure given that the person consensually turned over the information in the first place.

However, not all "consent" is legally (or morally) binding. For instance, if a person utters the words "I consent" while being coerced, forced, or exploited (or speaking the words as part of a theatrical performance), then one would not describe the words as actual consent given that the words were not uttered freely or as a speech act.

In a similar way, if consent is obtained by fraud or by misleading a person through opacity, then there would be no actual (moral or legally binding) consent. Normative principles regarding consent thus illuminate one of the fundamental problems with the third-party doctrine: the doctrine treats flawed consent as morally and legally binding consent. Since the *Smith* case (1979), courts have taken the position that when one gives information to a third party one "assumes the risk" that it will be turned over to the police.

There is thus a direct link to the third-party doctrine and the normative principles of contract law. However, as the dissenting opinions note in *Carpenter* (2018), the assumption of the risk doctrine is typically relevant when one "expressly agrees to accept a risk of harm" or by "manifest[ing] . . . willingness to accept" that risk and thereby "take[s] his chances as to harm which may result from it." Accordingly, the assumption of the risk doctrine is not decisive in the context of third-party disclosures.

In short, there is a disconnect between, say, accepting a routine agreement with an electronic communications service provider (such as agreeing to

---

[38] See *Carpenter v. United States* (2018), in which Justice Gorsuch's dissenting opinion raises these examples under the third-party doctrine.

[39] Joel Feinberg, *Harm to Others* (Oxford: Oxford University Press, 1987).

provide information to a bank in order to open a bank account) and agreeing to accept any possible consequence regarding the government demanding that the bank turn over your information without your knowledge. The disconnect is based upon the nature of the consent provided to the service provider. Even if one understands that it is possible for the government to make some sort of third-party demand, consenting to provide information to an electronic service provider is markedly different from consenting to have that information secretly turned over to the government so the government can investigate you (without probable cause and a warrant).

The upshot is that the third-party doctrine opaquely promotes a state's blanket authority (broad authority to act lacking adequate oversight of specific actions), which is inconsistent with a state's general moral duty regarding governance by law. Even though the third-party doctrine is based upon one's consent (to disclose information), such consent is often inadequate and thus does not create a morally binding special obligation by the one who provides the "consent."

3. Case Study: Investigating "Anarchists" and "Abortionists"

As a former FBI agent, I have had the occasion to field questions such as this one: "Some of my friends say crazy political stuff on social media—if I interact with them online, is the FBI going to show up at my door and call me a terrorist?" Of course, the answer is "no" if that's all there is to it. The First Amendment protects political speech and one need not fear investigation (presumably) unless there is evidence suggesting criminal intent.

On the other hand, it is easy to see why one might ask this sort of question. In 2020, President Trump declared that the United States would designate ANTIFA (a group of far-left antifascism activists) as a terrorist organization.[40] Even though the federal government can only deem *foreign* entities terrorist organizations (there is no *domestic* terrorism law), such presidential declarations might make one think twice about bantering online with so-called ANTIFA "members."[41]

---

[40] Maggie Haberman and Charlie Savage, "Trump, Lacking Clear Authority, Says U.S. Will Declare Antifa a Terrorist Group," *The New York Times*, May 31, 2020.

[41] Strictly speaking, ANTIFA is not even an organization because it does not have formal structures, leaders, or membership roles; it is instead a nebulous movement of people with similar protest tactics and targets.

Having made the natural career transition from FBI agent to academic philosopher (there's the joke—again), I routinely find myself teaching courses on legal and political philosophy. One topic that I cover is *philosophical anarchism*, which stands for the proposition that all states are illegitimate. However, the illegitimacy of a state implies only that it has no right to command and that its citizens have no obligation to obey; in contrast to *political anarchism* (or the bomb-throwers), then, philosophical anarchism does not imply that the state's illegitimacy must be opposed and (if possible) eliminated.[42]

This topic leads to a rich discussion with my students of the distinction between a state's legitimacy and its justification. A philosophical anarchist might construe the United States as a good and beneficial state all things considered (or simply better than the alternatives). Accordingly, such an anarchist may think we have good reasons to obey the law of the United States. There may be both prudential reasons (e.g., punishment avoidance) and moral reasons (e.g., because US law often tracks "natural law").

Notwithstanding this sort of justification, the philosophical anarchist may find the United States illegitimate to the extent that it has no authority to command obedience—for instance, because one didn't consent to the state's authority. A simple example: My neighbor, a dentist, may be giving good and beneficial advice when she tells me to floss, but she has no authority to command me to floss and any attempt to compel me to floss would be illegitimate. I'll continue to floss because it's the right thing to do and it's good for me, not because of her command to floss.[43]

Now consider the recent US Supreme Court decision (*Dobbs v. Jackson Women's Health Organization*) overturning *Roe v. Wade*. States may now enact laws that make all abortion illegal, no matter the circumstances. The decision to enact such legislation might be based (in many states) on the position that all abortion is murder. Whatever one's views are on the matter, it goes without saying that abortion is both an important moral issue and

---

[42] See A. John Simmons, *Justification and Legitimacy* (Cambridge: Cambridge University Press, 2001).

[43] Of course, we could tweak this example to make it more difficult. Suppose the dentist is in fact *my* dentist and says: "Unless you start flossing and brushing more regularly, or taking the medication you've been prescribed, I'm afraid I'm not willing to treat you anymore." Does she have the authority to do that? Yes, she can refuse to treat me if I don't do what she says considering that I agreed to be her patient under her terms. The analogy to the state will eventually break down considering the state's various commitments, including constraints on power and the way it wields power (along with, arguably, a lack of authority given a lack of—for example—consent to authority).

an important legal, political, and medical issue. Because philosophical anarchists believe the state is illegitimate, they would say that one ought to consider the commands of the state regarding abortion bans (as with all commands of the state) and decide whether those commands have merit and whether one should comply with the commands. In other words, the philosophical anarchist decides whether to obey the law based upon some independent reason (prudential and/or moral reasons) other than *because it's the law*. Again, though, there is no goal to eliminate the state, whether violently or otherwise.

Nevertheless, consider the (plausible) future scenario of, say, law enforcement agencies using third-party data to secretly investigate *anarchist domestic terrorist professors promoting systematic murder by delegitimizing abortion law*.[44] Indeed, many people are already worried about the role that third-party fertility trackers and other apps (not to mention simple internet search histories and other digital records) could play in secret law enforcement investigations of violations of abortion law.[45] And there have already been unfounded presidential declarations regarding "radical-left anarchists,"[46] which might cause one to wonder whether harmless philosophy professors teaching philosophical anarchism might be lumped into that group, too. What legal and philosophical questions regarding transparency do these scenarios raise?

3.1. Legal and Philosophical Questions

Legal question: In what ways may law enforcement agencies opaquely investigate persons without predication (without establishing a basis for the investigation)?

---

[44] This is not exactly a hypothetical scenario. A group of professors, (including two philosophy professors), the Idaho Federation of Teachers, and the University of Idaho Faculty Federation, filed a lawsuit challenging a 2021 state law that prevents state funds from being used to "procure, counsel in favor, refer to or perform an abortion." The lawsuit argues that the breadth and vagueness of the law puts the faculty at risk of prosecution and imprisonment simply for teaching about abortion. See Nadine El-Bawab, "Idaho Professors Say They Change Syllabi, Self-Censor Abortion over Fears of Prosecution," *ABC News*, August 11, 2023.

[45] Cat Zakrzewski, Pranshu Verma, and Claire Parker, "Police Used Texts, Web Searches for Abortion to Prosecute Women," *The Washington Post*, July 3, 2022.

[46] Benjamin Swasey, "Trump Lays Blame For Clashes On 'Radical-Left' Anarchists," *NPR*, May 31, 2020.

Philosophical question: Do the police govern by rule of law principles when they use discretionary power to opaquely investigate persons without establishing a basis for the investigation?

3.2. Legal and Philosophical Analysis

Legal analysis: Consider the FBI's vast jurisdiction and authority to investigate criminal and national security matters. The FBI's operations are generally covered by the Domestic Investigations and Operations Guide (DIOG), which "applies to all investigative activities and intelligence collection activities conducted by the FBI within the United States" (DIOG, § 1.1). Given that the FBI is both an intelligence agency and a law enforcement agency within the Department of Justice, the DIOG has standardized the FBI's investigation policy in national security and criminal law cases.

The DIOG permits four types of investigations: (1) assessments, (2) preliminary investigations, (3) full investigations, and (4) enterprise investigations. I want to focus upon the most basic investigation: *assessments*. Note first that the other, more advanced types of investigations require significant predication (basis for the investigation). Preliminary Investigations are predicated based upon "'allegation or information' indicative of possible criminal activity or threats to the national security" (DIOG, § 6.1), while Full Investigations are predicated upon an "'articulable factual basis' of possible criminal or national threat activity" (DIOG, § 7.1). Enterprise Investigations are opened as Full Investigations, but with respect to "a group or organization that may be involved in the most serious criminal or national security threats to the public" (DIOG, § 8.1).

Remarkably, on the other hand, assessments require *no predication*. The DIOG simply prohibits assessments that would amount to unlawful, arbitrary, frivolous, and groundless investigations (DIOG, § 5.1). In other words, the FBI has the discretion to secretly investigate almost anything, and it does not need any particular factual predication to do so. Given that no predication (basis) is needed, there is no basis to hold the state accountable.

But it gets worse. The FBI is permitted to engage in a variety of secret investigative tactics *prior* to establishing an assessment. This includes public information and records and the use of online services and resources (DIOG, § 5.1.1.1.—5.1.1.4). Accordingly, the FBI may investigate persons and groups—without predication or supervisory approval, and without even opening an assessment—through "any publicly available on-line service or resource including those that the FBI has obtained by subscription or purchase for official use, including services available only to law enforcement entities" (DIOG, § 18.5.4.1).

The DIOG does not list (there is no transparency, in other words) which third-party services it uses. But, for example, it has been widely reported that the FBI—along with other law enforcement and intelligence agencies such as the CIA and National Security Agency (NSA)—uses the data analysis firm Palantir (founded by billionaire venture capitalist and political activist Peter Thiel), whose algorithms allow government agents to analyze online data and assess one's potential criminality.[47] The use of this sort of data-sifting capability can of course be used for good, but it is difficult to see how such permissive surveillance discretion (with no predication requirement) would be consistent with the commitment to moral and legal ideals regarding limited authority, accountability, and the rule of law.

Philosophical analysis: Identifying the justified limits of discretion to engage in opaque investigations is enormously difficult, and it may be implausible to outline bright-line rules given the unique features of each case.[48] Unjustified discretion unfortunately seems to fall into the category of "know it when you see it." A government agent following someone in a vehicle based upon reasonable suspicion clearly seems justified, but not the opaque, blanket discretion to engage in 24/7, electronic, warrantless surveillance at the push of a button.

From the last section, we know that agencies such as the FBI have the power to opaquely investigate the public through online services provided by third parties. Even if such information is "public" because it was obtained through "consent," there is good reason to think that such consent might be inadequate considering the issues that were raised in the prior section.

---

[47] Quentin Hardy, "The Risk to Civil Liberties of Fighting Crime with Big Data," *The New York Times*, November 6, 2016, describes how "Palantir first built up its business by offering products like maps of social networks of extremist bombers and terrorist money launderers, and figuring out efficient driving routes to avoid improvised explosive devices," and uses similar techniques to spot people associated with traditional crimes such as murder.

[48] Some legal scholars have proposed "guiding principles" and "bright-line rules" to limit the third-party doctrine. H. Brian Holland, "A Third-Party Doctrine for Digital Metadata," *Cardozo Law Review* 41 (2020): 1549–1600, proposes a limiting framework that considers factors relating to the nature of the metadata generated and collected, the ability to derive personal information from aggregated metadata, the necessity of the device/service to participation in a modern society, and the ability to control automated metadata generation and collection). These and other ideas are valuable contributions, though I of course favor my own broad framework—the prerogative power test—considering its emphasis on justified deviations from the rule of law.

One reason is simply that persons cannot hold the police accountable if they are not transparent about the kind of information they use to investigate a person—especially when there is no basis to establish that the person engaged in criminal activity. If we are to have a (third-party) rule of law, we need to consider third-party predication and transparency.

3.3. Other Examples and Applications

It is one thing to consider cases regarding what a philosophy professor teaches in the classroom, but quite another to consider cases in which a person could be imprisoned for making a (potentially life-saving) decision to have an abortion. After the Supreme Court's decision to overturn *Roe v. Wade*, this is no longer a theoretical issue. Although the prospect of being opaquely investigated regarding the decision to have an abortion is an issue that real people face in the real world today, let us consider a hypothetical (though realistic) scenario given the sensitivity of the topic.[49]

Jane is seventeen-year old junior in high school who uses a period-tracking app on her smart phone to track her menstrual cycle. The app stores sensitive information regarding when Jane's period stops and starts, as well as when a potential pregnancy starts and stops. Jane and her boyfriend, John, have an active sexual relationship. After experiencing nausea for several days, Jane learns from an at-home test that she is pregnant. She and John discuss the prospect of her getting an abortion, including because the pregnancy creates a high risk for serious complications given Jane's Type 1 diabetes and that Jane has very limited financial and healthcare support. Jane searches "abortion advice" on her smart phone internet browser, which lists a free clinic that provides medical advice (including advice about pregnancy and abortion) in the area. Jane and John travel to the clinic. While sitting

---

[49] Although this is hypothetical case study, the underlying issues are indeed real. The Federal Trade Commission reached a settlement with a well-known fertility and period-tracking app after allegations that it misled users about the disclosure of their personal health data—for example, informing Facebook when a user was having their period, as well as the user's pregnancy intentions. Sam Schechner, "You Give Apps Sensitive Personal Information. Then They Tell Facebook," *The Wall Street Journal*, February 22, 2019; Federal Trade Commission, "Developer of Popular Women's Fertility-Tracking App Settles FTC Allegations that It Misled Consumers About the Disclosure of their Health Data" (press release), January 13, 2021. Moreover, Alabama's attorney general has argued that the state has the power to bring conspiracy charges against those who help women travel to another state for an abortion. "Alabama's attorney general says the state can prosecute those who help women travel for abortions," *Associated Press*, August 31, 2023.

in the clinic waiting room, Jane plays an online game on her phone and the game app collects her location data. Jane ultimately decides to take an "abortion pill" (such as mifepristone) and this decision is reflected on her period-tracking app.[50]

Abortion was recently banned and criminalized in Jane's state. The state's law makes it a crime to have an abortion as soon as cardiac activity is detectable, which is typically around six weeks.

Although it was not clear to Jane when she downloaded her period tracker two years earlier, the app included a clause stating that some data stored on the app may be sold to third parties from time-to-time. In fact, the business model for the period-tracking app company is based on selling user data to private corporations—including Firm X. Firm X is a data mining company that sells comprehensive data packages to Law Enforcement Agency Y, which uses the data in support of various criminal and national security investigations. Likewise, when Jane downloaded the gaming app onto her phone one year ago, she was not aware that the app would sell her location data to Firm X—nor that a data set from her phone's search history (including the search term "abortion advice") was sold to Firm X.

Law enforcement Agency Y has been tasked to investigate abortion. Agency Y would need a search warrant (based on probable cause) to investigate any data stored directly on Jane's phone. However, all of the personal data about Jane from her apps are stored on the "cloud," which allows the app companies to sell her data to Agency Y. After purchasing data sets from Firm X, Agency Y uses computer software to search the data set for the term "abortion." Agency Y has no particular basis to search the data set in this way; instead, they just want to see what pops up in the search results. The search—coupled with a subpoena for additional information—ultimate leads Agency Y to Jane's doorstep. Jane opens the door and is shocked to learn that officers from Agency Y say they have evidence that she had an illegal abortion.

This is exactly the sort of difficult, sensitive case with which we must grapple in the foreseeable future. Identifying the justified limits of discretion to engage in opaque investigations of this nature will of course be controversial. I leave it to you, reader, to provide your own legal and philosophical analysis of Jane's case.

---

[50] See Patrick Adams, "The Other Abortion Pill," *The Atlantic*, September 19, 2022.

4. Case Study: Precrime

Steven Spielberg's 2002 film, *Minority Report*, is an ominous story about a futuristic police department ("PreCrime") that apprehends criminals based upon the precognition of psychics (or "precogs"). On one hand, predicting and stopping crime before it happens sounds pretty good. Who doesn't want to stop a murderer before he acts?

On the other hand, it would of course be frightening to think the police can show up at your door and arrest you for something you didn't do (yet), or something you hadn't even considered consciously (yet). As you can see, some of the primary philosophical issues raised in the film have to do with high-tech societies debating free will versus determinism. The film's premise might seem a bit far-fetched considering what we know about policing today. But that's just it: There is a lot about policing that the public (and the police themselves) *don't* know. Indeed, the central problem with real-world *predictive policing* is not about free will at all. It is about transparency.

Consider this hypothetical scenario that is eerily similar to contemporary, real-world policing.[51] An innovative police department purchases software from a private company that analyzes social media posts, police records, and other third-party data in order to predict persons who have a high risk of going missing. In other words, the software relies upon a sophisticated algorithm to predict who might become a "missing person." The algorithm thus allows the police to preemptively intervene in a person's life before something happens.

Sounds good, right? Maybe, but there are reasonable worries about such tactics. For example, if the police rely upon a person's patterns on social media (e.g., that a person's social media activity ceased) in a missing person case, does an unusual social media pattern mean that the case should be prioritized over other cases in which the missing person does not use social media at all? What about cases in which a person is *not* missing? Should the police *preemptively* intervene in one's life based on an algorithm's predictive model? If so, how worried should we be about the consequences of false positives (i.e., preemptively intervening in a person's life who in fact does *not* have an elevated risk to go missing)?

---

[51] This scenario draws on the real-world examples discussed in Nathan Munn, "Canadian Cops Will Scan Social Media to Predict Who Could Go Missing," *Motherboard Tech by Vice*, April 17, 2019.

These worries are based on familiar questions and concerns about algorithms, but the questions are difficult to answer because algorithmic policing is far from transparent. First, is the data on which the algorithm relies accurate? Or is it instead flawed, biased, and blind to cultural and socioeconomic differences? Second, does the police's use of the algorithm have the effect (either unwittingly, or intentionally based on pretext) of simply increasing the likelihood that the person is charged with a crime?

Suppose the police intervene in a person's life based on the prediction that the person will go missing, but the intervention simply leads to the person's arrest because the police learn that the person is in possession of illegal drugs. Or consider a different scenario in which the police use an algorithm not to identify missing persons, but instead people who are at a "high risk" of becoming "radicalized" (e.g., as part of a left-wing or right-wing organization)?

The difficulty of answering these questions gets us to the heart of the matter: If the police rely upon predictive algorithms, the basis on which the police *proactively* show up at one's door is *opaque*. Not only is the public in the dark about how the algorithm operates, but the police themselves are typically unable to explain or evaluate the algorithm's prediction. Indeed, the police have little control over the way that predictive policing algorithms are developed by designers because the technology is private intellectual property.[52] Sociologist Sarah Brayne summarizes the situation perfectly:

> Private vendors can hide behind trade secrecy and nondisclosure agreements, ultimately circumventing typical public-sector transparency requirements and lowering police accountability by making it harder for scholars to study, regulators to regulate, and activists to mobilize for or against specific practices."[53] Moreover, designers—not the police—make decisions regarding tradeoffs between optimizing accuracy versus optimizing fairness (e.g., whether to avoid discrimination based upon ethnicity) in predictions on test data.[54]

---

[52] I discuss this point in *The Police Identity Crisis—Hero, Warrior, Guardian, Algorithm* (New York: Routledge, 2021), 157–58.

[53] Sarah Brayne, *Predict and Surveil: Data, Discretion, and the Future of Policing* (New York: Oxford University Press, 2020), 140.

[54] Faisal Kamiran and Toon Calders, "Data Preprocessing Techniques for Classification without Discrimination," *Knowledge & Information Systems* 33 (2012): 1–33.

The upshot is that even though the aforementioned scenario is based (ostensibly) on the goal of using algorithmic policing to identify victims, there may be significant problems with the tactic considering the lack of transparency.

Now consider one more scenario—this time a scenario in which predictive policing is used to target criminality directly. The missing person scenario describes what we may call *person-based* predictive policing (when the police opaquely target and investigate specific individuals based upon algorithmically generated predictions). What about *place-based* predictive policing (opaquely predicting when and where a crime will occur based upon an algorithm).[55]

"Prediction box" is a predictive policing technique that has been described as "forecast[ing] individual crimes in the immediate future in order to direct patrol officers into 500-by-500 foot areas (i.e., boxes) that are at a higher risk of a crime occurring during a particular 8, 10, or 12 hour shift."[56] In other words, the *prediction box* technique directs the officers on each shift to report to—and move through—a specific geographic box with the goal of preventing a specific crime from occurring in that box.[57]

Now suppose an innovative police department purchases prediction box software to address property crime. The city has been struggling with statistically high property damage and vandalism in the preceding months. The newly implemented prediction box software forecasts that a particular city street will suffer from property damage and vandalism (based on historic data on which the software's algorithm relies). In other words, the street in question is in the prediction box. The police thus focus their resources (patrol, surveillance, and so on) on preventing a crime from occurring on the street within the box.

A seventeen-year-old Black male is observed walking down the sidewalk wearing a hoodie and carrying spray paint, along with a bulging object in his

---

[55] For example, the (now-defunct) operation LASER ("Los Angeles Strategic Extraction and Restoration") "targets and surveils specific individuals within select neighborhoods based off their recent history with the criminal justice system." Maha Ahmed, *Aided by Palantir, the LAPD Uses Predictive Policing to Monitor Specific People and Neighborhoods*, *The Intercept*, May 11, 2018. Under operation LASER, officers were "tasked with maintaining an ongoing list of community residents to monitor, by creating 'Chronic Offender Bulletins' for so-called persons of interest." The place-based technique on which this section focuses—"Prediction Box"—is one of the more common "predictive policing" tools.

[56] Rachel Boba Santos, "Predictive Policing: Where's the Evidence?" in *Police Innovation*, ed. David Weisburd et al. (Cambridge: Cambridge University Press 2019), 372.

[57] Ibid. This section draws from my examination of the prediction box technique in *The Police Identity Crisis*; and "The Limits of Reallocative and Algorithmic Policing."

hoodie pocket. The police are suspicious given the prediction that property damage and vandalism will occur in the area. Accordingly, the police stop the teen and attempt to frisk him (pat down his clothes to determine whether the bulge is a weapon).

The teen in fact works for a construction company and was sent to purchase spray paint to be used for markings in a construction project. However, given his past experience with the police, the teen panics and resists as the police try to detain him—throwing the can of paint at the police and running away. The police shoot him, fearing that the bulge in his hoodie was a gun (when in fact it was a second can of spray paint). By unquestioningly relying on the algorithm's opaque prediction, the police failed to consider other factors and developments (unique to the area) that made the prediction less reliable (including the active construction zone in the area). In any case, the police claim that they were justified in stopping the teen based in part on the algorithm's prediction that crime would occur in the prediction box.[58]

4.1. Legal and Philosophical Questions

Legal questions: First, do the police have the authority to use algorithms that rely on personal data about persons (social media posts, legal records, and other sensitive information) to predict which persons might become "missing persons" and then preemptively intervene? Second, under what circumstances can the police stop and frisk a person walking down the sidewalk?

Philosophical question: Are the police justified in their reliance on algorithmic and predictive policing tactics considering the degree of transparency in such tactics?

4.2. Legal and Philosophical Analysis

Legal analysis: First, based on the third-party doctrine discussed in section 2, the police have the authority to use algorithms that rely on personal data

---

[58] This scenario is informed by Andrew G. Ferguson, "Predictive Policing and Reasonable Suspicion," *Emory Law Journal* 62 (2012): 314; see also Hunt, *The Police Identity Crisis*, chapter 4, which discusses Ferguson's work and related issues.

about a person to preemptively intervene in the person's life based on algorithmic predictions that the person might go missing.

Second, as noted in section 2, the Fourth Amendment requires police searches to be reasonable, which generally means pursuant to a valid warrant based on probable cause. However, the US Supreme Court has interpreted the Fourth Amendment such that the police have the authority to "stop and frisk" a person (detain and pat them down briefly) without a warrant if the stop and frisk is based upon *reasonable suspicion* (defined as "specific and articulable facts," a level of proof less than "probable cause") that the person is involved in criminal activity and the police have a reasonable belief that the person "may be armed and presently dangerous."[59]

In the scenario regarding the teen with the cans of paint, it is possible that the police would be able to meet this (broad) standard by articulating facts that would support the claim that they reasonably believed the teen might be involved in criminal activity and that the bulge in his hoodie was a weapon—*which might be bolstered by the algorithm's opaque prediction that crime would occur in the area.*

Philosophical analysis: When moving from the legal to the philosophical, it first helps to consider the different ways that algorithmic policing can fail to be transparent. In an illuminating essay, Duncan Purves and Jeremy Davis argue that the central component of algorithmic opacity "is that something about the algorithm itself, or about the context in which the algorithm is implemented, makes it extremely difficult for an ordinary person to understand how or why it arrives at its determinations, and how those determinations figure in institutional decision-making."[60] The account has intuitive appeal: If the police are going to use algorithms to help make important decisions regarding one's liberty and rights, then it stands to reason that the average person should know how those decisions are reached so they can hold the police accountable. Purves and Davis go on to identify several sources of opacity:

Proprietary Opacity: the algorithm's code may not be made publicly available because of intellectual property protections and concerns about competitive advantage.

---

[59] Terry v. Ohio, 392 U.S. 1 (1968).

[60] Duncan Purves and Jeremy Davis, "Public Trust, Institutional Legitimacy, and the Use of Algorithms in Criminal Justice," *Public Affairs Quarterly* 36, no. 2 (April 2022). It was a pleasure to read and comment on an early draft of Professor Purves and Professor Davis's insightful article in the *Workshop on Ethics in Criminal Justice AI* hosted by the University of Florida on March 12, 2021.

Technical Opacity: understanding programming languages is a specialized skill, and few non-programmers are computationally literate in ways that would allow them to understand why an algorithm makes the determinations that it does.

Fundamental Opacity: the decision procedures of machine learning algorithms, which work by a mathematical process of iterative statistical optimization, resist interpretation in terms comprehensible to any human.

Implementation Opacity: algorithmic systems are often shrouded in secrecy, either on the grounds that secrecy is important for strategic advantage or because of concerns about public attitudes toward them.[61]

We have already considered cases in which these sources of opacity appear in policing. Recall that the "missing person" algorithm was purchased by the police from a private company, likely shrouded in proprietary opacity. Similarly, if the police stop (and ultimately arrest) a person in part because they are in a "prediction box," the person is unable to assess the fairness of the underlying algorithm.

Even if the average person had access to the algorithm, it is unlikely that it would be of much use considering that the police themselves often do not understand how the technology works. Here is how one officer has described predictive policing: it "'involves a mathematical equation I know nothing about.'"[62] Hence we see the problems of technical and fundamental opacity.

Finally, the examples we have covered illustrate implementation opacity. Consider the "FISA Fiasco" case study. We do not want to compromise investigations by requiring substantive transparency; when law enforcement agencies such as the FBI keep the substance of FISA investigations secret from the public, such secrecy ultimately promotes the public's epistemic goods. On the other hand, there is much stronger case to be made for procedural transparency (the procedures and processes by which state institutions wield their power) considering the goal of accountability.

The fact that opacity makes things easier for law enforcement agencies does not excuse failures of procedural transparency. If the police are concerned with fostering competency and trust, then the police institution must play an active a role in the process of addressing ethical questions raised by

[61] Ibid.
[62] Sarah Brayne, *Predict and Surveil*, 87.

various algorithmic policing technologies—including questions about the data collected and used in algorithms.[63]

This is not an onerous task or a particularly high expectation. At a minimum, it simply requires police departments to (1) think strategically about how to integrate algorithmic policing (if at all) in a way that is consistent with a broader range of goals beyond security and crime reduction (such as respecting rights and personhood), and (2) communicate (signal) their competency for using particular tactics (such as predictive policing) through well-established practices such as procedurally just community policing.[64]

This does not mean that every police officer (and member of the public) must become versed in the finer points of machine learning. However, it does mean that the police institution cannot simply hide behind proprietary and technical opacity. They should instead communicate the ways they fulfill their obligation of providing *human* analysis of crime problems (rather than blind, reckless reliance on algorithms).[65] This signals to the public their competency and good faith commitment to their obligations. Good faith in policing thus fosters trust by protecting the reasonable expectations of the communities being policed—including their ability to hold the police accountable.

* * *

It is not difficult to see how the failures of transparency discussed in this chapter can have a profound effect on whether the public trusts that the police are acting in good faith. There is simply no way for the public to know whether the police are holding up their end of the bargain honestly by providing security in a way that is consistent with the principles of good faith and the rule of law (among other principles of political morality). To put it another way, failures of transparency make it difficult for the public to evaluate institutional authority (and thus legitimacy). Following Chapter 2's discussion of Hobbes, Locke, and Shelby, it would be unreasonable for communities

---

[63] See Andrew D. Selbst, "Disparate Impact in Big Data Policing," *Georgia Law Review* 52, no. 1 (2017): 101 (examining how "algorithmic impact statements would require police departments to evaluate efficacy and potential discriminatory effects of all available choices for predictive policing technologies").

[64] See Emily Owens, David Weisburd, Karen L. Amendola, Geoffrey P. Alpert, "Can You Build a Better Cop? Experimental Evidence on Supervision, Training, and Policing in the Community," *Criminology and Public Policy* 17, no. 1 (2018): 41–87; George Wood, Tom R. Tyler, Andrew V. Papachristos, "Procedural justice training reduces police use of force and complaints against officers," *Proceedings of the National Academy of Sciences* (May 2020).

[65] I considered these points in Hunt, *The Police Identity Crisis*.

to trust illegitimate institutions (or institutions whose legitimacy cannot be assessed).

We have considered a variety of cases and contexts in this chapter—from national security cases to more traditional law enforcement cases. No one expects the FBI to disclose the details of its counterintelligence and counter-terrorism investigations—just as no one expects a state police department to disclose details of its violent street gang investigations. Complete transparency is unnecessary and counterproductive because complete transparency may *fail* to promote public epistemic goods such as knowledge and true belief for the whole society. However, it is reasonable to expect transparency regarding the institutional procedures with which law enforcement agencies must comply (including constraints on institutional power). And if we care about trust, it is certainly reasonable to expect that such agencies will not deceptively and dishonestly misrepresent (including through omission or reckless ignorance) details about their compliance with institutional constraints.

Accordingly, *procedural transparency* (the procedures and processes by which state institutions wield their power) will almost always be required given the goal of accountability. The philosophical foundation for this distinction is governance by rule of law principles, which is in part based on complying with regulations that impose constraints on institutional power. Acting outside those constraints is acting fraudulently and without authority—and thus without legitimacy. Disregard for procedural transparency makes it difficult or impossible for the public to hold institutions accountable to these principles. This connection to the rule of law is what ties transparency to the prerogative power test.

The PPT is well-suited to assess deviations from procedural transparency by law enforcement agencies. Recall that the test recognizes an *institutional context* (including through the prudential constraint), a *substantive context* (including through the purpose and emergency constraints), and a *philosophical context* (including through the personhood constraint). The PPT is thus tailored to assess failures of procedural transparency. It helps us determine whether instances of law enforcement opacity are consistent with governance by law that is free from bad faith that is on par with fraud:

(1) Is the procedural opacity used for the public good or national security (purpose constraint)?
(2) Is legislative action to sanction the procedural opacity not viable (prudential constraint)?

(3) Is the procedural opacity free from affronts to liberal personhood (personhood constraint)?

(4) Is the procedural opacity reserved for emergencies that involve an acute threat of serious bodily harm that cannot be averted without opacity (emergency constraint)?

It should now be clear that it is impossible to identify a bright-line rule for every case, but the hope is that the prerogative power test provides a principled framework for thinking about whether deviations from procedural transparency are consistent with rule of law principles.

We can conclude the chapter by reiterating the importance of practical concerns, in addition to the philosophical concerns that have been raised. There are indeed a variety of concrete reforms that could enhance transparency. Some reforms—such as those regarding algorithmic policing, discussed in this section—are specialized and will not apply to all law enforcement institutions. Other reforms are both straightforward and universally applicable, such as making police disciplinary processes transparent (and accompanying records regarding disciplinary action), making police use-of-force policies and procedures transparent (along with body camera footage), and so on.

When it comes to intimate third-party data that the police opaquely use for surveillance, law enforcement institutions can work to be transparent about the kind of data they purchase from third-party vendors and how they use the data (including the processes and constraints limiting that use). They can also change their policies such that predication (a basis for the investigation) or a search warrant is required before such personal data is used, thus ensuring the prospect of accountability.

As things stand, the police's lack of public accountability regarding their policies and procedures (coupled with misleading and incomplete public statements regarding compliance with policies and procedures) is a dishonest failure of transparency that erodes trust. It is also contrary to the very idea of democratic policing.

Epilogue

Beyond Basketball: From Proactive to Reactive

In a livestreamed news conference in September 2017, the FBI revealed details of an expansive, proactive investigation into one of the biggest threats facing contemporary society: *college basketball recruiting*. Although many of us were oblivious to the danger posed by college basketball coaches, law enforcement officials apparently considered them a significant public enemy. With flare and a keen sense for punnery, a senior FBI official warned potential cheater-coaches during the news conference: "we have your playbook." Also, the investigation's codename was "Ballerz."[1]

The US Securities and Exchange Commission had alleged that a financial advisor ("Blazer") engaged in fraud to bankroll his various investments. Seeking leniency, Blazer agreed to work as an informant for the FBI by gathering evidence in a different investigation: payments to college athletes to use his financial services firm when they turned professional. Such payments made college athletes ineligible to play under NCAA rules and opened their schools to NCAA sanctions.[2] College and youth coaches are obviously in a position to facilitate these and other forms of impermissible payments.

The FBI case agent for the Ballerz investigation (along with Blazer, an undercover FBI agent, and others) eventually brought over $100,000 of government money to Las Vegas for the investigation's big dance, as it were. The undercover team rented a penthouse at the Cosmopolitan hotel, which had a nicely stocked wet bar as well as a nicely hidden array of cameras to record the targets (basketball coaches) of their investigation.[3] Consider one example of the dangers the public narrowly dodged.

---

[1] The facts in this case study are based on reporting from Nathan Fenno, "How an FBI Agent's Wild Vegas Weekend Stained an Investigation into NCAA Basketball Corruption," *Los Angeles Times*, March 9, 2023.

[2] Ibid.

[3] Ibid.

Police Deception and Dishonesty. Luke William Hunt, Oxford University Press. © Oxford University Press 2024.
DOI: 10.1093/oso/9780197672167.003.0007

Over several days, Blazer, an undercover FBI agent (posing as a sports management investor), and others, met several coaches in the luxurious Cosmopolitan—including a youth basketball coach from Florida ("Augustine"), who was in town with his team for a youth basketball tournament. Augustine accepted an envelope from the undercover officer that included $12,700. He used some of the money to cover his players' flight home from Las Vegas (who were staying in a modest, budget hotel), and the rest of the money to pay down debt from running the team.

Augustine was later charged with several felonies (wire fraud, conspiracy to commit wire fraud, conspiracy to commit money laundering) and resigned from the youth team. He then "swept floors in his father-in-law's warehouse to make ends meet." Eventually, however, all charges against Augustine were dropped.[4]

There was of course more to the investigation than that (several people were charged and convicted for impermissibly accepting money, including several college assistant basketball coaches), and different people will of course reach different conclusions about the justification of the investigation. But a reasonable reaction is this: *What the hell was the FBI thinking?*

Is this really the sort of case on which vast amounts of time and (public) money should be spent? Is this really the sort of case over which it's worth wrecking careers and lives, including arresting basketball coaches at gunpoint? Is this really the sort of case in which law enforcement officers are justified in their use of vast deception and dishonesty—including the use of informants and undercover officers in highly constructed, artificial scenarios designed to ensnare basketball coaches?

Regardless of how you answer those questions, it should be noted that the FBI's lead agent on the case used the investigation as an opportunity to gamble (and drink) away government money. As it turns out—after the final undercover transaction was concluded—the case agent drank nearly a fifth of vodka and a number of beers before losing over $13,000 of government money playing blackjack in the hotel's casino. He eventually pled guilty to a misdemeanor charge of conversion of government money, was sentenced to three months home confinement, and lost his job.[5] So much for good-faith policing.

---

[4] Ibid.
[5] Ibid.

Beyond Law Enforcement

"Ballerz" was an idiosyncratic law enforcement investigation, and it certainly is not representative of most police work. On the other hand, the case evocatively illustrates one of the central themes of this book: *there is more to policing than law enforcement.* Some of the basketball coaches in the Ballerz investigation were engaging in fraudulent acts, but it is not obvious that their offenses justify vast deception and dishonesty by law enforcement officers.[6]

Cooperative relationships—relationships built on trust and free from fraud—are indispensable in political society. This applies to basketball coaches, sure, but it is especially important when it comes to state institutions with vast coercive power, such as the police. We have considered how good faith is a core value of contracts and that policing is contractual in nature—both in the context of social contract theory and in the context of concrete encounters between law enforcement officers and the public. This point led us to the conclusion that good faith is a normative foundation for the police as a political institution.

An understandable worry about this conclusion is that the practical nature of the police role entails enforcing the law through dishonesty and deception (the "Ballerz" investigation used almost every imaginable form of law enforcement deception), which is inconsistent with good faith. We have thus considered how dishonesty and deception are justified only as narrowly circumscribed investigative tools constrained by institutional commitments to the rule of law and the fair distribution of security—precluding dishonest and deceptive police tactics on par with fraud outside of emergency situations.

To be sure, this conclusion means that the police are not justified in pursuing many of the supposed security enhancements that we think are necessary, including many proactive tactics that rely upon lying, deception, and bad faith.[7] I hope the reasoning leading to this conclusion is

---

[6] As described in the reporting on this case, "81% of Division I athletic directors and 70% of men's basketball head coaches were white in 2017, 56% of their players were Black. If the 47% of assistant coaches who were Black had a prayer of landing a head coaching job—or remaining employed—they needed to land top-level players. The four college assistant coaches charged in Ballerz—and eight of the 10 initial defendants . . . are Black. The four Black coaches all worked for white head coaches." Ibid.

[7] It's worth remembering that—for every advocate of proactive policing—there are critics (and empirical data supporting their criticism) of proactive policing—even when the proactive tactics are not directly based on deception and dishonesty. See, for example, Rachel Boba Santos, "Predictive Policing: Where's the Evidence?" in *Police Innovations: Contrasting Perspectives,* ed. David Weisburd and Anthony Braga (Cambridge: Cambridge University Press, 2019), 366–98.

intuitive: Deceptively defecting from agreements—taking advantage of another's trust—is a correlative of force inasmuch as defecting from cooperative arrangements leads to enmity. In the domain of policing, proactive policing (including tactics that rely on dishonesty and deception to stop crime) can be a form of preemptive defection—a source enmity between the police and some members of the community that can be observed in each side's posture of anticipation and distrust. Authority is necessary for legitimacy, and authority cannot be obtained through dishonesty, deception, and fraud.

As philosophy and policing scholar Jake Monaghan aptly notes, there are significantly different legitimacy concerns with respect to proactive versus reactive policing:

> Exercising power proactively involves seeking out problems to address them without being invited to do so by citizens. Exercising power reactively, on the other hand, involves responding to existing problems, often at the request of citizens. Reactive police power, more often than not, amounts to third-party defensive force which faces no special justificatory burdens.[8]

There is a natural overlap with the arguments considered and the conclusions reached in this book: Proactive policing that involves deception and dishonesty (undercover and sting operations, for example) on par with fraud is more likely to be legitimate only when it is consistent with societal commitments to personhood, as well as the need for timely action regarding emergencies of serious harm to the public. We can compare such (justified) cases of proactive policing with the routine (and likely unjustified) use of proactive deception and dishonesty in cases involving, say, illegal narcotics (or cheating basketball coaches).

Reactive policing is inherently more constrained and democratic: it limits the police by giving citizens the power to authorize police action (through citizen calls for service, for example).[9] I am of course painting with a broad brush—the line between proactive and reactive policing is not always stark—but the underlying distinction is an important one.

Although the book's emphasis on good-faith policing means that the police institution should become more reactive and less proactive, the prerogative power test provides a reasonable framework for evaluating when

---

[8] Jake Monaghan, "Boundary Policing," *Philosophy and Public Affairs* 49, no. 1 (2020), 33.
[9] See David H. Bayley, *Police for the Future* (New York: Oxford University Press, 1996), 120.

deceptive, dishonest (even fraudulent) tactics may be justified. It is of course an imperfect framework, but it provides principled guidelines for balancing institutional trust and societal security. If we are concerned about the public's erosion of faith in the police institution, then it stands to reason that we should hold the police to a disposition of principled good faith.

If you are skeptical—if you think a more reactive police institution committed to good faith is radical—then, again, keep in mind that there are calls to drastically reduce and even *abolish* (literally) the police. Working to identify the normative limits of police deception and dishonesty—and then reforming the police institution in accordance with those limits—is a comparatively modest approach given the loud calls to eliminate the police institution altogether. Let me say a bit more about this hotly debated issue.

Beyond Defunding and Abolishing the Police

Notwithstanding my analysis of proactive versus reactive policing, one might think the emphasis on deception and dishonesty seems misplaced given the steady barrage of horrific, unjustified police shootings—not to mention other blatant forms of brutality such as the murder of George Floyd and Tyre Nichols. Twenty-one police officers (the highest in a single year) were charged with murder or manslaughter resulting from on-duty shootings in the United States in 2021.[10]

Of course, brutality and unjustified police shootings can occur in conjunction with deception and dishonesty. Officers have been convicted of fatal shootings in cases involving allegations of planted evidence, including officers alleged to have planted guns on victims to justify lethal shootings.[11] Nevertheless, if people are literally dying, it is understandable for one to think that reform should focus not on a more honest and transparent police institution, but instead on *getting rid of the institution altogether in order to stop brutality and killing*. This of course raises the issue of defunding and abolishing the police institution instead of reforming it.[12]

---

[10] Erik Ortiz, "More Officers Were Charged in Fatal Police Shootings in 2021. Not Everyone Sees Progress." *NBC*, January 22, 2022, https://www.nbcnews.com/news/us-news/officers-charged-fatal-police-shootings-2021-not-everyone-sees-progres-rcna12799

[11] See, e.g., Heather Hollingsworth, "White Missouri Officer Convicted in Black Man's 2019 Death." *Associated Press*, November 19, 2021.

[12] Roger Wertheimer, "Are the Police Necessary?" in *The Police in Society*, ed. E. Viano and J. Reiman (Lexington: D.C. Heath, 1975), 49–60; Alex S. Vitale, *The End of Policing* (Brooklyn: Verso, 2017);

There are several reasons why institutional reform—including re-form regarding deception and dishonesty—is the more justified approach. "Defunding the police" can be described as reallocating funding away from the police to other government institutions funded by the state.[13] For example, a city might shift funding from the police to social services so communities can respond to mental-health crises, addiction, and homelessness more ef-fectively. Some of these initiatives are politically possible (some cities have reallocated resources) and supported by research suggesting their efficacy (e.g., research suggesting that increased socioeconomic opportunity—not police—reduces crime).[14] I myself have argued that piecemeal reallocation is consistent with background assumptions regarding the demands of jus-tice: Core state functions (e.g., socioeconomic services) are handled by state agents with the relevant expertise, while other agents of the state (the police) retain core functions relating primarily to security.[15] But beyond that there are three central problems with *abolition*—in other words, the idea that we should get rid of the police completely (not merely reallocate some police funding).

First is the *definitional problem*: Who counts as the police? Given the diversity of police roles and responsibilities—as well as the diverse ad-ministrative and bureaucratic manifestations of the police—there can be equivocation about which state entities count as "police" and which ones should be abolished. It is plausible to think that law enforcement—some sort of policing—is indispensable in any actual, existing (nonideal, nonutopian) society. Arguments regarding police abolition, then, can often be more like debates about what is meant by the term "police."

Second, police abolition raises a *socioscientific problem*. It would be unu-sual to compare policing in the United States to, say, Denmark given the vast differences between the two countries. Unlike Denmark, the United States must contend with the reality that there are more civilian-owned firearms (393 million) than people (326 million) in the United States. This and other

Meghan G. McDowell and Luis A. Fernandez, "'Disband, Disempower, and Disarm': Amplifying the Theory and Practice of Police Abolition," *Critical Criminology* 26 (2018): 373–391.

[13] Rashawn Ray, "What Does 'Defund the Police' Mean and Does It Have Merit?" *Brookings*, June 19, 2020.

[14] Christopher Uggen and Sarah K. S. Shannon, "Productive Addicts and Harm Reduction: How Work Reduces Crime—But Not Drug Use," *Social Problems*, 61, no. 1 (2014): 105–130.

[15] Luke William Hunt, "The Limits of Reallocative and Algorithmic Policing," *Criminal Justice Ethics*, 41, no. 2 (2022).

important socioscientific issues raise difficult questions regarding police abolition in some countries but not others.[16]

Third, police abolition raises a *philosophical problem*: Would a reallocative
model abolishing (or drastically limiting) the police be politically possible,
effective, and morally justified given a polity's assumptions about justice?[17]
For example, even it were possible to, say, privatize policing, reliance on private security forces would raise serious questions about the equal distribution of security to which most states are committed. Would efforts leading
to the abolition of the police—rather than piecemeal reallocation and other
reform efforts—improve the lives of those who are most in need of security
(considering that affluent citizens could simply hire private security without
the police)?

The upshot is that any nonutopian account of justice must have something
to say about cases of unjust actions, such as those that create emergencies of
security that require good faith policing. From both a practical and moral
perspective, it is reasonable to take steps toward procedural and substantive
police reforms that are politically possible, effective, and morally permissible
given the assumption that states have a duty to promote the security of its
members. Accordingly, here is another way to look at one of the book's central implications: People (especially those who are impoverished and live in
areas of high violence and crime) need, want, and are entitled to having the
police around—it's just that they need, want, and are entitled to trustworthy
police who act in good faith.

To be sure, good-faith policing is not your typical reform. Indeed, the
conclusion reached in this book is that good-faith policing is a fundamental
component of political societies that are committed to trust and cooperation: good-faith policing is an *indispensable* institutional reform given some
very basic assumptions about the nature of political life. If we defer to social
institutions for recourse—to enforce rules and sanction the rule breakers—
then we must have some degree of confidence that the social institution itself
will act with a disposition of good faith. I hope it is clear that there would
not be much point in deferring to a social institution such as the police if
the police do not operate honestly—if the police themselves enhance human

---

[16] Ibid.
[17] Policing scholars have embraced a variety of methodologies to evaluate philosophical problems
in policing, which I have examined in my *The Retrieval of Liberalism in Policing* (New York: Oxford
University Press, 2019), chapters 1 and 2; and "Policing, Brutality, and the Demands of Justice,"
Criminal Justice Ethics 40, no. 1 (2021).

vulnerability by acting with brutality and bad faith, defrauding people and undermining the rule of law.

Beyond the Ivory Tower

I have tried to balance theory and practice in reaching the book's conclusions. It is thus appropriate to close with a word about concrete reform—not merely the philosophical foundation for reform.

We have seen that there are a variety of practical remedies for police dishonesty and deception. Regarding "testilying," criminal justice institutions (police, prosecutors, courts) could embrace stiff punishment for officers who commit perjury and significant rewards (career advancement) for officers who act honestly (and expose systemic dishonesty).[18] Regarding investigative lying, some states have enacted legislation prohibiting law enforcement officers from using deception and dishonesty when interrogating people who are under the age of 18. This sort of legislation could prohibit common deceptive tactics such as false promises of leniency and false claims about the existence of incriminating evidence.[19] Such legislation can and should be expanded.

As an intermediary step, states could minimally enact legislation that mitigates the danger posed to citizens (such as informants) who are subjected to the police's proactive operational use of deception and dishonesty. For example, some states have enacted legislation requiring law enforcement agencies to adopt operational policies and procedures prioritizing the safety of informants, law enforcement personnel, offenders, and the public. This sort of legislation requires transparency in agreements between the police and citizens who serve as police informants: the police must be transparent regarding their inability to promise inducements such as immunity and reduced charges or sentences in exchange for a person serving as an informant.[20] Law enforcement institutions should ultimately move toward the

---

[18] See Christopher Slobogin, "Testilying: Police Perjury and What to Do About It," *University of Colorado Law Review* 67 (1996): 1054–1059.

[19] See Illinois Senate Bill 2122 (2021), Oregon Senate Bill 418 (2021), and Indiana Senate Bill 415 (2023), for examples of such legislation.

[20] See Florida statute 914.29 for an example of such legislation. This statute is known as "Rachel's Law," which is named after a young woman who was leveraged by the police to engage in a dangerous undercover operation in which the woman was murdered. I discussed the case in *The Retrieval of Liberalism in Policing*, chapter 4.

use of operational deception and dishonesty that is more in line with the prerogative power test.

There are of course no easy solutions when it comes to reforming the police institution. Disagreement is inevitable, but the hope is that this book has taken a small step toward clarifying a puzzle. All philosophical analysis begins with a question. The question we have considered is the justification of police deception and dishonesty. Our focus in chapter 1 was descriptive analysis—the relationship between force and fraud in social and political life. That chapter involved both empirical generalizations about the nature of societal arrangements, as well as empirical data reflecting support for those generalizations—leading to the concept of *universalistic positive morality*. In short, societal issues regarding brutality (force) and dishonesty (fraud) are grounded in positive (social) morality that is universalistic in character.

Chapter 2 drew upon some very basic understandings of a contract—both abstract social contract theory and concrete agreements between persons and institutions—to integrate Chapter 1's descriptive analysis into a theory about policing, namely: *good-faith policing.*

Chapters 3 and 4 turned to case studies and applications of the theory, with the goal of highlighting the virtues of good faith policing. Importantly, we saw that a central component of the theory—the prerogative power test—provides escape clauses that justify police deception and dishonesty (even deception and dishonesty on par with fraud) under circumstances that are substantiated by the analysis in the Interlude.

All of this is far from perfect, but we must continue to seek solutions—even imperfect ones—to the problems of our imperfect world.

The Logic of Legitimacy

Five Justifications for Police Honesty

1. Anti-anticipatory

And from this diffidence from one another, there is no way for any man to secure himself, so reasonable, as Anticipation: that is, by force, or wiles, to master the persons of all men he can, so long, till he sees no other power great enough to endanger him.

Thomas Hobbes, *Leviathan*

2. Authenticity

We must look to the outward expression of a person as manifesting his intention rather than to his secret and unexpressed intention. The law imputes to a person an intention corresponding to the reasonable meaning of his words and acts.

Lucy v. Zehmer, 196 Va. 493 (1954)

3. Assent

[An implied in fact contract is] an agreement . . . founded upon a meeting of minds, which, although not embodied in an express contract, is inferred, as a fact, from conduct of the parties showing, in the light of the surrounding circumstances, their tacit understanding.

Baltimore & Ohio Railroad Co. v. United States, 261 U.S. 592 (1923)

4. Authority

The Liberty of Man, in Society, is to be under no other Legislative Power, but that established, by Consent, in the Common-wealth, nor under the Dominion of any Will, or Restraint of any Law, but what the Legislative shall enact, according to the Trust put in it.

John Locke, *The Second Treatise*

5. Accountability

In framing a government which is to be administered by men over men...you must first enable the government to control the governed; and in the next place oblige it to control itself.

James Madison, *The Federalist Papers*

Acknowledgments

This project had an inauspicious start as an unfunded grant application. However, the project was a finalist for the grant, and I received extremely helpful feedback that informed my thinking on the relationship between policing and (dis)honesty. Around the same time, I was invited by Stephen Galoob and Jake Monaghan to participate in a workshop on policing and political philosophy. The paper I wrote for that workshop—which converged with the ideas I had been considering in the grant application—inspired what would become Chapter 2 of this book. I received wonderfully thoughtful comments from all the workshop participants, and I am fortunate to have my paper included alongside their work in a special issue of *Criminal Law and Philosophy*.

I was also fortunate to receive funding from George Mason University's Institute for Humane Studies (IHS) to host a manuscript review workshop, and I am grateful for the continued grant support from IHS. The manuscript review workshop was especially helpful—allowing me to receive comments from some truly fantastic scholars: Tom Carson, Kyle Fritz, Stuart Green, Ben Jones, Chris Nathan, Kevin Tobia, and Kevin Vallier.

I thank my students at the University of Alabama, especially Eric Carr, Nathan Clar, Leah Humble, and Jason Daniels, who taught me as much as I taught them in my seminar, "Legal and Philosophical Problems in Policing." Jonathan Cumberland and I met at Tuscaloosa's Monarch Espresso Bar to discuss a vision for the book's cover art; I am inspired by the evocative and poignant illustration he created. And without a doubt, this book would not have been possible without the enthusiastic support and keen guidance from Lucy Randall at Oxford University Press.

I am fortunate to have the unending support of my family—my wife, Melissa; my two sons, Henry and Oliver; my brother, Wesley; my in-laws; and of course my parents, to whom this book is dedicated.

L.W.H., Tuscaloosa, Alabama, Summer 2023

Bibliography

Adams, Patrick. "The Other Abortion Pill," *The Atlantic*, September 19, 2022.

Ahmed, Maha. "Aided by Palantir, the LAPD Uses Predictive Policing to Monitor Specific People and Neighborhoods," *The Intercept*, May 11, 2018.

Alighieri, Dante. *The Divine Comedy*. Translated by John Ciardi. New York: New American Library, 2003.

Allan, James. "Is You Is or Is You Ain't Hart's Baby? Epstein's Minimum Content of Natural Law." *Ratio Juris* 20, no. 2 (June 2007): 213–229.

Archibald, John. "Police in This Tiny Alabama Town Suck Drivers into Legal 'Black Hole'," *AI.com*, January 19, 2022.

Augustine, "Lying." In *Treatises on Various Subjects*, edited by R.J. Deferrari, 47–60. New York: Catholic University of America Press, 1952.

Basic Principles on the Use of Force and Firearms by Law Enforcement Officials, adopted by the Eighth UN Congress on the Prevention of Crime and the Treatment of Offenders, August 27–September 7, 1990.

Baier, Annette, "Trust and Antitrust," *Ethics* 96, no. 2 (1986): 231, 235.

Bayle, David H. *Police for the Future*. New York: Oxford University Press, 1996.

Beerbohm, Eric. *In Our Name: The Ethics of Democracy*. Princeton, NJ: Princeton University Press, 2012.

Berlin, Isaiah. *Liberty*. Oxford: Oxford University Press, 2002.

Biba, Jason. "Her Son Needed Help. First, He Had to Help the Police," *The New Republic*, January 4, 2022.

Bicchieri, Cristina. *The Grammar of Society: The Nature and Dynamics of Social Norms*. Cambridge: Cambridge University Press, 2006.

Bix, Brian. "H. L. A. Hart and the 'Open Texture' of Language." *Law and Philosophy* 10, no. 1 (February 1991): 51–72.

Bix, Brian. "The Promise and Problems of Universal, General Theories of Contract Law." *Ratio Juris* 30, no. 4 (December 2017): 391–402.

Bloomfield, Paul. "The Character of the Hypocrite." *Journal of Philosophical Research* 43 (2018): 69–82.

Bok, Sissela Bok. *Lying: Moral Choice in Public and Private Life*. New York: Vintage Book, 1999 [1978]).

Brandeis, Louis D. *Other People's Money and How the Bankers Use It*. New York: Frederick A. Stokes, 1914.

Brayne, Sarah. *Predict and Surveil: Data, Discretion, and the Future of Policing*. New York: Oxford University Press, 2020.

Brooks, Richard R. W. "Good Faith in Contractual Exchanges." In *The Oxford Handbook of the New Private Law*, edited by Andrew S. Gold, John C. P. Goldberg, Daniel B. Kelly, Emily Sherwin, and Henry E. Smith, 497–512. New York: Oxford, 2020.

Bybee, Jay. "Standards of Conduct for Interrogation under 18 U.S.C. 2340-2340A." *Memorandum from the Justice Department's Office of Legal Counsel for Alberto R. Gonzales, counsel to President Bush* (August 1, 2002).

Byerly, T. Ryan. "Group Intellectual Transparency: A Novel Case for Non-Summativism." *Synthese* 200, no. 69 (2022).

Carson, Tomas L. *Lying and Deception: Theory and Practice*. Oxford: Oxford University Press, 2010.

Carson, Thomas L. "Lying, Deception, and Related Concepts: A Conceptual Map for Ethics." In *From Lying to Perjury*, edited by Laurence R. Horn, 15–40. Berlin: De Gruyter Mouton, 2022.

Carson, Thomas L. "The Range of Reasonable Views about the Morality of Lying." In *Lying: Language, Knowledge, Ethics, and Politics*, edited by Eliot Michaelson and Andreas Stokke, 145–160. Oxford: Oxford University Press, 2018.

Cassell, Paul G. "Explaining the Recent Homicide Spikes in U.S. Cities: The "Minneapolis Effect" and the Decline in Proactive Policing." *The Federal Sentencing Reporter* 33, no. 1–2 (2020): 83–127.

Coates, Ta-Nehisi. "The Myth of Police Reform," *The Atlantic*, April 15, 2015.

Code of Conduct for Law Enforcement Officials, adopted by UN General Assembly resolution 34/169, December 17, 1979.

Cohen, Felix S. "Transcendental Nonsense and the Functional Approach." *Columbia Law Review* 35, no. 6 (June 1935): 809–849.

Convention against Torture and Other Cruel, Inhuman or Degrading Treatment or Punishment, adopted by General Assembly resolution 39/46, December 10, 1984.

Cook, Karen S., Hardin, Russell, and Levi, Margaret. *Cooperation Without Trust*. New York: Russell Sage Foundation, 2005.

Declaration of Basic Principles of Justice for Victims of Crime and Abuse of Power, adopted by UN General Assembly resolution 40/34, November 29, 1985.

del Pozo, Brandon. *The Police and the State: Security, Social Cooperation, and the Public Good*. Cambridge: Cambridge University Press, 2023.

Dershowitz, Alan. *Why Terrorism Works: Understanding the Threat, Responding to the Challenge*. New Haven, CT: Yale University Press, 2002.

Donelson, Raff. "Blacks, Cops, and the State of Nature." *Ohio State Journal of Criminal Law* 15, no. 1 (2017): 193–210.

Drury, S. B. "H. L. A. Hart's Minimum Content Theory of Natural Law." *Political Theory* 9, no. 4 (November 1981): 533–546.

Duncan, Sam. "Why Police Shouldn't Be Allowed to Lie to Suspects." *Journal of the American Philosophical Association* 9, no. 2 (June 2023): 268–283.

Duus-Otterström, Göran and Kelly, Erin I. "Injustice and the Right to Punish." *Philosophy Compass* 14, no. 2 (February 2019).

Dworkin, Ronald. *Law's Empire*. Cambridge, MA: Belknap Press, 1986.

Dworkin, Ronald. "A Special Supplement: The Jurisprudence of Richard Nixon." *The New York Review of Books*, May 4, 1972.

Dworkin, Ronald. *Taking Rights Seriously*. Cambridge, MA: Harvard University Press, 1977.

Dwyer, Jim. "The True Story of How a City in Fear Brutalized the Central Park Five," *The New York Times*, March 30, 2019.

Edmonds, David. *Would You Kill the Fat Man?: The Trolley Problem and What Your Answer Tells Us about Right and Wrong*. Princeton, NJ: Princeton University Press, 2014.

Ehrenberg, Kenneth M. *The Functions of Law*. Oxford: Oxford University Press, 2016.

Epstein, Richard A. "The Not So Minimum Content of Natural Law." *Oxford Journal of Legal Studies* 25, no. 2 (Summer 2005): 219–255.

Fabre, Cécile. *Spying through a Glass Darkley: The Ethics of Espionage and Counter-Intelligence*. Oxford: Oxford University Press, 2022.

Fallis, Don. "What Is Deceptive Lying?" In *Lying: Language, Knowledge, Ethics, and Politics*, edited by Eliot Michaelson and Andreas Stokke, 25–42. Oxford: Oxford University Press, 2018.

Feinberg, Joel. *Harm to Others*. Oxford: Oxford University Press, 1987.

Fenno, Nathan. "How an FBI Agent's Wild Vegas Weekend Stained an Investigation into NCAA Basketball Corruption," *Los Angeles Times*, March 9, 2023.

Ferguson, Andrew G. "Predictive Policing and Reasonable Suspicion." *Emory Law Journal* 62 (2012): 259–325.

Fletcher, George P. *Basic Concepts of Criminal Law*. New York: Oxford University Press, 1998.

Ford, Ken. "A Guilty Verdict for Daniel Holtzclaw," *The Atlantic*, December 11, 2015.

Foucault, Michel. *Discipline and Punish: the Birth of the Prison* (New York: Vintage Books, 1995).

Fritz, Kyle G. "Hypocrisy, Inconsistency, and the Moral Standing of the State." *Criminal Law and Philosophy* 13, no. 2 (2019): 309–327.

Frowe, Helen. "Lesser-Evil Justifications for Harming: Why We're Required to Turn the Trolley." *Philosophical Quarterly* 68, no. 272 (2018): 460–480.

Fuller, Lon L. *The Morality of Law*. New Haven, CT: Yale University Press, 1969.

Gallie, W. B. "Essentially Contested Concepts." *Proceeding of the Aristotelian Society* 56 (1956), 167–198.

Galoob, Stephen R., and Leib, Ethan J. "The Core of Fiduciary Political Theory." In *Research Handbook on Fiduciary Law*, edited by D. Gordon Smith and Andrew Gold, 401–417. Northampton: Edward Elgar Publishing, 2018.

Goldstein, Joseph. "New York Detective Charged with Faking Lineup Results," *The New York Times*, February 27, 2018.

Goldstein, Joseph, and Surico, John. "New York Detective Guilty of Lying About Drug Arrest," *The New York Times*, January 24, 2018.

Gordon-Solmon, Kerah. "How (and How Not) to Defend Lesser-Evil Options." *Journal of Moral Philosophy* 20, no. 3–4 (July 2023): 211–232.

Green, Stuart P. *13 Ways to Steal a Bicycle*. Cambridge, MA: Harvard University Press, 2012.

Green, Stuart P. *Criminalizing Sex: A Unified Liberal Theory*. New York: Oxford University Press, 2020.

Green, Stuart P. "The Legal Enforcement of Integrity." In *Integrity, Honesty, and Truth Seeking*, edited by Christian B. Miller and Ryan West, 35–62. New York: Oxford University Press, 2020.

Green, Stuart P. *Lying, Cheating, and Stealing: A Moral Theory of White-Collar Crime*. Oxford: Oxford University Press, 2006.

Green, Stuart P. "The Universal Grammar of Criminal Law." *Michigan Law Review* 98, no. 6 (2000): 2104–2125.

Haberman, Maggie and Savage, Charlie. "Trump, Lacking Clear Authority, Says U.S. Will Declare Antifa a Terrorist Group," *The New York Times*, May 31, 2020.

Hale, Mike. "Revisiting the Facts, After the Convictions," *The New York Times*, July 20, 2014.

Hannikainen, Ivar R., Tobia, Kevin P., da F. C. F. de Almeida, Guilherme, Donelson, Raff, Dranseika, Vilius, Kneer, Markus, Strohmaier, Niek, Bystranowski, Piotr, Dolinina,

Kristina, Janik, Bartosz, Keo, Sothie, Lauraityt, Egle, Liefgreen, Alice, Próchnicki, Maciej, and Rosas, Alejandro. "Are There Cross-Cultural Legal Principles? Modal Reasoning Uncovers Procedural Constraints on Law." *Cognitive Science* 45, no. 8 (2021).

Hardin, Russell. *Trust and Trustworthiness.* New York: Russell Sage Foundation, 2002.

Hardin, Russell. "Trusting Persons, Trusting Institutions." In *Strategy and Choice*, ed. Richard Zeckhauser, 185–209 (Cambridge, MA: MIT Press, 1991).

Hardy, Quentin. "The Risk to Civil Liberties of Fighting Crime with Big Data," *The New York Times*, November 6, 2016.

Harris, Aisha Harris. "The Central Park Five: 'We Were Just Baby Boys.'" *The New York Times*, May 30, 2019.

Hart, H. L. A. *The Concept of Law.* Oxford: Oxford University Press, 2012 (1961).

Hart, H. L. A. "Positivism and the Separation of Law and Morals." *Harvard Law Review* 71 (1958): 593–629.

Hathaway, Oona. "Do Human Rights Treaties Make a Difference?" *Yale Law Journal* 111, no. 8 (June 2002): 1935–2204.

Hawley, Katherine. *How to Be Trustworthy.* Oxford: Oxford University Press, 2019.

Hays, Constance L. "Prosecuting Martha Stewart: The Overview; Martha Stewart Indicted by U.S. on Obstruction," *The New York Times*, June 5, 2003.

Hays, Tom. "Prosecutor: Lil' Kim Lied About Shootout," *AP News*, March 1, 2005.

Hill, Daniel J., McLeod, Stephen K., and Tanyi, Attila. "The Concept of Entrapment." *Criminal Law and Philosophy* 12 (2018): 539–554.

Hirschmann, Nancy J. *Gender, Class, and Freedom in Modern Political Theory.* Princeton, NJ: Princeton University Press, 2009.

Hobbes, Thomas. *Leviathan.* Introduction by W. G. Pogson Smith. Oxford: Clarendon Press, 1909 (1651).

Holland, H. Brian. "A Third-Party Doctrine for Digital Metadata." *Cardozo Law Review* 41 (2020): 1549–1600.

Hollingsworth, Heather. "White Missouri officer convicted in Black man's 2019 death," *Associated Press*, November 19, 2021.

Hunt, Luke William. "Good Faith as a Normative Foundation of Policing," *Criminal Law and Philosophy* (2023).

Hunt, Luke William. "Legal Speech and Implicit Content in the Law." *Ratio Juris* 29, no. 1 (2016): 3–22.

Hunt, Luke William. "The Legitimacy and Limits of Punishing 'Bad Samaritans.'" *University of Florida Journal of Law and Public Policy* 31, no. 3 (2022): 355–376.

Hunt, Luke William. "The Limits of Reallocative and Algorithmic Policing," *Criminal Justice Ethics* 41, no. 1 (2022): 21–44.

Hunt, Luke William. *The Police Identity Crisis: Hero, Warrior, Guardian, Algorithm.* New York: Routledge, 2021.

Hunt, Luke William. "Policing, Brutality, and the Demands of Justice." *Criminal Justice Ethics* 40, no. 1 (2021): 40–55.

Hunt, Luke William. *The Retrieval of Liberalism in Policing.* New York: Oxford University Press, 2019.

International Covenant on Civil and Political Rights, adopted by General Assembly resolution 2200A (XXI), December 16, 1966.

International Convention on the Elimination of All Forms of Racial Discrimination, adopted by UN General Assembly resolution 2106 (XX) on December 21, 1965.

Joh, Elizabeth. "Breaking the Law to Enforce It." *Stanford Law Review* 62, no. 1 (2009): 155–198.

Johnson, James and Orr, Susan. *Should Secret Voting Be Mandatory?* Cambridge: Polity Press, 2020.

Jones, Ben. "Police-Generated Killings: The Gap between Ethics and Law." *Political Research Quarterly* 75, no. 2 (2022): 366–378.

Jones, Karen. "Trustworthiness." *Ethics* 123, no. 1 (2012): 61, 70–71.

Kagan, Jeremy. *Director's Closeup 2*. Lanham, MD: Scarecrow Press, 2013.

Kakutani, Michiko. "James Comey Has a Story to Tell. It's Very Persuasive." *The New York Times* (April 12, 2018).

Kamiran, Faisal, and Toon Calders. "Data Preprocessing Techniques for Classification without Discrimination." *Knowledge & Information Systems* 33 (2012): 1–33.

Kant, Immanuel. "On a Supposed Right to Lie from Philanthropy." In *Practical Philosophy*. Translated by Mary Gregor, 605–616. Cambridge: Cambridge University Press, 1996.

Kant, Immanuel. *Lectures on Ethics*. Translated by Louis Infield. Indianapolis: Hackett Publishing, 1963.

Kassin, Saul. "False Confessions and the Jogger Case." *The New York Times* (November 1, 2002).

Kassin, Saul. *Duped: Why Innocent People Confess—and Why We Believe Their Confessions*. Lanham: Prometheus Books, 2022.

Kelly, Erin I. "The Ethics of Law's Authority: On Tommie Shelby's, Dark Ghettos: Injustice, Dissent, and Reform." *Criminal Law and Philosophy* 16, no. 1 (2022): 1–12.

Knobe, Joshua, and Nichols, Shaun. "Experimental Philosophy." *The Stanford Encyclopedia of Philosophy*, edited by Edward N. Zalta (Winter 2017).

Kogelmann, Brian. *Secret Government: The Pathologies of Publicity*. Cambridge: Cambridge University Press, 2022.

Krstić, Vladimir. "Can You Lie without Intending to Deceive?" *Pacific Philosophical Quarterly* 100 (2019): 642–660.

Lacey, Nicola. "Analytical Jurisprudence Versus Descriptive Sociology Revisited." *Texas Law Review* 84, no. 4 (2006): 945–982.

Lackey, Jennifer. *The Epistemology of Groups*. Oxford: Oxford University Press, 2020.

Lazar, Seth. "Necessity in Self-Defense and War." *Philosophy & Public Affairs*, 40, no. 3 (2012): 3–44.

Leiter, Brian. "Beyond the Hart/Dworkin Debate: The Methodology Problem in Jurisprudence." *The American Journal of Jurisprudence* 48, no. 1 (June 2003): 17–51.

Levinson, Sanford. "In Quest of a Common Conscience: Reflections on the Current Debate about Torture." *Journal of National Security Law & Policy* 1, no. 2 (2005): 231–252.

Lindsey, Treva. "The Media Failed Black Women By Not Covering This Rape Trial." *Cosmopolitan*, December 15, 2015.

Llewellyn, K. N. "The Normative, the Legal, and the Law-Jobs: The Problem of Juristic Method." *Yale Law Journal* 49, no. 8 (June 1940): 1355–1400.

Locke, John. *Two Treatises of Government*. Edited by Peter Laslett. Cambridge: Cambridge University Press, 1988 (1690).

Loeb, Vernon. "When Hoarding Secrets Threaten National Security." *The Washington Post*, January 26, 2003.

Lussenhop, Jessica. "Daniel Holtzclaw Trial: Standing with 'Imperfect' Accusers." *BBC News*, November 13, 2015.

MacAskill, William. *Doing Good Better*. New York: Avery, 2015.

Manin, Bernard. "Why Open Voting in General Elections is Undesirable." In *Secrecy and Publicity in Votes and Debates*, edited by Jon Elster, 209–214. Cambridge: Cambridge University Press, 2015.

Markovits, Daniel. "Good Faith Is Contract's Core." In *Philosophical Foundations of Contract Law*, edited by Gregory Klass, George Letsas, and Prince Saprai, 272–293. New York: Oxford, 2014.

Mazzetti, Mark, and Katie Benner. "Mueller Finds No Trump-Russia Conspiracy, but Stops Short of Exonerating President on Obstruction," *The New York Times*, March 24, 2019.

McDowell, Meghan G., and Luis A. Fernandez. "'Disband, Disempower, and Disarm': Amplifying the Theory and Practice of Police Abolition." *Critical Criminology* 26 (2018): 373–391.

Mikhail, John. "Universal Moral Grammar: Theory, Evidence, and the Future." *TRENDS in Cognitive Sciences* 11, no.4 (2007): 143–152.

Miller, Christian B. *Honesty: The Philosophy and Psychology of a Neglected Virtue*. New York: Oxford University Press, 2021.

Monaghan, Jake. "Boundary Policing." *Philosophy and Public Affairs* 49, no. 1 (Winter 2021): 26–50.

Monaghan, Jake. *Just Policing*. New York: Oxford University Press, 2023.

Munn, Nathan. "Canadian Cops Will Scan Social Media to Predict Who Could Go Missing," *Motherboard Tech by Vice*, April 17, 2019.

Murphy, Sean. "Ex-Oklahoma Officer Gets 263 Years for Rapes, Sex Assaults," *Associated Press*, January 21, 2016.

Nagel, Thomas. *Mortal Questions*. Cambridge: Cambridge University Press, 1979.

Nagourney, Adam, and Ian Lovett. "Whitey Bulger Is Arrested in California." *New York Times*, June 23, 2011.

Nathan, Christopher. *The Ethics of Undercover Policing*. New York: Routledge, 2022.

National Academies of Sciences, Engineering, and Medicine, Proactive Policing: Effects on Crime and Communities (Consensus Study Report). Washington, DC: National Academies Press, 2018.

Nguyen, C. Thi. "Transparency Is Surveillance." *Philosophy and Phenomenological Research* 105, no. 2 (2021): 331–361.

Nussbaum, Martha. *Hiding from Humanity*. Princeton, NJ: Princeton University Press, 2004.

Omand, David, and Mark Phythian. *Principled Spying: The Ethics of Secret Intelligence*. Washington, DC: Georgetown University Press, 2018.

O'Neill, Onora. *A Question of Trust: The BBC Reith Lectures 2002*. Cambridge: Cambridge University Press, 2002.

O'Neill, Patrick Howell, Ryan-Mosley, Tate, and Johnson, Bobbie. "A Flood of Coronavirus Apps Are Tracking Us. Now It's Time to Keep Track of Them." *MIT Technology Review*, May 7, 2020.

Ortiz, Erik. "More Officers Were Charged in Fatal Police Shootings in 2021. Not Everyone Sees Progress." *NBC*, January 22, 2022.

Owens, Emily, Weisburd, David, Amendola, Karen L., and Alpert, Geoffrey P. "Can You Build a Better Cop? Experimental Evidence on Supervision, Training, and Policing in the Community." *Criminology and Public Policy* 17, no. 1 (2018): 1–47.

Philipps, Dave. "Former Oklahoma City Police Officer Found Guilty of Rapes," *New York Times*, December 10, 2015.

Plato. *Complete Works*, edited by John M. Cooper. Indianapolis: Hackett, 1997.

Purves, Duncan and Davis, Jeremy. "Public Trust, Institutional Legitimacy, and the Use of Algorithms in Criminal Justice." *Public Affairs Quarterly* 36, no. 2 (April 2022): 136–162.

Quiroz, Nigel. "Five Facts about Police Deception and Youth You Should Know." *Innocence Project* (May 13, 2021).

Rachels, James. "The Challenge of Cultural Relativism." In *The Elements of Moral Philosophy*, chapter 2 (New York: McGraw-Hill, 1986).

Rakoff, Jed S. "Why Innocent People Plead Guilty." *The New York Review of Books* (June 20, 2014).

Rawls, John. *A Theory of Justice*. Cambridge, MA: Harvard University Press, 1999 (1971).

Rawls, John. *The Law of Peoples*. Cambridge, MA: Harvard University Press, 1999.

Rawls, John. *Political Liberalism*. New York: Columbia University Press, 2005.

Ray, Rashawn. "What Does 'Defund the Police' Mean and Does It Have Merit?" *Brookings*, June 19, 2020.

Raz, Joseph. "Legal Principles and the Limits of Law." *The Yale Law Journal* 81, no. 5 (April 1972): 823–854.

Raz, Joseph. *The Authority of Law*. Oxford: Oxford University Press, 2009 (1979).

Raz, Joseph. "On The Nature of Law." *ARSP: Archiv Für Rechts- Und Sozialphilosophie* 82, no. 1 (1996): 1–25.

Redden, Molly. "Daniel Holtzclaw: Former Oklahoma City Police Officer Guilty of Rape," *The Guardian*, December 10, 2015.

Restatement (Second) of Contracts § 205 (Am. Law Inst. 1981).

Ross, William David. *The Right and the Good*, Oxford: Oxford University Press, 2007 (1930),

Santos, Rachel Boba. "Predictive Policing: Where's the Evidence?" In *Police Innovations: Contrasting Perspectives*, ed. David Weisburd and Anthony Braga, 366–398. Cambridge: Cambridge University Press, 2019.

Saul Jennifer Mather. *Lying, Misleading, and What is Said: An Exploration in Philosophy of Language and in Ethics*. Oxford: Oxford University Press, 2012.

Saul, Josh. "What Do Michael Flynn and Martha Stewart Have in Common? A List of People Charged With Lying to the FBI," *Newsweek*, December 1, 2017.

Savage, Charlie, Adam Goldman, and Katie Benner. "Report on F.B.I. Russia Inquiry Finds Serious Errors but Debunks Anti-Trump Plot," *The New York Times*, December 9, 2019.

Savage, Charlie. "Problems in F.B.I. Wiretap Applications Go Beyond Trump Aide Surveillance, Review Finds," *The New York Times*, March 31, 2020.

Schauer, Frederick. "A Critical Guide to Vehicles in the Park." *New York University Law Review* 83 (2008): 1109–1134.

Schechner, Sam. "You Give Apps Sensitive Personal Information. Then They Tell Facebook." *The Wall Street Journal*, February 22, 2019.

Schwartz, Adina. "A Market in Liberty: Corruption, Cooperation, and the Federal Criminal Justice System." In *Private and Public Corruption*, edited by John Kleinig and William C. Hefferman, 173–224. Lanham: Rowman & Littlefield, 2004.

Searle, John R. *The Construction of Social Reality*. New York: Free Press, 1995.

Seidman, Ann, Robert B. Seidman, and Michael McCord. "Theory and Methodology for Investigating the Function of law in Relation to Governmental Institutions: The Case of the Development Bank of Southern Africa." *Acta Juridica* 1993 (1993): 263–278.

Selbst, Andrew D. "Disparate Impact in Big Data Policing." *Georgia Law Review* 52, no. 1 (2017): 109–195.

Shapiro, Scott. J. "The "Hart-Dworkin' Debate: A Short Guide for the Perplexed." In *Ronald Dworkin*, edited by Arthur Ripstein, 22–55. Cambridge: Cambridge University Press, 2007.

Shelby, Tommie Shelby. "Justice, Deviance, and the Dark Ghetto." *Philosophy & Public Affairs* 35, no. 2 (2007): 126–160.

Shelby, Tommie. *Dark Ghettos: Injustice, Dissent, and Reform.* Cambridge: Belknap Press, 2016.

Silver, Kenneth. "Group Action without Group Minds." *Philosophy and Phenomenological Research* 104, no. 2 (2022): 321–42.

Simmons, A. John. *The Lockean Theory of Rights.* Princeton, NJ: Princeton University Press, 1992.

Simmons, A. John. *Justification and Legitimacy.* Cambridge: Cambridge University Press, 2001.

Simmons, A. John. *Political Philosophy.* New York: Oxford University Press, 2007.

Simmons, A. John. "Ideal and Nonideal Theory," *Philosophy and Public Affairs* 38, no. 1 (Winter 2010): 5–36.

Shane, Scott, Nicholas Confessore, and Matthew Rosenberg. "How a Sensational, Unverified Dossier Became a Crisis for Donald Trump," *The New York Times*, January 11, 2017.

Shiffrin, Seana Valentine. "Is a Contract a Promise?" In *The Routledge Companion to Philosophy of Law*, edited by Andrei Marmor, 241–257. New York: Routledge, 2012.

Shiffrin, Seana Valentine. *Speech Matters.* Princeton, NJ: Princeton University Press, 2014.

Shoarian, Ebrahim, and Mahsa Jafari. "Good Faith Principle in Contract Law: A Comparative Study under Sharī'ah, Islamic Law Jurisdictions with Emphasis on Iranian Law." *Arab Law Quarterly* 35 (2021): 1–27.

Skolnick, Jerome H. "Deception by Police." *Criminal Justice Ethics* 1, no. 2 (1982): 40–54.

Slobogin, Christopher. "Deceit, Pretext, and Trickery: Investigative Lies by the Police." *Oregon Law Review* 76, no. 4 (Winter 1997): 775–816.

Slobogin, Christopher. "Testilying: Police Perjury and What to Do About It." *University of Colorado Law Review* 67 (1996): 1037–1060.

Solum, Lawrence B. "The Positive Foundations of Formalism: False Necessity and American Legal Realism." *Harvard Law Review* 127, no. 8 (2014): 2464–2497.

Srinivasan, Amia. "Stop the Robot Apocalypse." *London Review of Books* 37, no. 18 (September 24, 2015).

Starr, Douglas. "The Interview." *The New Yorker*, December 1, 2013.

Stillman, Sarah. "The Throwaways," *The New Yorker*, September 3, 2012.

Stohr, Karen. *Choosing Freedom: A Kantian Guide to Life.* New York: Oxford University Press, 2022.

Stokke, Andreas. "Lying, Deceiving, and Misleading." *Philosophy Compass* 8 (2013): 348–359.

Sullivan, Ronald. "Detective Says He Tricked Jogger Suspect." *The New York Times*, July 24, 1990.

Sunshine, Jason, and Tyler, Tom R. "The Role of Procedural Justice and Legitimacy in Shaping Public Support for Policing." *Law & Society Review* 37, no. 3 (2003): 513–548.

Surprenant, Chris W. "Policing and Punishment for Profit." *Journal of Business Ethics* 159, no. 1 (2019): 119–131.

Swasey, Benjamin. "Trump Lays Blame for Clashes on 'Radical-Left Anarchists,'" *NPR*, May 31, 2020.

Tamanaha, Brian. "What Is General Jurisprudence: A Critique of Universalistic Claims by Philosophical Concepts of Law." *Transnational Legal Theory* 2, no. 3 (2011): 287–308.

Testa, Jessica. "The 13 Women Who Accused a Cop of Sexual Assault, in Their Own Words," *BuzzFeed News*, December 8, 2015.

Tobia, Kevin. "Experimental Jurisprudence." *Chicago Law Review* 89 (2022): 735–802.

Twining, William L. *General Jurisprudence: Understanding Law from a Global Perspective.* Cambridge: Cambridge University Press, 2009.

Tyler, Tom R. "What Is Procedural Justice: Criteria Used by Citizens to Assess the Fairness of Legal Procedures." *Law & Society Review* 22 (1988): 301–355.

Uggen, Christopher and Shannon, Sarah K.S., "Productive Addicts and Harm Reduction: How Work Reduces Crime—But Not Drug Use," *Social Problems* 61, no. 1 (2014): 105–130.

United Nations Convention on Contracts for the International Sale of Goods, S. Treaty Doc. No. 98–9, art. 7 (1983).

Uslaner, Eric M. (ed.). *The Oxford Handbook of Social and Political Trust.* New York: Oxford University Press, 2017.

Vallier, Kevin, and Weber, Michael (eds.). *Social Trust.* New York: Routledge, 2021.

Vallier, Kevin. *Trust in a Polarized Age.* New York: Oxford University Press, 2020.

Vitale, Alex S. *The End of Policing.* Brooklyn: Verso, 2017.

Vitale, Alex S. "The Police Are Not Here to Protect You." *Vice News*, June 1, 2020.

Waldmann, Felix. "John Locke as a Reader of Thomas Hobbes's Leviathan: A New Manuscript," *The Journal of Modern History* 93, no. 2 (June 2021): 245–282.

Waldron, Jeremy. "How to Argue for a Universal Claim." *Columbia Human Rights Law Review* 30, no. 2 (Spring 1999): 305–314.

Waldron, Jeremy. *Torture, Terror, and Trade-Offs.* Oxford: Oxford University Press, 2010.

Waldron, Jeremy. *"Partly Laws Common to Mankind": Foreign Law in American Courts.* New Haven, CT: Yale University Press, 2012.

Waldron, Jeremy. "The Rule of Law and the Importance of Procedure," in *NOMOS— Getting to the Rule of Law*, ed. J. E. Fleming, 3–31. New York: New York University Press, 2011.

Waldron, Jeremy. *Political Political Theory.* Cambridge, MA: Harvard University Press, 2016.

Weber, Max. "The Power Position of the Bureaucracy." In *Economy and Society: An Outline of Interpretative Sociology*, 990–994. New York: Bedminister Press, 1968.

Wertheimer, Roger. "Are the Police Necessary?" in *The Police in Society*, ed. E. Viano and J. Reiman, 49–60. Lexington: D.C. Heath, 1975.

The White House, "Transparency and Open Government: Memorandum for the Heads of Executive Departments and Agencies," United States White House, January 21, 2009.

Wiegmann, Alex, and Jörg Meibauer. "The Folk Concept of Lying," *Philosophy Compass* 14, no. 8 (2019).

Williams, Bernard. *Morality.* Cambridge: Cambridge University Press (Canto Edition), 1993 (1972).

Williams, Bernard. *Truth and Truthfulness.* Princeton, NJ: Princeton University Press, 2002.

Wood, Allan. *Kantian Ethics.* Cambridge: Cambridge University Press, 2008.

Wood, George, Tom R. Tyler, and Andrew V. Papachristos. "Procedural Justice Training Reduces Police Use of Force and Complaints against Officers." *Proceedings of the National Academy of Sciences* 117, no. 18 (April 2020): 9815–9821.

Yoo, John, and Robert Delahunty. "Application of Treaties and Laws to Al Qaeda and Taliban Detainees." *Memorandum for William J. Haynes, General Counsel, United States Department of Defense* (January 9, 2002).

Zakrzewski, Cat, Verma, Pranshu, and Parker, Claire. "Police Used Texts, Web Searches for Abortion to Prosecute Women," *The Washington Post*, July 3, 2022.

Zeidman, Steven. "From Dropsy to Testilying: Prosecutorial Apathy, Ennui, or Complicity?" *Ohio State Journal of Criminal Law* 16 (2019): 423–439.

Index

For the benefit of digital users, indexed terms that span two pages (e.g., 52–53) may, on occasion, appear on only one of those pages.